Penguin Plays

DA, A LIFE and TIME WAS

Hugh Leonard was born in Dublin in 1926 and was educated at Presentation College, Dun Laoghaire, and then spent fourteen years as a clerk in the Land Commission. He was able to give up this job when he began to have some success as a playwright. He was Literary Editor of the Abbey Theatre from 1976 until 1977, and has been Programme Director of the Dublin Theatre Festival since 1978. His other plays include *A Leap in the Dark* (1957), *A Walk on the Water* (1960), *The Saints Go Cycling In* (1965), *The Au Pair Man* (1968), *The Patrick Pearse Motel* (1971), *Thieves* (1973), *Summer* (1974) and *Irishmen* (1975). His real breakthrough came with *Da*, which in the United States won a Tony Award for the Best Play of 1978, the Drama Desk Award and the New York Critics' Circle Award. He also won the Harvey Award for the best play of 1979/80 with *A Life*. He has also written a number of plays for television, including *Silent Song*, which won the Italia Award for 1967, and his adaptations for television include works by Emily Brontë, Dickens, Flaubert, Maugham and Saki. *Home Before Night*, his autobiography, was published in 1979. Hugh Leonard lives in Dublin where he writes a weekly satirical column for the *Sunday Independent* and has a regular Saturday morning radio show.

DA, A LIFE and TIME WAS

Hugh Leonard

Penguin Books

Penguin Books Ltd,
Harmondsworth, Middlesex, England
Penguin Books,
625 Madison Avenue, New York, New York 10022, U.S.A.
Penguin Books Australia Ltd,
Ringwood, Victoria, Australia
Penguin Books Canada Ltd,
2801 John Street, Markham, Ontario, Canada L3R 1B4
Penguin Books (N.Z.) Ltd,
182–190 Wairau Road, Auckland 10, New Zealand

Da first published 1973
Revised edition published simultaneously
in the U.S.A. by Atheneum and in Canada by McClelland and Stewart Ltd 1978
Copyright © Hugh Leonard, 1973, 1978

This collection first published 1981

Copyright © Hugh Leonard, 1981

Made and printed in Great Britain by
Richard Clay (The Chaucer Press) Ltd, Bungay, Suffolk
Filmset in Monophoto Bembo by
Northumberland Press Ltd, Gateshead, Tyne and Wear

CONTENTS

DA

TO MY DAUGHTER

This play was first produced outside the U.S.A. at the Olympia Theatre, Dublin, for the Dublin Theatre Festival, on 8 October 1973, with the following cast:

CHARLIE	KEVIN MCHUGH
OLIVER	FRANK KELLY
DA	JOHN MCGIVER
MOTHER	PHYL O'DOHERTY
YOUNG CHARLIE	CHRIS O'NEILL
DRUMM	EDWARD GOLDEN
MARY TATE	DEARBHLA MOLLOY
MRS PRYNN	PAMELA MANT

CHARACTERS

CHARLIE	YOUNG CHARLIE
OLIVER	DRUMM
DA	MARY TATE
MOTHER	MRS PRYNN

THE PLACE: A kitchen and, later, places remembered.

THE TIME: May 1968 and, later, times remembered.

THE SET: There are several playing areas. The main one is the kitchen. This is the kitchen–living room plus small hallway of a corporation house. An exit at the rear to the scullery. A hint of stairs running up from the hall. There are two areas at either side of the kitchen and a series of connecting steps and ramps which climb up and over, behind the kitchen. One of the two areas is the sea-front . . . it includes a park bench. Behind the sea-front, on the rising platforms, is the hilltop. On the other side of the stage is a neutral area, defined by lighting. This can be a number of locales as the script requires. (In the Second Act there is an ornamental bench there; the park bench is removed.) The kitchen, however, is the womb of the play.

ACT ONE

CHARLIE, *overcoat on, is at the kitchen table, sorting letters, family papers,
old photos, etc., into two piles. He finds one paper of interest and puts on
his glasses to examine it. He then goes to the range and pours boiling
water from the kettle into a teapot. He then picks up the teapot as* OLIVER
comes to the door.

He is CHARLIE'*s age — early 40s. His clothes are too neat for him to
be prosperous; youthful bouncy step, handkerchief exploding from his breast
pocket. He sees that the door is ajar. He knocks all the same.*

CHARLIE: Yes?
  [OLIVER *is about to come in, but stops to remove a crêpe bow from
  the door.*]
  Yes, who is it?
  [OLIVER *steps into the hall and coughs.*]
  [*Half to himself*] I didn't ask how you are, but who you are. [*Then,
  seeing him*] Oliver!
OLIVER: Instant recognition. Oh-yes, full marks.
CHARLIE: You ... good God.
OLIVER [*careful speech, equal emphasis on each syllable*]: Well, I'm still
  a native-you-know. Not a globe-trotter like some. [*Almost wagging
  a finger*] Oh, yes.
CHARLIE: Well, today's the day for it.
OLIVER: Par-don me?
CHARLIE: Old faces. They've turned up like bills you thought you'd
  never have to pay. I'm on my own ... come in. [*He puts the teapot
  down on the table.*]
OLIVER: Won't intrude. Thought I'd offer my ...
CHARLIE: Sure.
OLIVER: For your trouble. [*Holding up the wreath*] I took the liberty.
CHARLIE: That's damn nice of you, Oliver. Thank you.

OLIVER: It was –

CHARLIE: He would have liked that.

OLIVER: It's from the door.

CHARLIE: From . . . ? [*A loud laugh*] I thought it was a . . . gift-wrapped Mass card. I mean, Masses in English, the priest facing you across the altar like a chef at a buffet luncheon . . . I thought it was one more innovation. [*Taking it purposefully*] Yes, by all means. [*He drops it into the range.*]

OLIVER: Gwendolyn – the wife-you-know – saw the notice in the 'Press'. I would have gone to the funeral –

CHARLIE: What for!

OLIVER: But business-you-know.

CHARLIE: It's nice to see you. It must be ten . . . I don't know, fifteen years? Sit down . . . the mourners left a soldier or two still standing. [*He takes a bottle of stout out of a crate.*]

OLIVER: It's seldom I take a drink.

CHARLIE: I've made tea for myself, do you mind? I never drink in this house. Every Christmas the Da would say: 'Will you have a bottle of stout, son?' Couldn't. It was the stricken look I knew would come on my mother's face, as if I'd appeared in my first pair of trousers or put my hand on a girl's tit in her presence.

OLIVER [*dutifully*]: Ho–ho–ho.

CHARLIE: So I . . . [*Blankly*] What?

OLIVER: Joll–y good.

CHARLIE: My God, Oliver, you still think saying 'tit' is the height of depravity. You must find married life unbearably exciting.

OLIVER [*beaming*]: Haven't changed, haven't changed!

CHARLIE [*pouring the stout*]: Anyway, I kept meaning to take that Christmas drink and send her upstairs in tears with a frenzied petition to St Ann. Next thing I knew, there I was aged thirty-nine, the year she died, a child on my lap who was capable of consuming the dregs of everyone else's tawny port to wild grandparental applause, and my wife sitting where you are, looking with dis-believing nausea at the man she had half-carried home the previous night, as he shook his greying head virtuously and said: 'No, thanks, Da, I still don't.' [*He hands the stout to* OLIVER.] After she died, the not altogether frivolous thought occurred to me that the man who will deliberately not cause pain to his mother must be something of a sadist. I suppose I could have had a drink since then, but why spoil a perfect ... [*Looking down at* OLIVER] You've got a bald spot.

OLIVER: Me? No ... ha-ha, it's the wind. [*Producing a comb*] Breezy out. No, no: fine head of hair still-you-know.

  [CHARLIE *smiles and pours his tea, using a pot-holder.*]

  [*As he combs*] Warm for a coat, but.

CHARLIE: Yes.

OLIVER: Month of May-you-know.

CHARLIE [*an evasion*]: I was halfway out the door when I remembered this lot. Rubbish mostly. HP agreements, rent books, insurance, broken pipe ... [*He moves them to the bureau.*]

OLIVER: Now!

CHARLIE: What?

OLIVER [*bowing his head for inspection*]: Look, You see ... see?

CHARLIE: Mm ... you were right and I was wrong. Hair care is not an idle dream.

OLIVER: The old massage-you-know.

CHARLIE: Ah-hah.

OLIVER [*firmly*]: Oh, yes. [*Stroking his hair, he picks up his glass and drinks.*]

CHARLIE: Have you children?

  [*Drinking,* OLIVER *holds up four fingers.*]

  Ah?

  [OLIVER *jabs a finger towards* CHARLIE.]

CHARLIE: Um? [*Takes a sip of tea.* CHARLIE *points interrogatively towards himself and raises one finger.*]

OLIVER: Ah.

CHARLIE: What else?

OLIVER: What?

CHARLIE: Is new.

OLIVER: Oh, now.

CHARLIE: Long time. So?

OLIVER: Oh, now. [*He thinks.*

  Pause. CHARLIE *waits, then is about to go back to his sorting.*]

  Yes, by Jove, knew I had something to tell you. Six years ago ...

CHARLIE: Yes?

OLIVER: I finally got the theme music from 'King's Row'.

CHARLIE: Is that so?

OLIVER: Only electronically-simulated stereo-you-know. But still . . .

CHARLIE: Still . . .

OLIVER: That was a good fillum.

CHARLIE: Wasn't it.

OLIVER: I got billy-ho for going with you to that fillum. My mother wouldn't let me play with you over that fillum.

CHARLIE: Why?

OLIVER: Oh, pretend he doesn't know!

CHARLIE: Remind me.

OLIVER: You made me miss my elocution class.

CHARLIE [*remembering*]: So I did.

OLIVER: Ah, sappy days. Do you remember that expression we had, ah, sappy days? I was glad I kept up with the old elocution-you-know. A great stand-by. Always pronounce properly and look after your appearance: that's how you get on.

CHARLIE: *Did* you get on?

OLIVER: Oh-well-you-know.

CHARLIE: How fantastic.

OLIVER: No harm being ready and waiting.

CHARLIE: None.

OLIVER: That's why I was always smart in myself.

CHARLIE: And you got all the best girls.

OLIVER: I did, though, did-n't I?

CHARLIE: Betty Brady . . .

OLIVER: Oh, now.

CHARLIE: And that one who lived in the maze of buildings behind Cross Avenue. What was it we called her?

OLIVER: The Casbah.

CHARLIE: The Casbah. And Maureen O'Reilly.

OLIVER: Maureen . . . oh, don't-be-talking. There was a girl who took pride in her appearance. With the big — well, it was-you-know — chest.

CHARLIE: Tits.

OLIVER [*as before*]: Ho-ho-ho.

CHARLIE: She once told me ... she said: 'Oliver is going to be a great man.' Believed it.

[OLIVER's *smile crumples; it is as if his face had collapsed from inside.*]

Mad about you. They all were. What's up?

[OLIVER *shakes his head. He affects to peer closely at a wall picture.*] All I ever seemed to get was the kind of girl who had a special dispensation from Rome to wear the thickest part of her legs below the knees. [*Looking for reaction*] Yes?

OLIVER [*face unseen*]: Oh, now.

CHARLIE: Modelled yourself on Tyrone Power, right? I favoured Gary Cooper myself, but somehow I always came across as Akim Tamiroff. Jesus, Oliver, us in those days! We even thought Gene Autry could act.

OLIVER [*turning*]: He could sing 'Mexicali Rose', still and all.

CHARLIE: Least he could do.

OLIVER: Your drawback was you didn't take the Dale Carnegie course like I done.

CHARLIE: Too lazy.

OLIVER: Very worthwhile-you-know. Then, after you went over the Pond, as they say, I joined the Rosicrucians. That was a great comfort to me the time the mother died. It's all about the soul surviving-you-know in the Universal Consciousness. Do you think I should keep on with it?

CHARLIE: Of course if it helps.

OLIVER: Your da-you-know came to the mother's funeral. I never forgot that to him.

CHARLIE: Well, he was always fond of you.

[DA *comes in from the scullery and looks at* OLIVER.]

DA: Fond of him? Fond of that one? Jesus, will you give over, my grave's too narrow to turn in. [*He goes out again.*

CHARLIE, *in whose mind this has happened, winces.*]

CHARLIE: In his way.

OLIVER: In the end, was it ... 'em, if you don't mind me asking ...?

CHARLIE: No, it wasn't sudden. He got these silent strokes, they're called. Old age. What I mean is, it wasn't unexpected. He *went* suddenly.

OLIVER [*still delicately*]: You weren't, em ...

CHARLIE: I was in London: flew over yesterday, off tonight. Well, my middle-aged friend, now we're both parentless. We've gone to the head of the queue.

OLIVER: Queue for what? Oh, now. Long way to go yet, only getting started. [*He bounces to his feet.*] Well!

CHARLIE: Don't go. Finish your drink.

OLIVER: The wife-you-know.

CHARLIE: Let me finish here and I'll run you home.

OLIVER: No, must be riding the trail to the old hacienda.

CHARLIE [*a hint of urgency*]: Ten minutes.

OLIVER: The little woman ...

[OLIVER *moves to the door, takes gloves from his jacket pocket.*]

Queer-you-know how a house looks empty after a funeral. What will happen to it now, do you think?

CHARLIE: This place? It'll be re-let, I suppose.

OLIVER: I wondered – what was it I wondered? – do you happen to know anybody in the Corporation?

CHARLIE: Me?

OLIVER: Well, I hear you got on, so they tell me. Gwendolyn and me are on the list for a house this long time. If you had a bit of pull-you-know.

CHARLIE [*his manner cooling*]: No, I haven't. Sorry.

OLIVER: Oh, now. Man who's up in the world ...

CHARLIE: I haven't.

OLIVER: Oh. Well, ask not and you receive not.

CHARLIE: Dale Carnegie.

OLIVER: Ho-ho. Oh, now. Well, see you next time you're over. Sorry for the trouble. Sappy days, eh?

CHARLIE: Sappy days.

[OLIVER *goes.* CHARLIE *closes the door.*]

Fucking vulture. [*He faces the empty room. He returns the teapot to the range with* OLIVER'S *unfinished tumbler of stout. He looks briefly at* DA'S *chair and then goes to the bureau and begins to sort papers.*

He finds a wallet and puts on his glasses to examine a photograph in it.

    DA *comes in. He wears workingman's clothes: Sunday best.*]

[*Refusing to look at him*] Hoosh. Scat. Out.

DA: That wasn't too bad a day.

CHARLIE: Piss off.

    [DA *sits in his chair,* CHARLIE *looks at him.*]

Sit there, then! No one is minding you.

DA: I knew it would hold up for you. You were lucky with the weather when you came over at Christmas, too.

    [CHARLIE *ignores him and returns the papers to the table and goes on sorting them.*]

Mind, I wouldn't give much for tomorrow. When you can see the Mountains of Mourne, that's a sure sign it'll rain. Yis, the angels'll be having a pee.

CHARLIE [*whirling on him*]: Now that will do!

DA: That's a good expression. Did you ever hear that expression?

CHARLIE: Did I? Thanks to you, until I was twelve years of age every time the rain came down I had a mental picture of a group of winged figures standing around a hole in the clouds relieving themselves. Go away; I'm working, I'm clearing up. [*Working, half to himself*] Oh, yes, that was him. A gardener all his life, intimately associated with rainfall: i.e., the atmospheric condensation of warm air which, when large enough to fall perceptibly to the ground, constitutes precipitation. Hot air rises, the rain falls; but as far as he was concerned that kind of elementary phenomenon was . . .

DA: Codology.

CHARLIE: Codology. No, it was easier and funnier and more theologically orientated to say that the angels were having a pee.

[*He goes to the range and drops a large pile of papers in.*]

DA: You ought to put that down in one of your plays.

CHARLIE: I'd die first.

    [DA *rises and, without moving more than a step or two, takes a look at* CHARLIE's *teacup, then turns towards the range.*]

What are you doing?

DA: Sitting there without a cup of tea in your hand.

CHARLIE: I've a cupful.

DA: It's empty.

CHARLIE: It's full.

DA [*dismissively*]: G'way out that.

CHARLIE: Now don't touch that teapot. Do you hear me? For forty-two years I've been through this, you and that bloody teapot, and I know what's going to happen. So don't touch it!

DA: Not a drop of tea in his cup ... no wonder he's delicate.

CHARLIE: Look, will you – [*He watches dumbly, almost tearfully, as* DA *picks up the teapot and starts with it across the room. Halfway across he sets the teapot down on the floor.*]

DA [*agonized*]: Jesus, Mary and Joseph. [*He hugs his hand.*]

CHARLIE: I knew it.

DA, CHARLIE [*together*]: That's hot.

CHARLIE: Too damn headstrong. Couldn't you have waited until my ma came in and let her – [*Softly*] Jesus.

[DA *begins to stalk the teapot.*]

DA: Bad cess to it for an anti-Christ of a teapot. The handle must be hollow. Whisht, now ... say nothing. [*He takes* CHARLIE'*s cup from the table and looks contemptuously into it.*] Empty! [*He pours the contents – it is three-quarters full – into a scuttle, then kneels down, placing the cup in front of the teapot. He holds the handle of the pot between fingers and thumb, using the end of his necktie as a pot-holder, and pours the tea. Wincing*] The devil's cure to it, but it's hot. [*Rising*] Oh, be the hokey. [*He sets the cup before* CHARLIE.] There you are, son.

CHARLIE [*controlling himself*]: Thanks.

DA [*hovering*]: That'll put the red neck on you.

CHARLIE: Right!

DA: Where's the sugar?

CHARLIE: I have it. [*Beating him to the sugar and milk.*]

DA: Is there milk?

CHARLIE: Yes!

DA: If you don't want tea I'll draw you a bottle of stout.

CHARLIE: No! [*More composed*] You know I never ... [*Correcting himself*] I don't want a bottle of stout. Now sit.

DA: Sure there's no shaggin' nourishment in tea. [*Returning to his chair, he is brought up short by the sight of the teapot.*] How the hell are we going to shift it? Hoh? If herself walks in on us and sees that on the floor there'll be desolation. The gee-gees let her down today, and if the picture in the Picture House was a washout as well she'll come home ready to eat us. That's a right conundrum, hoh?

CHARLIE [*coldly*]: Cover it with a bucket.

DA: The handle is hot for the night. [*A solution*] Don't stir. Keep your ear cocked for the squeak of the gate.

CHARLIE: Why? What . . .

[DA *goes to the range, picks up a long rusting pair of tongs and starts to use them to lift the teapot.*]

Oh, God. [CHARLIE *rushes over, grabs the teapot and puts it back on the range. He sucks his scorched hand.*]

Now will you get out and leave me be. You're dead. You're in Dean's Grange, in a box, six feet under . . . with her. I carried you . . . it's over, you're gone, so get out of my head.

[DA *sits in the armchair, unperturbed, filling his pipe with tobacco.*]

Or at least stay quiet. Eighty miserable years of you is in this drawer, and as soon as I've sorted out the odds and ends, I'm slamming that front door and that's *it*. Your nephew Paddy got the TV set, I gave the radio to Maureen and Tom, and Mrs Dunne next door got my sincere thanks for her many kindnesses and in consequence thereof has said she'll never talk to me again. The junkman can have the rest, because I've got what *I* want. An hour from now that fire will go out and there'll be no one here to light it. I'll be rid of you. I'm sweating here because I couldn't wait to put my coat on and be off. So what do you say to that?

DA [*amiably*]: Begod, son, you're getting as grey as a badger.

CHARLIE: Old Drumm was right about you. The day he came here to give me the reference.

DA: Drumm is not the worst of them.

CHARLIE: He had *you* taped.

DA: Was he here today?

CHARLIE: He was at the Mass . . . next to the pulpit.

DA: Was that him? I wouldn't recognize him. God, he's failed greatly.

CHARLIE: You can talk.

DA: Decent poor bugger, but.

CHARLIE: Do you know what he called you? The enemy.

MOTHER [*off*]: Charlie, will you come down when I tell you.

CHARLIE: Who's that?

MOTHER [*off*]: Charlie! [*She comes in from the scullery. At this time she is in her late 50s; DA is fours years older.*]
[*Looking towards the ceiling*] Do you want me to come up to you?

CHARLIE: I'd forgotten what she looked like.

MOTHER [*to DA*]: Will you get off your behind and call him. He's in the lavatory with his curse-o'-God books again.

DA [*galvanized into action, yelling*]: Do you hear your mother? Come down out of there. You pup, come when you're called. If I put my hand to you ...

MOTHER: That will do.

DA [*now wound up*]: Slouching around ... skipping and jumping and acting the go-boy. Mr Drumm is halfway up the path!

MOTHER: I said that will do. Read your paper.

DA [*a grotesque imitation of a boy leaping about*]: With your hopping and-and-and leppin' and your playing cowboys on the Green Bank. Buck Jones.

CHARLIE: You were always behind the times. I hadn't played cowboys in five years.

DA: Hoot-shaggin' Gibson, Tim McCoy and Randaloph Scott.

MOTHER: You'd give a body a headache.

DA [*subsiding*]: And-and-and-and Jeanie Autry.

MOTHER: When Mr Drumm comes in this house you're not to say yes, aye or no to him, do you hear me?

DA: Sure *I* know Drumm. Who was it pruned his rose-trees?

MOTHER: No passing remarks. [*She picks up the teapot.*]

DA: Mag, that teapot is ...

MOTHER: Say nothing. [*She takes the teapot into the scullery.*]

CHARLIE: I never knew how she did it.

DA: 'Tynan,' says he to me, ''clare to God, I never seen the beating of you for roses.' That's as true as you're standing there, Mag. Never seen the beating of me. [*Ruddy with pleasure*] Hoh?

CHARLIE: Throw you a crumb and you'd call it a banquet.

DA: 'I hear,' says he to me, 'you're a great man for the whist drives.'
Do you know, I nearly fell out of my standing. 'Who told you
that?' says I, looking at him. 'Sure,' says he, 'there's not a dog or
divil in the town doesn't know you!' [*He laughs.*

> YOUNG CHARLIE *comes downstairs. He is 17, shabbily dressed.
> He carries a book.*]

[*To* YOUNG CHARLIE] Charlie, I was saying, sure I know old
Drumm these donkey's years.

CHARLIE: Oh, God: not that little prick.

> [YOUNG CHARLIE *looks at him, smarting at the insult. Their
> contempt is mutual.*]

You were, you know.

YOUNG CHARLIE: And what are you, only a big –

CHARLIE: Careful, that could lead to a compliment.

> [YOUNG CHARLIE *sits at the table and opens his book.*]

DA: Oh, Drumm will give you a grand reference.

> [MOTHER *returns with the teapot and pours boiling water into it.*]

And if he didn't itself, what odds? Aren't we all grand and
comfortable, owing nothing to no one, and haven't we got our
health and strength and isn't that the main thing?

CHARLIE: Eat your heart out, Oscar Wilde.

MOTHER [*to* YOUNG CHARLIE]: Don't lie over the table ... You'll
get a hump-back like old Totterdel.

DA: Old Totterdel was a decent man.

CHARLIE: What's the book?

YOUNG CHARLIE [*surly*]: 'Story of San Michele'. [*He pronounces it
'Michelle' as in French.*]

CHARLIE [*Italian*]: Michele, you thick.

MOTHER: The state of that shirt. I'll give you a fresh one.

YOUNG CHARLIE: It's only Tuesday.

MOTHER: Take it off.

YOUNG CHARLIE: How am I to wear one shirt all week?

MOTHER: You can go easy on it, can't you? Do as you're told.
[*Going into the scullery*] More you do for them, the less thanks you
get.

> [YOUNG CHARLIE *removes his shirt: under it is a singlet.*]

DA: You could plant seed potatoes on that shirt, son.

YOUNG CHARLIE [*muffled, the shirt over his head*]: Ah, dry up.

DA [*singing to himself: the tune is 'The Girl I Left Behind Me'*]:

'Oh, says your oul' wan to my oul' wan,

"Will you come to the Waxie Dargle?"

And says my oul' wan to your oul' wan,

"Sure I haven't got a farthin'."'

The Waxies were tailors and the Waxie Dargle was a fair they used to have beyant in Bray in old God's time. You never knew that. Hoh?

[YOUNG CHARLIE, *shivering, ignores him.*]

CHARLIE [*glaring*]: Answer him.

YOUNG CHARLIE [*to* DA]: Yeah, you told me. [*To* CHARLIE] You're a nice one to talk about being polite to him.

CHARLIE: Privilege of age, boy.

DA [*pinching* YOUNG CHARLIE's *arm*]: Begod, son, there's not a pick on you. 'I'm thin,' the fella says, 'and you're thin'; but says he: 'Y'r man is thinner than the pair of us put together!'

[MOTHER *has returned with the shirt.*]

MOTHER: This is newly-ironed. Put it on. [*She holds it for him. It has been lengthened by the addition of ill-matching pieces from another shirt to the tail and sleeves.*]

YOUNG CHARLIE: What's that?

MOTHER: Put it on you.

YOUNG CHARLIE: Look at it.

MOTHER: There's not a brack on that shirt, only it's gone a bit small for you. There's many a poor person 'ud be glad of it.

YOUNG CHARLIE: Then give it to them.

MOTHER: You cur.

YOUNG CHARLIE: God, look at the tail.

MOTHER: Who's going to see it?

YOUNG CHARLIE: I'm not wearing it.

MOTHER [*flinging the shirt down*]: Leave it there, then, Don't. [*Picking it up at once*] Put that shirt on you.

YOUNG CHARLIE: I won't.

MOTHER [*turning to* DA]: Nick . . .

DA [*a half-feigned, half-real, rather frightened anger*]: Do like the woman tells you. Can we not have a bit of peace and quiet in the house the one day of the week? Jasus Christ tonight, do you want old Drumm to walk in on top of you?

MOTHER [*quietly*]: That will do with your Sacred Name. [*To* YOUNG CHARLIE] Lift your arms.

YOUNG CHARLIE [*already beaten*]: I'm not wearing that –

[*She slaps his face briskly and, almost in the same movement, thrusts the shirt over his head. She pulls his arms into the sleeves, jerks him to her and fastens the buttons.*]

DA [*relieved*]: That's the boy. Herself cut up one of my old shirts for that, son: didn't you, Mag?

CHARLIE: You were always there with the good news.

MOTHER [*coldly, wanting to hurt back*]: The day you bring money in, you can start being particular. Time enough then for you to act the gentleman. You can do the big fellow in here then, as well as on the sea front. Oh, it's an old saying and a true one: the more you do for them ...

DA: Sure that looks grand.

MOTHER: How bad he is .... And at the end of it they'd hang you.

[YOUNG CHARLIE *puts his jacket on. He sits and picks up his book.*]

CHARLIE: You always give in. Too soft to stand up to them. No guts.

[MOTHER *is at the door looking out.*]

It could have been worse. Like the time you had the date with Ita Byrne and you asked her [MOTHER] to press your navy-blue trousers: told her it was for the altar boys' outing. She'd never pressed a pair of trousers in her life, and she put the creases down the side. And every little gurrier in the town followed you and Ita that night singing 'Anchors Aweigh'. Remember?

YOUNG CHARLIE [*now grinning*]: Sappy days.

[*The gate squeaks.*]

MOTHER: There he is now. [*To* YOUNG CHARLIE, *fearfully, the quarrel forgotten*] God and his holy Mother send he'll find you something.

[DA *starts towards the door. She yanks him back.*]

Will you wait till he knocks.

DA [*almost an incantation*]: Sure I know old Drumm.

MOTHER: And keep that mouth of yours shut. Have manners.

YOUNG CHARLIE: He's only a clerk, you know.

[*She looks at him venomously.* DRUMM *comes into view: he is in his mid-50s, thin, acerbic. He knocks.* MOTHER *and* DA *go to the door. The greetings are mimed.*]

CHARLIE: He was a chief clerk.

[YOUNG CHARLIE *looks towards the door, anguish on his face, fists clenched.*]

Five-fifty a year . . . not bad for nineteen-forty . . . what?

YOUNG CHARLIE: Four . . . November.

CHARLIE: What's up?

YOUNG CHARLIE: Nothing.

CHARLIE: Don't be proud with me, boy.

YOUNG CHARLIE: Listen to them: they always *crawl*.

CHARLIE: Blessed are the meek: they shall inherit the dirt. The shame of being ashamed of them was the worst part, wasn't it? What are you afraid of?

YOUNG CHARLIE: Tell us . . . That day.

CHARLIE: When?

YOUNG CHARLIE: Then. Now. Today. Did they . . . say anything to him?

CHARLIE: About what?

[DRUMM *is shown in.*]

MOTHER: Still, we're terrible, dragging you out of your way.

DRUMM: Is this the young man? [*Shaking hands*] How do you do?

DA [*belatedly*]: Shake hands, son.

DRUMM: A bookworm like myself, I see.

MOTHER [*to* DA]: Move out and let the man sit down.

DA [*offering his chair, saluting with one finger*]: Here you are, sir!

CHARLIE [*angry*]: Don't call him sir.

MOTHER: Now you'll sit there and have a cup of tea in your hand.

[*She sets about pouring the tea.*]

DRUMM [*quite sternly*]: No, I will not.

DA [*aggressive*]: Don't mind him. Yes, he will. You will!

DRUMM: You're a foolish woman. In these times we may take hospitality for granted. A ration of a half-ounce of tea per person per week doesn't go far.

MOTHER [*serving him*]: Now it won't poison you.

DA: And them's not your tea-leaves that are used and dried out and used again, sir. Get that down you. There's your milk and there's your sugar.

DRUMM: Look here, my dear man, will you sit. I'm not helpless.

MOTHER: Nick ...

DA: Sure what the hell else have we only for the cup of tea? Damn all ... amn't I right?

DRUMM [*ignoring him, to* YOUNG CHARLIE]: Your name is ... ?

MOTHER: Charles Patrick.

DRUMM: And you've done with school?

MOTHER: He's got a scholarship to the Presentation Brothers. There was many a one got it and took the money; but no, we said, let him have the education, because it'll stand to him when we're gone.

DA: Oh, Charlie's the boy with the brains.

DRUMM: Bright are you? Who's your favourite author?

YOUNG CHARLIE: Shakespeare.

CHARLIE: You liar.

DRUMM: And where do your talents lie?

YOUNG CHARLIE: Dunno.

DRUMM: An authority on Shakespeare shouldn't mumble. I asked, what kind of post do you want?

MOTHER: He'll take what he's offered. He's six months idle since he left school. He won't pick and choose.

DA: And if there's nothing for him, sure he can wait. There'll be any amount of jobs once the war's over.

DRUMM: Past history says otherwise. There's usually a depression.

DA: Not at all.

DRUMM: You're an expert, are you?

DA [*a stock phrase*]: What are you talking about, or do you know what you're talking about? The Germans know the Irish are their friends, and sign's on it, when the good jobs are handed out in England they'll give us the first preference.

DRUMM: Who will?

DA: The Jerries, amn't I telling you ... when they win.

DRUMM: You support the Germans, do you?

CHARLIE [*to* DA]: Shut up. [*To* YOUNG CHARLIE] Don't go red. Smile.

[YOUNG CHARLIE *summons up an unnatural grin. He laughs. At once* DRUMM *looks at him bad-temperedly.*]

DRUMM: Is something amusing you?

YOUNG CHARLIE: No.

DA: Hitler's the man that's well able for them. He'll give them lackery, the same as *we* done. Sure isn't the greatest man under the sun, himself and De Valera?

MOTHER [*not looking at him*]: Now that will do ...

DA: What the hell luck could the English have? Didn't they come into the town here and shoot decent people in their beds? But they won't see the day when they can crow it over Heil Hitler. He druv them back into the sea in 1940, and he'll do it again now. Sure what's Churchill anyway, bad scran to him, only a yahoo, with the cigar stuck in his fat gob and the face on him like a boiled shite.

[*Pause.* DRUMM *just looks at him.*]

MOTHER: There's plenty more tea in the –

DRUMM: No, I must be going.

MOTHER [*with a false smile*]: You oughtn't to mind him.

DRUMM: I don't at all. I thought the boy might walk with me, and I could ask him what it is I need to know.

MOTHER: Charlie, do you hear? Go and comb your hair and give your face a rub.

[YOUNG CHARLIE *goes upstairs, glad to get away.*]

I know you'll do your best for him. You will.

DRUMM: It would be a poor best. There's nothing here for anyone. Have you thought of letting him go to England?

DA: England!

DRUMM: There's work there.

MOTHER: Ah, no.

DRUMM: It might be for his good.

MOTHER: No, we'd think bad of losing him.

DA: There's good jobs going here if you keep an eye out. I'm gardening above in Jacob's these forty-six years, since I was a young lad ... would you credit that?

DRUMM: Yes, I would.

MOTHER: What is there in England only bombs and getting into bad health? No, he'll stay where he's well looked after. Sure, Mr Drumm, we're all he has. His own didn't want him.

DRUMM: His own?

MOTHER [*bitterly*]: Whoever she was.

DRUMM: Do you mean the boy is adopted?

[YOUNG CHARLIE *comes downstairs at a run, anxious to be off. He hears what* DRUMM *has said and hangs back on the stairs.*]

MOTHER [*purely as punctuation*]: Ah, don't talk to me.

CHARLIE: And I listened, faint with shame, while you delivered your party-piece.

MOTHER: I took him out of Holles Street Hospital when he was ten days old, and he's never wanted for anything since. My mother that's dead and gone, the Lord have mercy on her, said to me: 'Mag, he's a nurse-child. You don't know where he was got or how he was got, and you'll rue the day. He'll turn on you.'

DA [*a growl*]: Not at all, woman.

MOTHER: Amn't I saying! [*To* DRUMM] You try rearing a child on thirty shillings a week then and two pounds ten now after forty years of slaving, and see where it leaves you.

CHARLIE: Stand by. Finale coming up.

MOTHER: And a child that was delicate. She tried to get rid of him.

DRUMM: Get rid?

CHARLIE: Roll of drums, *and* ...!

MOTHER: Before he was born. Whatever kind of rotten poison she took. Dr Enright told me; he said, 'You won't rear that child, ma'am, he'll never make old bones.' But I did rear him, and he's a credit to us.

CHARLIE: Band-chord. Final curtain. Speech!

MOTHER: He's more to us than our own, so he is.

CHARLIE: Thunderous applause. [*To* DRUMM] Hand her up the bouquet.

DRUMM: You're a woman out of the ordinary. The boy has cause to be grateful.

CHARLIE: Well done. House-lights.

[YOUNG CHARLIE, *his lips pressed tight together to suppress a howl, emits a high-pitched half-whimper, half-squeal, and flees into the garden.*]

And the scream seemed to come through my eyes.

MOTHER: Charlie?

DRUMM [*looking out*]: I see he's leading the way. Goodbye, Mrs Tynan: I'll do what little I can.

MOTHER: Sure I know. God never let me down yet.

DRUMM [*He looks at* DA *and then at* MOTHER]: You surprise me.

MOTHER: Nick, say goodbye.

DA: Are you off? Good luck, now. [*Giving him a Nazi salute*] We shall rise again. Begod, we will.

DRUMM: You're an ignorant man. [*He nods to* MOTHER *and goes out.*

DA *laughs softly and shakes his head, as if he had been complimented.*]
[*Off*] Young man, come here.

DA [*as* MOTHER *comes in from hall*]: There's worse going than old Drumm. A decent man. 'I never seen the beating of you,' says he, 'for roses.'

[*She glares at him, too angry to speak, and takes* DRUMM's *teacup out to the scullery.*]

CHARLIE [*to* DA]: You could have stopped her. You could have tried. You never said a word.

DA [*calling to* MOTHER]: I think I'll do me feet tonight, Mag. I have a welt on me that's a bugger.

CHARLIE: All those years you sat and looked into the fire, what went through your head? What did you think of? What thoughts? I never knew you to have a hope or a dream or say a half-wise thing.

DA [*rubbing his foot*]: Aye, rain tomorrow.

CHARLIE: Whist drive on Wednesday, the Picture House on Sundays and the Wicklow regatta every first Monday in August. Bendigo plug-tobacco and 'Up Dev' and 'God bless all here when I get in meself'. You worked for fifty-eight years, nine hours a day, in a garden so steep a horse couldn't climb it, and when they got rid of you with a pension of ten shillings a week you did hand-springs for joy because it came from the Quality. You spent your life sitting on brambles, and wouldn't move in case someone took your seat.

DA [*softly*]: You're a comical boy.

CHARLIE [*almost an appeal*]: You could have stopped her.
  [MOTHER *comes in.*]

MOTHER: Ignorant, he said you were, and that's the word for you.

DA [*taken aback*]: What?

MOTHER: With your 'Up Hitler' in front of him and your dirty expressions. Ignorant.

DA: What are you giving out about?

MOTHER: You. You sticking your prate in where it's not wanted, so's a body wouldn't know where to look. I said to you: 'Keep that mouth of yours shut,' I said. But no . . . it'd kill you.

DA: Sure I never said a word to the man, good, bad or indifferent.

MOTHER: You're not fit to be let loose with respectable people. I don't wonder at Charlie running out of the house.

DA: What? Who did?

MOTHER: It wouldn't be the first time you made a show of him and it won't be the last. God help the boy if he has you to depend on.

DA [*upset*]: Ah now, Mag, go easy. No . . . sure Charlie and me is –

MOTHER: *Anyone* would be ashamed of you.

DA: No, him and me is –

MOTHER: He's done with you now. Done with you. [*She goes out.*]

CHARLIE: Serves you right. You could have stopped her.
  [*The lights go down on the kitchen and come up on the promenade. The sound of seagulls.* DRUMM *and* YOUNG CHARLIE *appear. They stand in front of a bench.*]

DRUMM: The wind has moved to the east. Do you take a drink?

YOUNG CHARLIE: Not yet.

DRUMM: You will, please God. Do you chase girls?

YOUNG CHARLIE: Pardon?

DRUMM: Female persons. Do you indulge?

YOUNG CHARLIE: The odd time.

DRUMM: As a diversion I don't condemn it. Henry Vaughan, an otherwise unremarkable poet of the seventeenth century, summed it up happily when he wrote 'How brave a prospect is a bright backside.' Do you know Vaughan?

YOUNG CHARLIE: 'They are all gone into the world of light.'

DRUMM: So you do read poetry! Listen to me, my friend: if you and I are to have dealings you had better know that I do not tolerate liars. Don't try it on with me ever again.

YOUNG CHARLIE: I didn't . . .

DRUMM [*firmly*]: Shakespeare is nobody's favourite author. [*He gives* YOUNG CHARLIE *a searching look.*] We'll say no more about it. Yes, chase away by all means and give them a damn good squeeze if you catch them, but be slow to marry. The maximum of loneliness and the minimum of privacy. I have two daughters myself . . . no boys.

YOUNG CHARLIE: I know your daughters.

DRUMM: Oh?

YOUNG CHARLIE: To see. Not to talk to.

DRUMM: I would describe them as . . . bird–like.

YOUNG CHARLIE [*trying to say the right thing*]: Yes, I suppose they –

DRUMM: Rhode Island Reds. You may laugh . . .

YOUNG CHARLIE: I wouldn't.

DRUMM: I say you may. *I* do. No . . . no boys. [*He sits on the bench and motions for* YOUNG CHARLIE *to sit beside him.*] There will be a vacancy in my office for a filing clerk. I don't recommend it to you: jobs are like lobster pots, harder to get out of than into, and you seem to me to be not cut out for clerking. But if you want to sell your soul for forty-five shillings a week I daresay my conscience won't keep me awake at nights.

YOUNG CHARLIE: Do you mean I can have it?

DRUMM: If you're fool enough. My advice –

YOUNG CHARLIE: A job. A job in an office, in out of the cold. Oh, Jancy, I think I'll go mad. [*He jumps up.*] Yeow!

[DRUMM *taps the umbrella on the ground.*]

God, I think I'll split in two. I'm a millionaire. Mr Drumm . . . any time if there's e'er an oul' favour I can do for you over this –

DRUMM: You can speak correct English.

YOUNG CHARLIE: Honest to God, Mr Drumm, I'm so delighted, if you asked me to I'd speak Swahili. A job!

DRUMM [*sourly*]: And this is how we throw our lives away.

YOUNG CHARLIE [*grins, then*]: Beg your pardon?

DRUMM: You'll amount to nothing until you learn to say no. No to jobs, no to girls, no to money. Otherwise, by the time you've learned to say no to life you'll find you've swallowed half of it.

YOUNG CHARLIE: I've been looking for a job since school, Mr Drumm. I couldn't refuse it.

DRUMM: To be sure.

YOUNG CHARLIE: I mean, I'm the only one at home ...

DRUMM: I'm aware of that. [*Considers it settled.*] So be it. There's a grey look about your face: I suggest you begin to wash yourself properly. And I'll need a copy of your birth certificate. What's your name?

YOUNG CHARLIE [*surprised*]: Tynan.

DRUMM: I mean your real name. You overheard what your foster-mother told me, didn't you? That you're illegitimate. Don't give me that woe-begone look. It's a fact, you're going to have to live with it and you may as well make a start. Bastardy is more ignominious in a small town than in a large one, but please God it may light a fire under you. Do your friends know?

[YOUNG CHARLIE *shakes his head.*]

Probably they do. So don't tell them: they won't thank you for spiking their guns. What ails you? Look here, my friend: tears will get no sympathy from me. I said we'll have done with it ... people will take me for a pederast. Your nose is running: wipe it.

YOUNG CHARLIE: I haven't got a handkerchief.

DRUMM: Well, you can't have mine. Use something ... the tail of your shirt.

[YOUNG CHARLIE *is about to comply when he remembers.*]

Well?

YOUNG CHARLIE: I won't.

DRUMM [*bristling*]: Won't?

YOUNG CHARLIE [*loftily*]: It's a disgusting thing to do.

DRUMM: You think so?

[*They outglare each other.* YOUNG CHARLIE *sniffs deeply. Brass band music is heard in the distance.*]

Well, perhaps there's hope for you yet.

YOUNG CHARLIE: There's a band on the pier.

DRUMM [*rising to look*]: Hm? Yes, the Artane Boys, by the sound of them.

[YOUNG CHARLIE *whips out his shirt-tail, wipes his nose and readjusts his dress as* DRUMM *turns to face him.*]

Your ... mother, shall we call her? ... is a fine woman.

YOUNG CHARLIE: Yeah. Except she tells everyone.

DRUMM: About you?

YOUNG CHARLIE: All the old ones. Then they say to her: isn't she great and how I ought to go down on my bended knees. Even the odd time I do something right, it's not enough ... it's always the least I could do. Me da is different: if you ran into him with a motor car he'd thank you for the lift.

DRUMM: I'm fond of him.

YOUNG CHARLIE [*disbelieving*]: Of me da?

DRUMM: I can afford that luxury: I'm not obliged to live with him. You are. That's why he's the enemy.

YOUNG CHARLIE: The what?

DRUMM: Your enemy.

YOUNG CHARLIE [*straight-faced, trying not to laugh*]: I see.

DRUMM: Don't be polite with me, my friend, or you'll be out of that job before you're into it. Once at a whist drive I heard him say that the world would end in 1940. It was a superstition that had a fashionable currency at one time among the credulous. Well, 1940 came and went, as you may have noticed, and finding myself and the county of Dublin unscathed, I tackled him on the subject. He was unruffled. He informed me that the world hadn't ended because the German bombs had upset the weather.

[YOUNG CHARLIE *laughs boisterously. He bangs his fists on his knees.* DA *enters the neutral area and rings a doorbell.*]

Yes, the dangerous ones are those who amuse us.

[*The bell is rung again.* DA *puts his pipe in his pocket and waits.*]

There are millions like him: inoffensive, stupid, and not a damn bit of good. They've never said no in their lives or to their lives, and they'd cheerfully see the rest of us buried. If you have any sense, you'll learn to be frightened of him.

[*A light is flashed on* DA*'s face as if a door had been opened.*]

DA [*saluting*]: That's a hash oul' day, ma'am. Certainly you know me ... Tynan, of Begnet's Villas, sure I'm as well known as a begging ass. And do you know what I'm going to tell you? ... that back field of yours, the meadow: if you was to clear that field of the rocks that's in it and the stumps of trees and had it dug up with a good spreading of manure on the top of it, begod, you wouldn't know yourself. There's bugger-all you couldn't grow in it.

DRUMM: From people too ignorant to feel pain, may the good God deliver us!

DA: The young lad, do you see, he's starting work. Oh, a toppin' job: running an office, sure he's made for life. And the way it is, I'd think bad of him starting off without a decent suit on his back or the couple of good shirts. Sure you couldn't let him mix with high-up people and the arse out of his trousers. Have you me?

DRUMM: I'm advising you to live in your own world, not with one foot in his.

DA: I'll come to you so on Sundays and do the field ... sure it won't take a feather out of me. [*Embarrassed by mention of money*] Very good, yis ... I'll leave that to yourself: sure whatever you think. [*Saluting*] Thanks very much, more power. [*He starts off, then bobs back again.*] More power, says oul' Power when young Power was born, wha'?

[*The door-light snaps off. As he moves away, the lights on the neutral area go down.*]

DRUMM: Are we still on speaking terms?

YOUNG CHARLIE [*hating him*]: Yes.

DRUMM: You aren't angry?

YOUNG CHARLIE: No!

DRUMM: Indeed, why should you be! Shall we stroll down and listen to the Artane Boys?

[*They walk off. Lights come up quickly on* CHARLIE *and* DA *in the kitchen as before.*]

CHARLIE: And I went off with him like a trollop.

DA: Drumm is a decent skin. Came in here once to see how I was managing after herself died. Three years ago this month, yis. Gev me a packet of cigarettes. 'No,' says I, 'I won't.' 'You will,' says he; 'take them when you're told to.' So I did. Wait now till I see where I have them.

CHARLIE: We listened to the band and I even made excuses for you. Told him about your grandfather and two uncles starving to death in the Famine.

DA: Oh, aye. Them was hard times. They died in the ditches.

CHARLIE: What ditches? I made it up!

DA: Fierce times they were. Where the hell did I put them? You can smoke them in the aeroplane. [*Going to the dresser*]

CHARLIE: I don't want them.

DA [*searching*]: Yes, you do.

CHARLIE: Don't make a – [*He takes a packet of 'Player's' from his pocket.*] It's all right ... look, I found them.

DA: Hoh?

CHARLIE: Look.

DA: Good lad. Yis, it was in the month of – [*He breaks off.*] Drumm smoked 'Sweet Aftons' ... that's not them. [*He resumes the search.*]

CHARLIE: Messer!

DA: It was in the month of May herself died, and it was in the month of May I went. Would you credit that? [*He climbs on a chair.*]

CHARLIE: Congratulations. I should have stuck up for you and told him to keep his job. Then I could have hated you instead of myself. Because he was dead on: he described you to a – [*Seeing him*] Oh, get down.

[DA *finds the cigarettes on top of the dresser. He begins to climb down.*]

You destroyed me, you know that? Long after I'd quit the job and seen the last of Drumm, I was dining out in London: black dickie-bow, oak panelling, picture of Sarah Bernhardt at nine o'clock: the sort of place where you have to remember not to say thanks to the waiters. I had just propelled an erudite remark across the table and was about to shoot my cuffs, lose my head and chance another one, when I felt a sudden tug as if I was on a dog-lead. I looked, and there were you at the other end of it. Paring your corns, informing me that bejasus the weather would hold up if it didn't rain, and sprinkling sugar on my bread when Ma's back was turned.

[DA *gives him the cigarettes as if he was passing on contraband.*]

DA: Say nothing. Put this in your pocket.

CHARLIE: So how could I belong there if I belonged here?

DA: 'Take them,' says Drumm to me, 'when you're told to.'

CHARLIE: And it was more than a memory. She was dead then, and at that moment I knew you were sitting here on your own while the daylight went. Did you think bad of me? I wish I were a fly inside your head, like you're a wasp inside of mine. Why wouldn't you come and live with us in London when we asked you?

DA: What would I do that for?

CHARLIE: You were eighty-one.

DA: Sure I was a marvel. 'Begod, Tynan,' says Father Kearney to me, 'we'll have to shoot you in the wind-up.' What a fool I'd be to leave herself's bits and pieces here where any dog or divil could steal them. And for what? To go to England and maybe land meself in an early grave with the food they serve up to you.

CHARLIE: No, you'd rather stay here instead, like a maggot in a cabbage, and die of neglect.

DA: I fended for meself. No better man.

CHARLIE: In sight or out of it, you were a millstone. You couldn't even let me lose my virginity in peace.

DA: Lose your what?

CHARLIE: Nothing. It's a slang word, now obsolete.

[MARY TATE *walks on. She is 25, a loner.*]

DA: Who's that? That's a fine figure of a girl. What's she doing around here?

CHARLIE: She's not here: she's on the sea-front. And she wasn't a fine girl. She was known locally as the Yellow Peril.

[YOUNG CHARLIE *and* OLIVER — *younger now* — *are lounging in the neutral area.* MARY *walks by. They pay her no obvious attention.*]

YOUNG CHARLIE [*suddenly, singing*]: 'Underneath the lamplight . . .'

OLIVER: 'By the barracks gate . . .'

YOUNG CHARLIE: 'Darling, I remember . . .'

OLIVER: 'The way you used to wait.'

YOUNG CHARLIE, OLIVER [*together*]:

'I heard you walking in the street,
I smelt your feet,
But could not meet,
My lily of the lamplight,
My own Lily Marlene.'

[MARY's *step falters as she hears the lyrics. She continues on to the bench, where she sits and opens a copy of 'Modern Screen'.*
The two youths go on singing – quietly now and to themselves. YOUNG CHARLIE *looks covertly at her once or twice.*]

CHARLIE [*to* DA]: We all dreamed, privately and sweatily, about committing dark deeds with the Yellow Peril. Dark was the word, for if you were seen with her, nice girls would shun you and tell their mothers, and their mothers would tell yours: the Yellow Peril was the enemy of mothers. And the fellows would jeer at you for your beggarman's lust – you with your fine words of settling for nothing less than Veronica Lake. We always kept our sexual sights impossibly high: it preserved us from the stigma of attempt and failure on the one hand, and success and mortal sin on the other. The Yellow Peril never winked, smiled or flirted: the sure sign of an activist. We avoided her, and yet she was a comfort to us. It was like having a trusty flintlock handy in case of necessity.

[YOUNG CHARLIE *and* OLIVER *both look at* MARY.]

YOUNG CHARLIE: They say she's mustard.

OLIVER: Oh, yes. Red-hot-you-know.

YOUNG CHARLIE: And she has a fine-looking pair.

OLIVER: Of legs-you-mean?

YOUNG CHARLIE: Well, yeah: them, too.

OLIVER: Oh. Ho-ho-ho. Oh, now. Joll-y good.

[MARY *looks up from her book as* OLIVER *raises his voice: a calm direct look, neither friendly nor hostile.*]

YOUNG CHARLIE: She's looking. [*To* MARY, *bravely*] 'Evening.

OLIVER [*embarrassed*]: Don't.

YOUNG CHARLIE: Why?

OLIVER: We'll get ourselves a bad name. Where was I? Yes ... I was telling you about Maria Montez in 'Cobra Woman'. Now there's a fine figure of a –

YOUNG CHARLIE: They say she'd let you. All you have to do is ask.

OLIVER: Maria Montez? Is that a fact?

YOUNG CHARLIE [*pointing*]: Her.

OLIVER: Ah, yes: but who is that hard up for it?

CHARLIE: I was.

OLIVER: I mean, who wants to demean himself?

CHARLIE: I did.

YOUNG CHARLIE: God, I wouldn't touch her in a fit. I'm only –

OLIVER: And she would make a holy show of you, you-know, like she done with the man who tried to interfere with her in the Picture House.

YOUNG CHARLIE: When?

OLIVER: I think it was a Bette Davis. The man sat down next to her and as soon as the big picture came on the screen he started tampering with her in some way. And she never said a word, only got up and dragged him to the manager by his wigger-wagger.

YOUNG CHARLIE [*stunned*]: She never.

OLIVER: True as God. He felt very small, I can tell you.

YOUNG CHARLIE: Still, if she minded she can't be all that fast.

OLIVER: Oh-I-don't-know. If she wasn't fast she'd have dragged him by something else.

[YOUNG CHARLIE *looks at* MARY *in awe*.]

CHARLIE: Lust tied granny-knots in my insides. I wanted the Yellow Peril like I wanted no girl before or no woman since. What was worse, I was wearing my new suit for the first time and I had to do it now, now or never, before the newness wore off.

OLIVER [*who has been talking*]: So will we trot up to the billiard hall?

YOUNG CHARLIE: You go.

OLIVER: Me?

YOUNG CHARLIE: I'll follow you. [*He looks almost tragically at* OLIVER.

Pause. Then OLIVER *stares from him to* MARY.]

OLIVER: Her?

YOUNG CHARLIE [*agonized*]: Go on.

OLIVER: Ho-ho-ho-ho. Oh, now. [*Dismay*] You wouldn't.

YOUNG CHARLIE: Olly ... fizz off.

OLIVER: But you don't want to chance your arm with her; she'd *let* you. [*Then*] Where will you take her?

YOUNG CHARLIE: I dunno: down the back.

OLIVER: I'll see you, then.

YOUNG CHARLIE: Yeah.

OLIVER: I suppose you know you'll destroy your good suit.

YOUNG CHARLIE: Will you go on. See you.

[OLIVER *does not move. Hostility forms on his face.*]

OLIVER: I was the one you came out with-you-know.

[YOUNG CHARLIE *waits for him to go.*]

They say it's very disappointing-you-know, very over-rated. [*Pause. Angrily*] Well, don't salute me in the town when you see me, because you won't be saluted back. [*He goes.*

YOUNG CHARLIE *goes towards the bench. He stops, suddenly panic-stricken.*

CHARLIE *has by now moved out of the kitchen area.*]

CHARLIE: Do you want a hand?

[*Still looking at* MARY, YOUNG CHARLIE *motions to him to be quiet.*]

If they think you're afraid to ask them they attack you. You said yourself, all you have to do is ask.

YOUNG CHARLIE: Dry up, will you.

[MARY *looks at him.*]

CHARLIE: Now ... quick!

YOUNG CHARLIE: 'Evening.

MARY: You said that.

CHARLIE: Sit.

[YOUNG CHARLIE *sits beside her. What follows is ritual, laconic and fast.*]

MARY: Didn't ask you to sit down.

YOUNG CHARLIE: Free country.

MARY: Nothing doing for you here.

YOUNG CHARLIE: Never said there was.

MARY: Ought to have gone off with that friend of yours.

YOUNG CHARLIE: Who ought?

MARY: You ought.

YOUNG CHARLIE: What for?

MARY: Nothing doing for you here.

YOUNG CHARLIE: Never said there was.

> [*Pause. Phase Two in conversation.*]

MARY: What's your name, anyway?

YOUNG CHARLIE: Bruce.

MARY [*a sceptical grin*]: Yeah?

YOUNG CHARLIE: It is. [*He crosses his eyes and thumbs his nose at* CHARLIE *by way of defiance.*]

MARY: Bruce?

YOUNG CHARLIE: Mm.

MARY: Nice name.

YOUNG CHARLIE [*pointing off*]: He's Oliver.

MARY: That so?

YOUNG CHARLIE: He's from the town.

MARY: Where *you* from?

YOUNG CHARLIE: Trinity College.

MARY: That right?

YOUNG CHARLIE: English Literature.

MARY: Must be hard.

YOUNG CHARLIE: Bits of it.

> [*She goes back to her reading. A lull. End of Phase Two.*]

CHARLIE: Ask her.

YOUNG CHARLIE: She's not on.

CHARLIE: Ask.

> [*Instead,* YOUNG CHARLIE *clamps his arm heavily around* MARY. *She does not look up from her magazine during the following.*]

MARY: Wouldn't Edward G. Robinson put you in mind of a monkey?

YOUNG CHARLIE: Let's see. Do you know, he does.

MARY: One of them baboons.

YOUNG CHARLIE: Yes. Yes, yes, yes, yes. [*At each 'yes' he slaps her vigorously on the knee.*

She stares as if mesmerized at his hand as it bounces up and down and finally comes to rest on her knee in an iron grip. As she returns to her magazine he begins to massage her kneecap.]

CHARLIE [*staring*]: You insidious devil, you.

MARY: It doesn't screw off.

YOUNG CHARLIE: What?

MARY: Me leg.

[*His other hand now slides under her armpit, intent on touching her breast. He is unaware that he is kneading and pinching her handbag, which is tucked under her arm. She watches this hand, fascinated.*]

CHARLIE: I think you're getting her money all excited.

MARY [*having returned to her reading*]: You needn't think there's anything doing for you here.

YOUNG CHARLIE: I don't.

MARY: Dunno what you take me for ... sort of person who'd sit here and be felt with people passing. If you won't stop I'll have to go down the back. [*She looks at him directly for the first time.*] If you won't stop.

YOUNG CHARLIE [*not stopping; hoarsely*]: All right.

MARY [*looking off*]: Wait till that old fella goes past.

YOUNG CHARLIE: Who?

MARY [*fondling his knee*]: Not that you're getting anything.

YOUNG CHARLIE [*dazed with lust*]: I know.

CHARLIE: My silver-tongue eloquence had claimed its helpless victim. Defloration stared me in the face. My virginhood swung by a frayed thread. Then ...!

DA [*off*]:
    'Oh, says your oul' one to my oul' one:
    "Will you come to the Waxie Dargle?"
    And says my oul' one to your oul' one:
    "Sure I haven't got a farthin'."'
        [YOUNG CHARLIE's *kneading and rubbing comes to a halt.*
        As DA *walks on at a good stiff pace, he tries to extract his hand from under* MARY's *armpit but she holds it fast.*]
    [*Passing*] More power. [*He walks a few more paces, stops, turns and stares.*] Jesus, Mary and Joseph.

YOUNG CHARLIE [*his voice cracking*]: Hello.

42

MARY: Don't talk to him.

> [DA *looks at* MARY's *hand on* YOUNG CHARLIE's *knee.* YOUNG CHARLIE *removes her hand; she replaces it.*]

DA: Sure the whole world is going mad.

MARY: Don't answer him.

> [DA *sits next to her.*]

DA: The whist drive was cancelled, bad scran to it. Only four tables. Says I: 'I'm at the loss of me tram fare down, but I won't be at the loss of it back, for I'll walk.' [*He looks at* YOUNG CHARLIE's *hand flapping helplessly.*] I dunno. I dunno what to say.

MARY: He'll go away. Don't mind him.

CHARLIE: If my hand was free I'd have slashed my wrists.

DA: Oh, the young ones that's going nowadays would eat you. I dunno.

MARY: He doesn't know much.

DA: He knows too shaggin' much. [*To* YOUNG CHARLIE] If your mother was here and seen the antrumartins of you, there'd be blood spilt.

MARY: Much she'd care.

DA: Much who'd care.

MARY: Me ma.

YOUNG CHARLIE: He's talking to me.

DA: Certainly I'm talking to him, who else? That's my young lad you're trick-acting with.

MARY [*to* YOUNG CHARLIE]: Is he your –

DA: Oh, that's Charlie.

MARY: Who?

YOUNG CHARLIE: Bruce is me middle name.

DA: That's Charles Patrick.

YOUNG CHARLIE: Oh, thanks.

DA [*to* MARY]: You mind me, now. What is it they call you?

MARY [*a little cowed*]: Mary Tate.

YOUNG CHARLIE: Leave her alone.

DA: You hold your interference. From where?

MARY: Glasthule ... the Dwellin's.

> [DA *makes a violent gesture, gets up, walks away, turns and points at her dramatically.*]

43

DA: Your mother was one of the Hannigans of Sallynoggin. Did you know that?

MARY: Yes.

DA: And your uncle Dinny and me was comrades the time of the Troubles. And you had a sister that died of consumption above in Loughlinstown.

MARY: My sister Peg.

DA: And another one in England.

MARY: Josie.

DA: Don't I know the whole seed and breed of yous! [*To* YOUNG CHARLIE] Sure this is a grand girl. [*He nudges* YOUNG CHARLIE *off the bench and sits down next to* MARY.] Tell me, child, is there news of your father itself?

MARY [*her face clouding*]: No.

DA: That's hard lines.

MARY [*bitterly*]: We don't *want* news of him. Let him stay wherever he is – we can manage without him. He didn't give a curse about us then, and we don't give a curse about him now.

DA: There's some queer people walking the ways of the world.

MARY: Blast him.

[DA *talks to her. She listens, nods, wipes her eyes.*]

CHARLIE: And before my eyes you turned the Yellow Peril into Mary Tate of Glasthule, with a father who had sailed off to look for work in Scotland five years before, and had there decided that one could live more cheaply than seven. The last thing I'd wanted that evening was a person.

[DA *rises, about to go.*]

DA [*to* YOUNG CHARLIE]: You mind your manners and treat her right, do you hear me. [*To* MARY] Don't take any impudence from him. Home by eleven, Charlie.

YOUNG CHARLIE: Yes, Da.

DA: 'Bye-'bye, so. Mind yourselves.

MARY: 'Bye . . .

[*They watch until he is out of sight.*]
Your old fellow is great gas.

YOUNG CHARLIE [*sourly*]: Oh, yeah. A whole bloody gasometer.

MARY [*pause, then*]: Well, will we go down the back?

YOUNG CHARLIE: Uh ... down the back ... yeah.

MARY: He's gone, he won't see us. [*Affectionately, mocking*] Bruce!

YOUNG CHARLIE: The thing is, I promised Oliver I'd see him in the billiard hall.

MARY: Oh, yeah?

YOUNG CHARLIE: Maybe some evening next week, if you're around, we can –

MARY: Mm ... sure.

YOUNG CHARLIE: Oliver's holding a table for us. Got to run. Well ... see you.

MARY: Suppose you will. [*As he goes*] Y'ought to wrap yourself in cotton wool. [*Chanting*] Daddy's little baby ... Daddy's little b—

[*She stops and begins to cry, then goes off.*]

CHARLIE: I stayed away from the sea-front for a long time after that. [*He finds an object on the table in front of him.*] Is this yours? [*He sees that he is alone. He looks at it more closely.*] Tug-o-war medal. Nineteen ... God almighty, nineteen-twelve. It was different then. It was even different when ... when? When I was seven. You were an Einstein in those days.

[DA *comes in from the scullery. He is thirty years younger: in his prime.*]

DA [*a roar*]: Hup out of that! Put up your homework, get off your backside, and we'll take the dog for a run around the Vico.

CHARLIE [*happily*]: Yes, Da.

DA [*summoning the dog*]: Come on, Blackie ... who's a good dog? That's the fella ... hup, hup! [*He crouches as if holding a dog by the forepaws, and allows his face to be licked.*] Give us the paw ... give. Look at that ... begod, wouldn't he near talk to you? Get down. Are you right, son? [*He extends his hand.*

CHARLIE *takes it.*

MOTHER *comes in from the scullery with a woollen scarf.*]

MOTHER: No, he's not right. [*She puts the scarf around* CHARLIE's *neck, tucking it in tightly.*] You have as much sense in you as a don't-know-what. Dragging him out with his chest exposed. Do you want to get him into bad health?

CHARLIE: Ah, Ma ...

MOTHER: Ah, Ma! Go on. Bless yourselves going out, the pair of you.

[CHARLIE *and* DA *go into the hall.* DA *dips his fingers into a holy-water font and flicks the water at* CHARLIE.]

DA [*opening the front door: to the dog, stumbling*]: Blast you, don't trip me up ... hoosh owa that!

[*They stop on the doorstep,* DA *looking at the sky.*

During this scene, CHARLIE *does not attempt to imitate a child. He is an adult re-enacting a memory. Trust is evident in his attitude towards* DA.]

That's a fine mackerel sky. Sure isn't it the best bloody country in the world!

CHARLIE: Da, say it.

DA: Say what?

CHARLIE: What you always say. Ah, you know ... what the country mug in the army said. Say it.

DA [*feigning innocence*]: What did he say?

CHARLIE: Ah, do ...

DA: Yis, well, he joins up. And sits down to his dinner the first night, and says he ...

CHARLIE: Yeah, yeah!

DA: Says he: 'Yes, sir; no, sir; sir, if you please. Is it up the duck's arse that I shove the green peas?'

[CHARLIE *laughs delightedly.*

They walk hand in hand up and around the stage, both singing 'Waxie Dargle'.

Lights go down on the kitchen. They stop at an upper level. DA *reaches back to help* CHARLIE *up.*]

Come on, now ... big step.

CHARLIE: I can't, Da.

DA: Yes, you can.

CHARLIE: I'll fall.

DA: You won't fall. Catch a hold of me hand. That's the lad ... and there you go! Looka that, looka them mountains. There's a view, if you were rich enough you couldn't buy it. Do you know what I'm going to tell you? ... there's them that says that view is better nor the Bay of Naples.

CHARLIE: Where's Naples, Da?

DA: Ah, it's in Italy.

CHARLIE: What's Italy like, Da?

DA [*pause, then gravely*]: Sticky, son ... sticky.

CHARLIE: Da ...

DA: What?

CHARLIE: Will I go to Italy when I grow up?

DA [*comforting*]: Not a fear of it ... we wouldn't let you.

CHARLIE [*looking out and down*]: There's a ship. Is that it, Da? ... is that our ship coming in?

DA: Where? No ... no, son, that one's going out.

CHARLIE: Will ours come in tomorrow, Da?

DA: Begod now it might.

CHARLIE: We'll be on the pig's back then, Da, won't we? When we're rich.

DA: We won't be far off it.

CHARLIE: And what'll we do?

DA: Do?

CHARLIE: <u>When we win the Sweep.</u>

DA [*the standard answer*]: We won't do a shaggin' hand's turn.

CHARLIE [*awe and delight*]: Gawny!

DA [*deadpan*]: Sure the girl drew out me ticket the last time, and bad cess to her, didn't she drop it.

CHARLIE [*dismay*]: She didn't?

DA: She did.

CHARLIE: The bloomin' bitch.

DA: The what? Where did you hear that expression?

CHARLIE: I dunno, Da.

DA: Don't ever again let me hear you saying the like of that. That's a corner-boy expression.

CHARLIE: Sorry, Da.

DA: Women is different from you and me: y'ought to grow up to have respect for them. No, never call a woman a name like that, son, not even if she was a right oul' whoor. [*Pause*] Do you know where we are now?

CHARLIE: Dalkey Hill, Da.

DA: Not at all. In my day this was called Higgins' Hill, and oul'

Higgins used to chase us off it and him up on a white horse. He never set foot in church, chapel or meeting, and sign's on it when he died no one would have him, and [*Pointing off*] that's where he's buried, under that stump of what's left of a cross after it was struck by lightnin'. Sure they say he sold his soul to the Oul' Fella himself.

CHARLIE: What oul' fella?

DA [*pointing down*]: Your man. Isn't the mark of his hoof on the wall below on Ardbrugh Road where he tripped running down to the mailboat to go back to England?

CHARLIE: Da, let's go home.

DA: What ails you?

CHARLIE: I'm afraid of old Higgins.

DA: Are you coddlin' me?

CHARLIE: And it's getting dark. I want to go home.

DA: Sure ghosts won't mind you if you don't mind them.

CHARLIE: Da ... [*Reaching for his hand*]

DA: Wait now till I light me pipe and then we'll go.

CHARLIE: Da, you know the thing I'm worst afraid of?

DA: What's that?

CHARLIE: Well, you know me mother? ... not Ma: me real one.

DA: What about her?

CHARLIE: Me Aunt Bridgie says when it gets dark she comes and looks in at me through the window.

DA: Looks in at you?

CHARLIE: And she says she's tall and with a white face and a black coat, and she comes out from Dublin on the tram, and she wants me back.

DA: Is that a fact?

CHARLIE: And me Aunt Bridgie says it wasn't true what you told me when I was small, about me mother being on Lambay Island where she wasn't able to get hold of me, and living on pollack and Horny Cobblers.

DA: Not true? Did I ever tell you a word of a lie?

CHARLIE: I don't believe she's on Lambay Island.

DA: No. No, she's not there. That wasn't a lie, son: it was ... a makey-up. Because you were too young, do you follow me . . . you wouldn't have understood.

CHARLIE [*apprehensive*]: Understood what? Why, where is she?

[DA *looks impassively out to sea.*]

Da, tell us.

DA [*seeming to change the subject*]: Do you see that flashing light?

CHARLIE: That's the Kish lightship.

DA: Well, that's where she is.

CHARLIE [*stunned*]: On the Kish?

DA: God help her.

CHARLIE: What's she doing on the Kish?

DA: She . . . cooks.

CHARLIE: For the lightshipmen?

DA: Yis.

CHARLIE: What does she cook?

DA: Ah, pollack, son, and Horny Cobblers.

[CHARLIE *gives him a suspicious look, then peers out to sea.*]

CHARLIE: Gawny.

DA: So now you know.

CHARLIE: Da . . . what if she got off the Kish? What if she's at home now before us and looking through the window?

DA: Well, if she is, I'll tell you what we'll do. I'll come up behind her and I'll give her the biggest root up in the arse a woman ever got.

CHARLIE [*pleased*]: Will you, Da?

DA: I will. And bejasus it'll be nothing compared to the root I'll give your Aunt Bridgie. [*Rising, brushing his trousers-seat*] Now where the hell is that whelp of a dog?

CHARLIE: Da, I love you.

DA [*staring at him in puzzlement*]: Certainly you do. Why wouldn't you? [*Moving away*] Blackie, come here to me!

[DA's *reply has the effect of causing* CHARLIE *to revert to his present-day self.*]

CHARLIE [*fuming*]: Why wouldn't I? I'll tell you why bloody wouldn't I. Because you were an old thick, a zombie, a mastodon. My God . . . my mother living on a lightship, trimming the wick and filleting Horn Cobblers. What a blazing, ever-fertile imagination you had – Cobblers aren't even edible!

DA [*whistles*]: Blackie!

CHARLIE: And pollacks!

DA: You're right son, a bollix, that's what he is.

CHARLIE: The black dog was the only intelligent member of the family. He died a few years later. He was poisoned, and no one will convince me it wasn't suicide. God knows how Ma ever came to marry you.

[*Lights come up in the kitchen.* MOTHER *looks on while* YOUNG CHARLIE *is writing a letter.*]

Oh, I know how, sort of . . . she told me. I mean why.

MOTHER: He was called Ernie Moore. He used to be on the boats . . . the B and I. The 'Lady Hudson-Kinahan' it was. I was very great with him for a while. Then himself came to the house one day and said how he had the job above in Jacob's and he wanted to marry me. So that was that.

YOUNG CHARLIE: How?

MOTHER: It was fixed.

YOUNG CHARLIE: How fixed?

MOTHER: My father told him I would, so it was fixed. Things was arranged in them days.

YOUNG CHARLIE: Did you want to?

MOTHER: I had no say in it.

YOUNG CHARLIE: How well did you know him?

MOTHER: Well enough to bid the time of day to.

YOUNG CHARLIE: That was handy.

MOTHER: A body's not put into this world to pick and choose and be particular. I was seventeen, I done what I was told to.

YOUNG CHARLIE: What about Popeye the Sailor?

MOTHER: Who?

YOUNG CHARLIE: The other one.

MOTHER: Mr Moore in your mouth. When your time comes and you have to answer to God in the next world it makes no differ who you married and who you didn't marry. That's when everything will be made up to us.

YOUNG CHARLIE: You mean they hand out free sailors?

MOTHER: What? You little jeer, you. [*She aims a blow at him which he wards off.*] Well, God send that you never have to get married young for fear that if you stayed at home you might die, like many another died, of consumption for want of proper nourishment.

[YOUNG CHARLIE *affects to ignore her. He resumes writing and sings 'Popeye the Sailorman' under his breath in derisive counterpoint.*]

Waited on hand and foot, never wanting for nothing. Well, when you do get married, to whatever rip will have you, I only hope you'll be half the provider for her as himself has been for me. Is that letter done?

YOUNG CHARLIE: Yeah.

MOTHER: Read it out.

YOUNG CHARLIE: The Jacobs don't care whether I got a job or not.

MOTHER: It's manners to tell them, they ask after you. Go on.

YOUNG CHARLIE: 'Dear Nelson and Jeanette . . .'

[*She gives him a look. He amends.*]

'Dear Mr and Mrs Jacob: My father has told me how often you have been so good as to inquire as to whether I have yet found employment. I am grateful for your interest and am glad to say that I have now been given a clerical position. So, happily, I am no longer like Mr Micawber, constantly expecting something to turn up. Thanking you for your –'

MOTHER: What sort of codology is that?

YOUNG CHARLIE: What?

MOTHER: You're no longer like who?

YOUNG CHARLIE: It's an expression out of a book.

MOTHER: Write it out again and do it proper.

YOUNG CHARLIE: What for?

MOTHER: Because you're told to.

YOUNG CHARLIE: Look, there's this character in a book. He's always hard up, but he's an optimist. He –

MOTHER: Do as you're bid.

YOUNG CHARLIE: There's nothing wrong with it. Maybe you don't understand it, but the Jacobs will. It's meant to be funny, they'll laugh when they read it.

MOTHER: Aye, to be sure they will. At you, for setting yourself up to be something you're not.

YOUNG CHARLIE: It's my letter. You're not writing it: I am.

MOTHER: Then write it proper.

YOUNG CHARLIE: Proper-*ly*!

MOTHER: Don't you pull *me* up. Don't act the high-up lord with *me*, not in this house. They said I'd rue the day, and the gawm I was, I didn't believe them. He'll turn on you, they said. My own mother, me good neighbours, they all –

YOUNG CHARLIE: Oh, play another record.

MOTHER: Don't you back-answer me, you cur.

YOUNG CHARLIE: Whatever it is, if you don't understand it, it's rubbish. To hell with Charles Dickens and the rest of them: Nat Gould and Ruby M. Ayres made the world.

MOTHER: Are you going to write that out again, yes or no?

YOUNG CHARLIE: No, because there's nothing the –

MOTHER: Are you not! [*She looks up at* DA, *who with* CHARLIE *is still standing in the hill area.*] Nick ...

DA: Ah, son, write it out the way she wants you to.

MOTHER: Don't beg him: tell him.

DA [*violently*]: Will you do as you're bloody well told and not be putting the woman into a passion! Can we not have a solitary minute's peace in the house with you and your curse-o'-God Jack-acting?

MOTHER: Do that letter again.

YOUNG CHARLIE [*in a rage*]: All right, all right! I'll do it. [*He crumples up the letter, takes the notepad and writes furiously.*] 'Dear Mr and Mrs Jacob ... I am very well. My parents hope you are well, too, as it leaves them. I have a j-o-b now. I do not know myself, I am that delighted. Thanking you and oblige ...' [*He signs it.*] Now are you happy?

MOTHER: Hand it here. I wouldn't trust you to post it. [*She takes the letter and puts it into an envelope. He cannot quite believe that she is taking it seriously.*]

YOUNG CHARLIE: You're not going to send –

DA [*turning to* CHARLIE]: Begod, son, you always made a great fist of writing a letter.

YOUNG CHARLIE [*barely in control*]: I'm going to the billiard hall.

MOTHER: Go wherever you like.

> [YOUNG CHARLIE *storms out, loudly singing 'Popeye the Sailorman'. He emits a last mocking 'Boop-boop!' as he vanishes.*
> *We hear the far-off barking of a dog.*]

CHARLIE: It was a long time before I realized that love turned upside down is love for all that.

DA: There's the whoorin' dog gone down ahead of us in the finish. And the lights is on in the town. [*Pointing*] That's the Ulverton Road, son, where we frightened the shite out of the Black-and-Tans. And the lamp is lit in your uncle Paddy's window.

CHARLIE: If it is, he didn't light it: he's dead these donkey's years. Uncle Paddy, Kruger Doyle, Gunjer Hammond, Oats Nolan – all your cronies – and old Bonk-a-bonk with his banjo and Mammy Reilly in her madhouse of a shop, with her money, so they said, all in sovereigns, wrapped up inside her wig. All dead. Like yourself . . . and, trust you, last as usual.

DA: That's a hash old wind starting up. We'll need a couple of extra coats on the bed tonight, son.

CHARLIE: We will.

DA: Mind your step now. If you slip and cut yourself she'll ate the pair of us. Give me your hand. Let the light from the Kish show you where the steps are.

CHARLIE: That's it, Mother: light us home. Least you can do.

[*Curtain*]

ACT TWO

CHARLIE *and* YOUNG CHARLIE *appear, walking towards the front door. There is a slightly exaggerated vivacity in* CHARLIE's *manner: the result of having had a few drinks.*

CHARLIE: Ikey Meh? I remember the *name* ...

YOUNG CHARLIE: The tram conductor. We used to yell Ikey Meh at him when the tram went past, and he'd pull the emergency stop and lep off after us –

CHARLIE: Leap off.

YOUNG CHARLIE: ... And leave the passengers high and dry. God, he could run.

CHARLIE: Of course: yes! Ikey Meh. ['*Meh' is drawn out in imitation of a goat.*] He – [*He catches sight of* DA, *who is trailing along behind them.*] I told you to stop following me. Now go away.

YOUNG CHARLIE: Leave him alone.

CHARLIE: I go out for a bite to eat and a quiet jar, to get away from him, and what happens? He's in the pub ahead of me. Fizz off.

[DA *hangs back and lurks in the shadows.*]

YOUNG CHARLIE: You might be civil to him. I mean, it's his day.

CHARLIE: It was. The funeral's over.

YOUNG CHARLIE [*coldly*]: Oh, that's exquisite. You're a gem, you are.

CHARLIE: Don't get uppish with me, sonny Jim: you're as dead as he is. Come in and keep me company while I finish up.

YOUNG CHARLIE: I think I'll hump off.

CHARLIE [*aggressively*]: You'll hump nowhere. You'll stay in my head until I choose to chase you out of it.

YOUNG CHARLIE: Oh, will I?

CHARLIE: There's only room in there for one of you at a time, and if I let you leave he'll come back like a yo-yo. Look at him, lurking. Get in there when you're told to. [*He has opened the front door with a key and pushes* YOUNG CHARLIE *in ahead of him.*]

YOUNG CHARLIE: Mind who you're shaggin' pushin'.

CHARLIE: Shag*ging*. Pushi*ng*. Get in.

　[DA *comes up to the door, moving fast.*]

Oh, no you don't. Out, and stay out. [*He shuts the door.*]

　[DA *promptly walks through the fourth wall and sits in his armchair filling his pipe.*]

YOUNG CHARLIE: Someone to see you.

CHARLIE: Who? [*He stares angrily at* DA.]

DA: God, they done wonders with the public house, son. I wouldn't recognize it. All the metally bits and the red lights ... it'd put you in mind of a whoorhouse.

YOUNG CHARLIE: When were you ever in a –

CHARLIE: Say nothing. Ignore him. [*He searches through the bureau drawers.*]

DA: That pub used to be called Larkin's ... you didn't know that. [*He fetches a jug from the dresser and empties it. It is filled with old keys, bits of yarn and thread, receipts, newspaper clippings, odds and ends.*]

YOUNG CHARLIE: If you hadn't gone out you could have been finished and away by now. But no, you couldn't wait to get maggoty drunk.

CHARLIE: Maggoty? On three small ones?

DA: I never seen you take a drink before, son. But sure what odds? Aren't you old enough?

YOUNG CHARLIE [*primly*]: *I* never needed artificial stimulets.

CHARLIE: Stimulants.

YOUNG CHARLIE: Booze. Look at you.

DA [*placidly*]: The way you swally-ed them. Begod, says I to meself, that fellow would drink Lough Erin dry.

CHARLIE: Shut up. [*To* YOUNG CHARLIE] What's wrong with me?

YOUNG CHARLIE: Well, you're a bit of a disappointment.

CHARLIE: Oh, yes?

YOUNG CHARLIE: I mean, I'd hoped to do better for meself.

CHARLIE: What had you in mind?

YOUNG CHARLIE: Don't get huffy. It's not that I amn't glad to see you: at least it means I'll live till I'm forty: that's something.

CHARLIE: Thanks.

YOUNG CHARLIE [*looking at* CHARLIE's *wrist*]: And I like the watch.

CHARLIE: Oh, good.

YOUNG CHARLIE: I suppose I could have done worse: but you can't deny you're a bit ordinary. It gives a fellow the creeps, seeing himself at your age: everything behind him and nothing to look forward to.

CHARLIE: I get the old-age pension next year: there's that.

YOUNG CHARLIE: Yesterday I was thinking: I'm only eighteen, anything can happen to me ... anything. I mean, maybe a smashing girl will go mad for me. Now I dunno.

[CHARLIE *puts on his glasses to read a receipt.* YOUNG CHARLIE *looks at him.*]

Ah, God.

CHARLIE: What?

YOUNG CHARLIE: Glasses. I'm blind as well.

CHARLIE: I'm sorry about that. The time I was castrated in a car crash, it affected my eyesight.

YOUNG CHARLIE [*horrified*]: You weren't. [*Then*] You're so damn smart.

DA: Oh, them motor cars is dangerous.

YOUNG CHARLIE: Everything's a laugh, isn't it? Anyone I see who's your age ... same thing. All lah-de-dah and make a joke of it. God if something good happens to me, I jump up in the air, I let out a yell, I run. Your sort just sits there.

CHARLIE: Arthritis.

YOUNG CHARLIE: You're dried up. Dead.

CHARLIE: I'm a seething torrent inside.

YOUNG CHARLIE: You? You're jizzless.

CHARLIE: I'm what?

YOUNG CHARLIE: There's no jizz in you. The fun's gone out of you. What's worse, you're no good ... wouldn't even take him with you to London when me ma died.

CHARLIE: I asked him.

YOUNG CHARLIE: Instead of forcing him.

CHARLIE: Him? Who could force him to do anything?

YOUNG CHARLIE: Did you try?

CHARLIE: Don't get righteous with me, my pasty-faced little friend. It doesn't become you. Were *you* any good? Who was it once gave him a packet of six razor blades for Christmas?

YOUNG CHARLIE: I was broke.

CHARLIE: Yeah, and why? Because you'd bought a pair of nylons for that typist from Cappoquin who let you grope her up against the railings of the Custom House. Six Gillette blades!

DA: Oh, there was great shaving in them blades.

YOUNG CHARLIE: You weren't even here when he died.

CHARLIE: It was sudden.

DA [*rising*]: I think I have one of them still. Hold on.

CHARLIE, YOUNG CHARLIE [*together*]: Sit down.

CHARLIE: It was sudden. I'm not clairvoyant.

YOUNG CHARLIE: You were glad it was sudden, though, weren't you?

CHARLIE: Why not? It's the best way. No pain ...

YOUNG CHARLIE: No pain for you, you mean. No having to go to him and wait and watch him and say things. All the dirty bits over with when you got here.

CHARLIE: Do you think I planned it?

YOUNG CHARLIE: No, but it suited you. Didn't it?

CHARLIE: I was ...

YOUNG CHARLIE: Relieved.

CHARLIE [*nodding*]: Mm.

YOUNG CHARLIE: Look at me, you with your lousy watch. I haven't got a tosser, but at least I've got a few principles. Where's yours?

CHARLIE: Principles? You mean like when you took that job Drumm offered you?

YOUNG CHARLIE: That's a stop-gap.

CHARLIE: I see.

YOUNG CHARLIE: I'll be out of it in a month and doing what I want to.

CHARLIE: A month?

YOUNG CHARLIE: A month!

[DRUMM *appears in the neutral area, a letter in his hand.*]

DRUMM: My friend ... [*As* YOUNG CHARLIE *looks around*] Come in here.

YOUNG CHARLIE: Now what? [*He leaves the kitchen through the fourth wall and goes over to* DRUMM.] Yes, Mr Drumm?

DRUMM: How long have you been employed here?

YOUNG CHARLIE: Thirteen years, Mr Drumm.

DRUMM: In those thirteen years it may not have escaped your notice that there is one filing drawer for names with the initial letter 'M', and another for those which are adorned with the prefix 'Mac', whether written M-a-c, M-c or M-apostrophe. This letter pertains to one James Maguire. I found it, after a forty-minute search, in the 'Mac' drawer. Spell 'Maguire', would you?

CHARLIE, YOUNG CHARLIE [*together*]: M-a-g-u-i-r-e.

DRUMM [*slowly, as if it were a death sentence*]: M-a-g.

YOUNG CHARLIE: I must have –

DRUMM: M-a-g.

YOUNG CHARLIE: Yes.

DRUMM: You will concede that this was incorrectly filed?

YOUNG CHARLIE: Technically, yes ...

DRUMM [*with venom*]: Don't use words you don't know the meaning of. A barely literate child could have filed this letter where it belongs. But not, apparently, a man thirty years of age, with a wife, the beginnings of a family and pretensions towards intellectual superiority.

YOUNG CHARLIE: That has nothing to do with – [*He stops.*]

DRUMM [*dangerously*]: With whom? [*He nods towards the other, unseen members of the staff.*] Get on with your work. [*To* YOUNG CHARLIE] With whom?

YOUNG CHARLIE [*a retreat*]: With this place.

[DRUMM *smiles at him scornfully.*]

DRUMM: File this where it –

YOUNG CHARLIE: Or with you either, Mr Drumm.

DRUMM: Don't get insolent with me, my friend. If you don't like it here, be off with you. No one is holding you. But while you remain you will stay awake and do your work. Accurately. Do you understand?

[YOUNG CHARLIE *holds out his hand for the letter.*]

I asked if you understood.

YOUNG CHARLIE: Yes. [*He takes the letter.*]

DRUMM: We all know that you think your position here is beneath you. But you must try and put up with it and with us, Mr Tynan. Or whatever your name is.

[YOUNG CHARLIE *looks at him, then goes.* DRUMM *remains standing during the following.*]

DA: Oh, Old Drumm is a decent man.

CHARLIE: For years he'd taken me in hand like a Victorian father. He taught me, not by his enthusiasms – he had none – but by his dislikes.

DRUMM: Women, Mr Tynan, should be given a damn good squeeze at the earliest opportunity, and thereafter avoided.

CHARLIE: Perhaps he wanted a son or had a fondness for strays. He made me his confidant.

DRUMM: That man Kelly is known to be a pervert. Shun him. What's more, he spits as he talks. I move away from him, and he follows me and spits on me again.

CHARLIE: One evening, I was in a hurry somewhere – to meet a girl, go to a film: I don't know. I saw him coming towards me. I didn't want to stop and talk, so I crossed over. He'd seen me avoid him. It was that simple. Except at work, he never spoke to me again.

[*The light fades on* DRUMM. DA *gets the razor blade from the bureau.*]

DA: Ah.

CHARLIE: What?

DA: I dunno is this one of the blades you gev me, son.

CHARLIE: Show. [*He sniffs at it.*] A Gillette, definitely. Sheffield, I'd say ... nineteen-forty-three. An impudent blade, sharpish after-taste ... precocious, but not presumptuous. Damn it, I bet this *is* one of them. Anything I ever gave you, you took and wouldn't use. Wouldn't be under a compliment to me.

[DA *slips the blade into* CHARLIE's *pocket.*]

DA: Say nothing ... take them home with you.

CHARLIE: It's a wonder you cashed the cheques I sent you for tobacco.

DA: Certainly I cashed them. Wasn't that how I got thrun out of that home you put me into last January?

CHARLIE: Home? Blast your impudence, that was a private hotel.

DA: Whatever it was.

CHARLIE: I'm telling you what it was. An hotel.

DA [*carelessly*]: Yis.

CHARLIE: Because you'd gone dotty. Shouting out to Ma, who was two years dead. Going around to my cousin Rosie for your Christmas dinner at two in the morning. Do you know how hard it was to get you into that hotel?

DA: Hotel my arse. Sure they wouldn't let me go up to the bank to cash that cheque you sent me. But begod, says I, I'll bate them yet. Do you know what I done?

CHARLIE: I heard.

DA: I got out over the shaggin' wall. And these two big impudent straps of country ones cem after me. 'Come back,' says they. 'Leave go of me,' says I; 'The divil's cure to the pair of yiz.' Then doesn't one of them put her mawsy red hands on me be the collar. 'Be a good boy,' says she to me. Well ... [*He laughs fondly.*] I drew out with me fist and I gev her a poke for herself in the stomach.

CHARLIE: They told me it was on the breast.

DA: It was in the pit of the stomach ... I wouldn't poke a woman in the breast. Yis, I drew out with me fist ...! That wasn't bad for eighty-three, wha'?

CHARLIE: So they threw you out.

DA: And after that you had me put into the Union.

CHARLIE: Into the what?

DA [*ashamed to say it*]: You know ... the ... the ... the poorhouse.

CHARLIE: Oh, you malignant, lop-sided old liar. It was a private room in a psychiatric hospital.

DA: I know, I know.

CHARLIE: A hospital.

DA: Yis.

CHARLIE [*incredulous*]: Poorhouse!

DA: Sure it's greatly improved since I was a young lad. You wouldn't know a bit of it.

CHARLIE [*beginning to shout*]: It was not the p—

DA: I amn't saying a word again' it. Sure hadn't I the best of everything, and wasn't I better off there than I was where you put me before that – in the home?

CHARLIE [*giving up*]: Jesus.

DA: Do you know what I'm going to tell you? If the oul' heart hadn't gone on me the evenin' before last, I'd be alive today.

CHARLIE: Is that so?

DA: It is.

CHARLIE: There are no shallows to which you won't sink, are there?

DA [*proudly*]: There aren't! [*Reminiscent*] I drew out with me fist and I give her a poke. You never seen me when I was riz, did you, son?

CHARLIE: No. [*Then*] Yes ... once.

DA: You did not.

CHARLIE: Nineteen-fifty-one. You were sixty-seven ... She was sixty-three then, and I still don't believe I saw it happen.

[*There is a squeak of the gate and* MOTHER *appears. She is carrying a shopping bag.*]

DA [*looking out*]: There she is at long last. It's gone half-past six; I thought she was run over. [*He opens the door.*

MOTHER *comes in. She is in a good mood, humming to herself.*]

I say, we thought you were under the wheels of a bus. Where were you at all? The boy is home before you, with his stomach roaring for his tea.

MOTHER [*unruffled*]: He'll get it when it's put in front of him, not before. [*She takes off her coat and hangs it up, then puts on her apron.*]

DA [*grumbling*]: We didn't know *what* happened to you. Was the picture any good itself?

MOTHER: It was an old love thing, all divorces and codology. A body couldn't make head or tail of it. Charlie, clear that rubbidge off the table and be a bit of help to me.

[CHARLIE *puts the odds and ends back in the jug.*

MOTHER *begins to lay the table.*]

DA: It's seldom we hear a song out of you.

MOTHER: I ought to cry to suit you.

DA: I'm only saying, any other time the picture is a washout you come home to us raging. [*Pause*] And your horse finished down the field today as well.

MOTHER: Did it? [*Nodding, not caring*] The going was too soft.

[*She goes on with her work, still humming.*

CHARLIE *and* DA *exchange puzzled looks.*]

DA [*curious, fishing*]: I suppose Dun Laoghaire was packed.

MOTHER: Crowds.

DA: Nothing strange or startling, so?

MOTHER [*almost coyly*]: Mm ...

DA: Well, tell us or don't tell us, one or the other.

[MOTHER *turns. She cannot keep her adventure to herself.*]

MOTHER: I was treated to a glass of port in the Royal Marine Hotel.

DA: You were what?

MOTHER: Someone I met in Lipton's.

CHARLIE: The grandeur of you!

DA [*laughing*]: Was he good-looking itself?

MOTHER: It wasn't a 'him' at all – don't be such a jeer. This woman comes up to me. 'Excuse me,' says she, 'for asking. Are you not Margaret Tynan ... Maggie Doyle, that was?' 'I am,' says I; 'Do I know you?' 'You do,' says she.

DA [*in disgust*]: Ah.

MOTHER: Well, to cut a long story, who was she but Gretta Moore out of the Tivoli in Glasthule.

DA: I never heard tell of her.

MOTHER: Ah, Gretta Nolan that married Ernie Moore off of the B and I.

CHARLIE [*remembering*]: Who?

MOTHER: He's retired these two years.

CHARLIE [*it comes to him; singing*]: 'I'm ... Popeye the Sailorman!'

MOTHER: Hold your tongue.

[DA *is staring at her, numbed.*]

So in with the pair of us into the Royal Marine Hotel. Says she to me: 'Sure we're as good as the best of them.' And the style of all the old ones there, with their dyed hair and the fur coats on them. Tea, they were all having, and sweet cake. 'Sure,' says Gretta, 'we can have *that* at home in the house.' [*To* CHARLIE] So this waiter comes up in a swalla-tail coat. Oh, she was well able for him. 'We want two large glasses of port wine,' says she, and off he went like a hare to get them!

DA: Making a show of yourself.

CHARLIE: What show?

DA: High-up people looking at you.

MOTHER [*loftily*]: Pity about them!

DA: The whole town'll have it tomorrow.

CHARLIE [*to* MOTHER]: Then what?

MOTHER: Three shillings for two glasses of port wine you'd be hard put to it to wet your lips with ... and sixpence on top of that for the waiter. Oh, it was scandalous. Says I to her –

DA: Sure Ernie Moore is dead these donkey's years.

MOTHER: What?

DA [*dogged*]: I know he's dead.

MOTHER: How do you know?

DA: I know.

MOTHER: The man's wife says different.

DA: Oh aye, ask me brother am I a liar! Oh, she must be a right good thing. And you're worse. Pouring drink into you in the Royal Marine Hotel, and the crowds of the world looking at you and ... and ... laughing.

CHARLIE: What crowds?

MOTHER: Don't mind him.

DA: And I say he's dead and long dead.

MOTHER: Is he? Well, I'll soon tell you next Thursday whether he's dead or no.

DA: What's next Thursday?

MOTHER [*almost coquettishly*]: I'm invited down for me tea.

DA: Down where, for your tea?

MOTHER: To the Tivoli. [*To* CHARLIE] Gretta was telling me her eldest is beyant in Canada, and she has a grandson nearly your age, and –

DA: Well, you'll go there by yourself if you go, because I'm staying where I am.

MOTHER: You can stay wherever you like, for you weren't invited.

DA: Am I not!

MOTHER: Your own tea will be left here ready for you.

DA: Well, it needn't be, because you're not going.

MOTHER: Why amn't I?

DA: You aren't setting foot outside of here.

MOTHER: You won't stop me.

DA: Will I not!

MOTHER [*her fury mounting*]: You were always the same and you always will be the same. The one time I'm invited to a person's house, you begrudge it to me. [*Beginning to shout*] Well, I'll go *wherever* I like and see *whoever* I like.

DA: Do, and you'll go out of this. I'm the boss in this house and I'll stay the boss in it.

CHARLIE: She's only going for a cup of tea.

DA [*wildly*]: Oh aye ... aye, that's what she'd like us to think. But it's to see him ... *him*.

MOTHER: To see who?

DA: You faggot, you: don't let on you don't know. It's Ernie ... Ernie ... curse-o'-God Ernie! [*His fist crashes on the table*.] May he die roaring for a priest ... curse-o'-God Ernie!

[*Even* MOTHER, *who knows him, is alarmed by the violence of his rage. She stares at him. He strikes the table again.*]

CHARLIE [*remembering*]: And the floorboards barked like dogs, and the cups went mad on their hooks.

DA: You set one foot in the Tivoli, you look crossways at a whoor-master the like of him, and be Jesus, I'll get jail for you, do you hear me? I won't leave a stick or a stone standing in the kip.

MOTHER [*recovering, still a little afraid*]: Look at you ... look at the yellow old face of you.

DA [*savagely, almost skipping with rage*]: With your ... your port wine, and your sweet cake, and your Royal Marine Hotel.

MOTHER: The whole town knows you for a madman ... aye, and all belonging to you.

DA: Ernie ... Ernie! You'll stay clear of him, Thursday and every other day.

MOTHER: Because you know I preferred him over you, and that's what you can't stand. Because I never went with you. Because you know if it wasn't for me father, God forgive him, telling me to –

[DA *makes a violent rush at her, his fist raised.*]

CHARLIE: Hey ...

[DA's *fist comes down and stops, almost touching her face, where it stays, trembling, threatening.*]

MOTHER [*quietly*]: Go on. Go on, do it. And that'll be the first time and the last. I'll leave here if I was to sleep on the footpath.

[*Pause.* DA *starts past her towards the scullery.*]

[*Half to herself*] You went behind my back to him because you knew I wouldn't have you.

[DA *runs to the table and raises a cup as if to dash it to pieces. Instead, he takes his pipe from the table and throws it on the ground. It breaks. He goes into the scullery.* CHARLIE *stoops to pick up the pieces of the pipe as* MOTHER *faces away from him to wipe her eyes.*]

CHARLIE [*still stooping*]: Will you go? On Thursday?

[*She faces him. Although tears are coming, there is a wry, almost mocking attempt at a smile.*]

MOTHER: The jealous old bags.

[*The lights fade. Then we see a woman enter and sit on a rustic seat in the neutral area. She is* MRS PRYNNE, *50, Anglo-Irish accent, dressed for the country.*]

YOUNG CHARLIE [*off, singing: the tune is 'Blaze Away'*]:

'Tight as a drum,
Never been done,
Queen of all the fairies!'

[MRS PRYNNE *opens her eyes. Through the following,* YOUNG CHARLIE *comes on carrying two quart cans.*]

'Bolicky Biddy had only one diddy
To feed the baby on.

Poor little fucker had only one sucker
To grind his teeth up . . .' [*He stops on seeing* MRS PRYNNE.]

MRS PRYNNE: Good evening. Do you know where Tynan is? The gardener.

YOUNG CHARLIE: He's in the greenhouse. Will I tell him you want him?

MRS PRYNNE: If you would.

YOUNG CHARLIE: Sure [*He goes across the stage.*] Da! Hey . . .
    [DA *appears, carrying a basket of tomatoes.*]
  You're wanted.

DA: Who wants me?

YOUNG CHARLIE: I dunno. Posh-looking old one.

DA [*a mild panic*]: It's the mistress. Hold this for me . . . will you hold it! [*He thrusts the basket at* YOUNG CHARLIE *and getting his coat from offstage struggles to put it on.*]

YOUNG CHARLIE: Easy . . . she's not on fire, you know. [*Helping him*] How much do you think?

DA: How much what?

YOUNG CHARLIE: Money.

DA [*confidently*]: I'll get me due. Poor oul' Jacob wouldn't see me stuck, Lord ha' mercy on him . . . no, nor none of us. Says he many's the time: 'Yous'll all be provided for.' The parlourmaid and Cook got their envelopes this morning. [*A sob in his throat*] A decent poor man.

YOUNG CHARLIE: Don't start the waterworks, will you?

DA [*voice breaking*]: God be good to him.

YOUNG CHARLIE: Hey, is it true they bury Quakers standing up?

DA: Jasus, you don't think they do it sitting down, do you? Where's the mistress?

YOUNG CHARLIE: Yours or mine? [*As* DA *looks at him*] By the tennis court. [*He calls after him*] Da . . . how much was the cook left?

DA: A hundred.

YOUNG CHARLIE: Pounds? [*He emits a quiet 'Yeoww!' of pleasure. Exits.*
    DA *makes his way painfully, carrying the basket of tomatoes. He salutes* MRS PRYNNE.]

MRS PRYNNE: Oh, Tynan, isn't this garden beautiful? Mr Prynne and I shall hate not to see it again. I'm sure you'll miss it too. Sit down, Tynan: next to me.

[DA *salutes and sits beside her.*]

We loathe selling 'Enderley', but with my dear father gone and the family with homes of their own, there's no one left to live in it.

DA: I picked you the best of the tomatoes, ma'am.

MRS PRYNNE: Aren't you the great man. We'll take them back to Mountmellick with us in the morning. And the rose-trees.

DA [*authoritative, tapping her knee*]: Yis ... now don't forget: a good pruning as soon as you plant them. Cut the hybrids – the Peer Gynts, the Blue Moons and the Brasilias – cut them well back to two buds from the bottom, and the floribundas to five buds.

MRS PRYNNE: The floribundas to five buds.

DA: The harder you cut, the better the bloom: only don't cut into a stem that's more than a year old.

MRS PRYNNE [*attentive*]: I'll remember.

DA [*slapping her knee*]: I'll make a rose-grower out of you yet, so I will. And feed the buggers well in July, do you hear, if you want a good second blush.

MRS PRYNNE: I do hope they take: my father loved the Enderley roses. Did you hear we have a buyer for the house, Tynan? A schoolteacher and his wife. She owns a fashion business in the city ... I daresay that's where their money is. Catholics, I believe.

DA [*contemptuous*]: Huh!

MRS PRYNNE: I'm sure they'll want a gardener.

DA: Let them. Catholics with money, letting on they're the Quality: sure they're the worst there is. No, I wouldn't work for me own: they'd skin you. The way it is, the legs is gone stiff on me, and the missus says it's time I gev meself a rest.

MRS PRYNNE: What age are you now, Tynan?

DA: I'm sixty-eight, and I'm here since I was fourteen.

MRS PRYNNE: Fifty-four years?

DA: The day yourself was born, the boss called me in. Nineteen-hundred-and-three, it was. 'Take this in your hand, Tynan,' says he to me, 'and drink it.' Begod, I never seen a tumbler of whiskey the size of it. 'And now,' says he, 'go off to hell home for the rest of the day.'

MRS PRYNNE: The world is changing, Tynan, and not for the better. People are growing hard; my father's generation is out of fashion.

[DA*'s eyes are moist again. She takes an envelope from her handbag.* DA *gets to his feet.*]

In his will he asked that Mr Prynne and I should attend to the staff. We think you should have a pension, Tynan: you're entitled to it. We thought twenty-six pounds per annum, payable quarterly.

DA [*saluting automatically*]: Thanks, ma'am; thanks very much.

MRS PRYNNE: Nonsense, you've earned it. Now, the lump sum. Poor Cook is getting on and will have to find a home of her own, so we've treated her as a special case. But I'm sure you and Mrs Tynan won't say no to twenty-five pounds, with our best wishes and compliments.

[DA *takes the envelope and again salutes automatically. He looks at it dumbly.*]

You're a great man for the work, and whatever you may say, we know you wouldn't give it up for diamonds. And there's that boy of yours. Once he leaves school he'll be a great help to you. You did well to adopt him.

DA: The way it is, do you see, the young lad is saving up to get married . . .

MRS PRYNNE: Married?

DA: So we'd think bad of asking him to —

MRS PRYNNE: How old is he?

DA: Sure didn't yourself send him up to get me.

MRS PRYNNE: Was that he? But he's a young man.

DA [*calling*]: Charlie! Come here to me. [*To* MRS PRYNNE] Sure he's working these six years. Only every shilling he earns, do you see, has to be put by. So herself and me, we couldn't ask him to —

MRS PRYNNE: You mustn't encourage him to be selfish. Young people can live on next to nothing.

[*As* YOUNG CHARLIE *arrives*] Hello. How d'you do?

YOUNG CHARLIE: 'Evening.

DA: Shake hands now, son. [*To* MRS PRYNNE] He cem to pick the loganberries. Sure we couldn't leave them to go rotten.

MRS PRYNNE: You are thoughtful. I'll ask Cook to make jam and send it to us in Mountmellick. [*To* YOUNG CHARLIE] I hear you're getting married.

YOUNG CHARLIE: I hope to.

MRS PRYNNE: Well done. But you must look after this old man. Remember how much you owe him, so be good to him, and generous. [*She looks in her handbag and finds a five-pound note.*] Mr Prynne and I would like you to have this. A wedding gift. Perhaps you'll buy something for your new home.

YOUNG CHARLIE: No ... thank you. I –

DA: Yes, he will. Take it.

YOUNG CHARLIE: Well ... [*Taking it*] I'm sure we could do with a Sacred Heart picture for over the bed.

DA [*missing the sarcasm*]: That's the boy!

MRS PRYNNE: I see you've reared an art-lover, Tynan. And now the most important thing. I know my father would want you to have a keepsake ... one of his treasures. [*She picks up a loosely-wrapped package from the seat.*

    DA *and* YOUNG CHARLIE *are intrigued.*]

[*To* YOUNG CHARLIE] Have you travelled?

YOUNG CHARLIE: Not much.

MRS PRYNNE: You must. In these days of aeroplanes, young people have no excuse. When my father was your age he'd been around the world. In nineteen-hundred-and-six he was in San Francisco at the time of the earthquake. That's on the west coast of America, you know.

YOUNG CHARLIE: Yes, I saw the film.

MRS PRYNNE: After the great fire, he was passing a gutted jewellery shop when he saw this, lying on the ground for the taking. A find in a thousand, Tynan. [*She reverently lifts the paper, unveiling a mass of tangled bits of wire mounted on a metal base.*] What do you think of that? Thirty or more pairs of spectacles, fused together by the heat of the fire. [*Pause*] My father had them mounted.

DA: Sure, what else would he do with them?

MRS PRYNNE: Extraordinary, yes?

DA: That's worth having.

MRS PRYNNE: It is, and there you are. [*She gives it to him; then shaking hands*] Goodbye, Tynan. Take care of yourself and we'll call to see you when we're in town. [*To* YOUNG CHARLIE] See that he doesn't overdo things, won't you? Goodbye ... our best to your intended. [*She goes off, taking the various cans with her.*
    DA *salutes her, tears in his eyes.*]

YOUNG CHARLIE: It's a miracle she didn't take the bench. When she said he found it in the ruins of a jeweller's shop, I thought for sure it was the Star of India. Thirty pairs of spectacles.

DA: You hold them: me hands is dirty. Don't drop them.

YOUNG CHARLIE: Don't what?

DA: They're worth money.

YOUNG CHARLIE [*irate*]: Ah, for – What are you bawling for?

DA: A great man, she said I was. Sure I am, too.

YOUNG CHARLIE: How much did you get?

DA: Fifty-four years in the one place. I laid that tennis court ... aye, and rolled it, too.

YOUNG CHARLIE: I don't care if you knitted the net. How much?

DA [*looking up*]: And I planted them trees.

YOUNG CHARLIE [*realizing*]: You've been diddled.

DA: What diddled? Sure she needn't have gev me anything. The work I done, wasn't I paid for it ... every Friday like a clockwork. I got me week off in the summer ...

YOUNG CHARLIE: Give me that. [*He takes the envelope and opens it.*]

DA [*unheeding, ranting away*]: And me two days at Christmas, with an extra pound note put into me fist, and the sup of whiskey poured and waiting for me in the pantry. Wasn't I –

YOUNG CHARLIE [*looking at the cheque*]: Twenty-five?

DA [*snatching it back*]: Don't go tricking with that.

YOUNG CHARLIE: Is that *it*?

DA: Isn't it money for doing bugger-all? And sure haven't I the offer of work from the people that's bought the house.

YOUNG CHARLIE: What work? You're giving it up.

DA: Ah, time enough to give it up when I'm going downhill.

Catholics, yis. They own a dress shop. Sure if your own won't look after you, who will?

YOUNG CHARLIE: My God, she'll kill you.

DA: Who will?

YOUNG CHARLIE: She will, when you bring that home to her. [*Meaning the cheque*] Here, put this with it. [*He offers him the five-pound note.*]

DA: What for?

YOUNG CHARLIE: It'll save you a couple of curses.

DA: Go 'long out of that ... that's for yourself and Polly, to buy the holy picture with. Are you off into town to see her?

YOUNG CHARLIE: Well, I'm not going home, that's for sure. Blast her anyway, and her twenty-five quid and her Californian wire puzzle.

DA: Sure the Quakers was the only ones that was good to us the time of the Famine. Oh, the mistress is a decent skin. [*He laughs.*] 'Tynan,' says she to me, 'aren't you the greatest man that ever trod shoe-leather!' And I planted them hyacinths, too.

[YOUNG CHARLIE *has gone off, taking the parcel with him.*
DA *goes into the house.*]

Mag ... Mag. Do you know what the mistress said to me?

[*Lights up.* CHARLIE, *his glasses on, is writing. The jug, with its contents, is back on the table.*]

CHARLIE: Twenty-five pounds divided by fifty-four. I make it that your gratuity worked out at nine shillings and threepence per year of service. No wonder she didn't talk to you for a week.

DA: Who didn't?

CHARLIE: She didn't.

DA: Are you mad? In fifty-nine years there was never a cross word between us.

CHARLIE: Oh, dear God.

DA: There was not.

CHARLIE: 'Ernie, Ernie, curse-o'-God Ernie!'

DA: Sure I was only letting on I was vexed with her. [*With relish*] Oh, I put a stop to her gallop, her and her ... high tea! Son, do you remember them spectacles from San Francisco?

CHARLIE: Do I?

DA: Herself took them down to the pawn office. 'How much will you give me on these?' says she. 'I'll give you nothing at all on them, ma'am,' says he, 'for they're too valuable for me to keep under this roof.' And you saying I was diddled: you thick, you!

CHARLIE: Where are they?

DA: What?

CHARLIE: The spectacles.

DA [*shiftily*]: I musta lost them.

CHARLIE: Liar. [*Searching*] They're in this house, and if I find them I'll pulp them and bury them. You ignorant, wet, forelock-tugging old crawler. [*Mimicking him*] 'Begod, ma'am, sure after fifty-four years all I needed to be set up for life was a parcel of barbed wire.' And then you put in another four years, toiling for the Catholic but somewhat less than Christian Diors of Grafton Street.

DA: 'Tynan,' says that bitch's ghost to me, and him only a schoolmaster, 'I want more honest endeavour from you and less excuses.' 'Do you see this fist?' says I to him –

CHARLIE [*still searching*]: I asked you where they were.

DA: I disrecall.

CHARLIE: You probably had them buried with you. I can hear St Peter now – 'Hey God, there's an old gobshite at the tradesmen's entrance with thirty pairs of spectacle-frames from the San Francisco earthquake. What'll I tell him?' [*God's voice, with a Jewish accent*] 'Tell him we don't want any.' [*He scoops up the contents of the jug and moves to dump them in the range.*] Mind up: this is the last.

DA [*seizing on an article*]: That pipe is worth keeping.

CHARLIE: It's in bits. You broke it.

DA: Sure a piece of insulating tape would –

CHARLIE: No. Move. [*He goes past* DA *and drops the lot in the range.*]

DA: You could have smoked that, and you'll folly a crow for it yet. What else did you throw out? [*He opens* CHARLIE's *dispatch case and goes through the papers.*]

CHARLIE: At the funeral this morning I heard one of your old cronies muttering what a great character you were and how I'll never be the man me da was.

DA: Don't belittle yourself: yes, you will. What's this?

CHARLIE: Death certificate. Tell me, what was it like?

DA: What?

CHARLIE: Dying.

DA [*offhand*]: Ah, I didn't care for it. [*Peering at a document*] Eighteen-hundred-and-

CHARLIE: ... Eighty-four. Birth certificate.

DA [*annoyed*]: You kept nothing worth keeping at all. There was more to me than this rubbidge. Where's me old IRA service certificate? And the photograph of the tug-o'-war team? I still have the mark under me oxter where the rope sawed into it. And the photo herself and meself had took in the Vale of Avoca.

CHARLIE: I threw them out.

DA: And yourself the day of your first Communion with me beside you.

CHARLIE: I burned them. I don't want them around.

[DA *stares blankly at him.*
CHARLIE *waits, almost daring him to be angry.*]

DA: You wha'?

CHARLIE: I got rid of them. You're gone, now they're gone. So?

DA [*nodding*]: Ah, sure what the hell good were they anyway.

CHARLIE: Eh?

DA: Bits of paper. Sure they only gather dust.

CHARLIE: I burned all that was left of you and you can't even get angry. You were a sheep when you lived: you're still a sheep. 'Yes, sir; no, sir; sir, if you please –'

DA [*chuckling*]: 'Is it up the duck's arse that I shove the green peas?' Oh, that was a good poem. [*Singing*] 'Is it up the –'

CHARLIE: Where's my coat? I'm going to the airport.

DA: Yis. [*Calling*] Mag ... Mag, the lad is off.

CHARLIE: She won't answer you. Goodbye.

[MOTHER *comes in quickly from the scullery. She pays* CHARLIE *no attention.*]

MOTHER [*briskly*]: Where is he? [*Calling upstairs*] Charlie, you'll be late. [*To* DA] Call him.

DA [*yelling*]: You pup, will you come down before the shaggin' aeroplane is off up into the air and you're left standin'!

MOTHER: Charlie!

DA: If he misses that aeroplane they'll be no whoorin' weddin'

Then he'll be nicely destroyed. Jasus, come when you're called!
[YOUNG CHARLIE, *carrying a suitcase, is on the stairs, followed by*
OLIVER.]

MOTHER: That will do. He won't miss it.

YOUNG CHARLIE [*coming in*]: Will you quit roaring. I'm not deaf.

MOTHER: It's the last time you'll have to put up with it, so hold your
tongue. Have you everything?

YOUNG CHARLIE: Yes.

MOTHER: Smarten yourself. Anyone'd think it was Oliver that was
getting married.

OLIVER: Oh, now. Ho-ho. Oh, now.

YOUNG CHARLIE: I left Oliver's wedding present upstairs. Will you
keep it for me?

OLIVER: It's just a bowl to float rose-petals in-you-know. Maybe
your da will give you some of his roses.

DA: I only grow the shaggers. I don't learn 'em to swim.

MOTHER: You're to mind yourself in that aeroplane and bless yourself
when it starts.

YOUNG CHARLIE: Yes.

DA: Oh, Charlie won't crash.

MOTHER [*half snapping*]: No one is saying to the contrary.

DA: Divil a fear of him.

MOTHER [*aggrieved*]: Going off to the other side of the world
to get married.

YOUNG CHARLIE: Five hundred miles ...!

MOTHER: It's far enough. Too far.

YOUNG CHARLIE: It's where she lives.

DA: Oh, Belgium is a great country.

MOTHER: It's little you or I will ever see of it. No matter.

YOUNG CHARLIE [*angrily*]: Don't start. You were both invited –

MOTHER: Oh, aye. Aye, I'm sure we were.

YOUNG CHARLIE [*To* OLIVER]: They damn well were. But no,
it's too far, it's too foreign, his legs won't let him ...

MOTHER: I said it's no matter.

[YOUNG CHARLIE *gives her a hostile look.*]

OLIVER: When he gets time during the honeymoon, Charlie is going
to drop you a line and give me all the details.

[*As they look at him*]
About going in an aeroplane-you-know.
  [*Pause.* YOUNG CHARLIE *is chafing to be off and trying to conceal it.*
  CHARLIE *moves to be near him.*]
MOTHER: You may as well be off, so. There's nothing to keep you.
YOUNG CHARLIE [*protesting*]: I'll be back in a fortnight.
  [*She nods, upset.*]
MOTHER: Please God.
CHARLIE: Now. Goodbye, and out.
YOUNG CHARLIE: Yeah, well, mind yourselves.
MOTHER: You mind yourself. [*She reaches for him blindly.*
  He half-resists the kiss, half-accepts it.
  She steps back and looks at him, eyes large.
  He reaches for his case as DA *comes forward, hand extended.*]
CHARLIE: Hang on . . . one to go.
DA [*shaking hands*]: Good luck now, son. Sure you'll get there in great style. Oh, aeroplanes is all the go these days.
YOUNG CHARLIE: Yeah. 'Bye, now.
DA [*not letting go*]: Have you your tickets?
YOUNG CHARLIE: Yes.
CHARLIE [*to* DA]: Let go.
DA: Have you your passport?
YOUNG CHARLIE: Yes.
CHARLIE: It's the Beast with Five Fingers.
DA: Have you your –
YOUNG CHARLIE: I've got to go. [*He prises his hand free and starts out.*]
MOTHER: Bless yourself!
  [*He dips his fingers in the holy-water font and hurries out.*
  MOTHER *and* DA *come to the door.*
  OLIVER *is caught behind them. He coughs.*]
OLIVER: I'm going with him. As far as the bus-you-know.
YOUNG CHARLIE [*agonized, waiting for him*]: For God's sake.
OLIVER: Well, 'bye-'bye now and sappy days. That's an expression him and me have-you-know. Oh, yes.
YOUNG CHARLIE [*half to himself*]: Oliver!

OLIVER [*turning to wave*]: Cheerio, now.

CHARLIE [*from the house*]: Well, at least wave to them.

[YOUNG CHARLIE *raises a hand without turning and climbs across to an upper level where he rests, waiting for* OLIVER.]

OLIVER: That went well, I thought. I mean, they can get very sentimental-you-know. Often with my mother I can't feel anything because I'm trying to stop *her* from feeling anything. How do *you* feel?

[YOUNG CHARLIE *makes a huge gesture of relief.*]

They're all the same-you-know. I dread the roars of my mother when I get married. She cries even if I go to a late-night dance.

YOUNG CHARLIE: Come on before we meet someone.

OLIVER: Oh-ho. Off to the altar. Can't wait.

YOUNG CHARLIE: Dry up.

OLIVER: The eager bridegroom. Oh, yes.

YOUNG CHARLIE: Well, it's the beginning, isn't it?

[*They go off.*]

MOTHER: Well, that's the end of him. [*She and* DA *return to the kitchen.*]

DA: Still and all, mebbe we ought to have gone, Mag, when we were asked.

[*She gives him a sour look.*]

Sure it'd have been a . . . a . . . a change for us.

MOTHER: I never hindered him. I wasn't going to start now.

DA: What hinderment? Weren't we asked?

MOTHER [*it is not a disparagement, but evasion*]: You'd be a nice article to bring to a foreign country. [*Then*] I think I'll make his bed now and have done with it. [*She goes upstairs. She is in view during part of the following.*]

DA [*laughing, watching her*]: Oh, a comical woman.

CHARLIE: She died an Irishwoman's death, drinking tea.

DA: Do you want a cup?

CHARLIE: No! Two years afterwards, I told a doctor in London about you, on your own and getting senile. I said you'd have to be made to come and live with us. He said: 'Oh, yes. Then he can die among strangers in a hospital in Putney or Wandsworth, with nothing Irish around him except the nurses. But with your luck you'd probably have got Jamaicans.' It's always pleasant to be told what you half-want to hear. So when I came to see you – the last time – there was no talk of your going to London. I was solicitous: asked you how you were managing, were you eating regularly ...

[DA *is in his 80s, stooped and deaf.* CHARLIE's *attituded is paternal.*]

DA: Hoh?

CHARLIE: I said are you eating regularly?

DA: Sure I'm getting fat. I go to Rosie for me tea and Mrs Dunne next door cooks me dinner. Are *you* eating regular.

CHARLIE: She's a widow. I'd watch her.

DA: Hoh?

CHARLIE: I say I'd watch her.

DA: I do.

CHARLIE: You reprobate. Do you need extra cash, for whist drives?

DA: I gave up going. Me hands is too stiff to sort the cards into suits. The last time I went, oul' Drumm was there. Do you remember oul' Drumm?

CHARLIE: Yes.

DA: He accused me of renegin'. 'Why don't you,' says he, 'join the Old People's club and play there?' Says I to him back: 'I would,' says I, 'only I'm too shaggin' old for them!' [*He laughs.*]

CHARLIE: That was good.

DA: Sure I have the garden to do ... fine heads of cabbage that a dog from Dublin never pissed on. I'm kept going. I say I blacked the range yesterday.

CHARLIE: You're a marvel.

DA: I am. How's all the care.

CHARLIE: They're great. Send their love.

DA [*rising*]: I was meaning to ask you ...

CHARLIE: What?

DA [*saluting him*]: I do often see your young one in the town.

CHARLIE: What young one?

DA: Her ... Maggie. Your eldest. 'Clare to God, Mr Doyle, I never seen such shiny bright hair on a girl.

[CHARLIE *stares at him.*

Note: this is not a flashback to DA *as a young man; it is* DA *in his 8os, his mind wandering.*]

Sure she's like a young one out of the story books. The way it is, Mr Doyle, I'm above at Jacob's these six years, since I was fourteen. I have a pound a week and the promise of one of the new dwellin's in the square. I'd think well of marrying her, so I would.

CHARLIE: Da, no, she's —

DA: You can ask anyone in the town about me. And, and, and she wouldn't want for an'thing. The job is safe, we won't go short. I'm learning roses, do you see. To grow them. Oh, yis: Polyanthas and Belles de Crecys and Cornelias and Tuscanys and Amy Robsarts and Janet's Pride and —

CHARLIE: Da, stop.

DA: And, and, and Portlands and Captain John Ingrams and Heidelbergs and Munsters and Shepherdesses and Golden Jewels and Buccaneers and New Dawns and King's Ransoms and —

CHARLIE: Jesus Christ, will you stop. [*In despair*] You old get, what am I going to do with you?

DA: A rainbow of roses. I never seen a young one like her ... so I know you'd think bad of refusing me. [*Looking at* CHARLIE] But sure you wouldn't.

CHARLIE: No.

DA: And you'll put in a good word for me? She wouldn't go again' you.

CHARLIE: I'll talk to her.

DA [*happy now*]: I'm on the pig's back, so. On it for life. Oh, she won't be sorry. [*Looking up at the ceiling*] Mag! Mag, are you up there?

CHARLIE: Da, sh. [*He seats* DA.]

DA [*begins to sing aimlessly*]:

'I've just been down to Monto Town
To see the bould McArdle,
But he wouldn't give me half a crown
To go to the Waxy —'

CHARLIE: Stop it: it's not then any more, it's now. [*Picking up a paper*] See that? Death certificate ... yours.

[DA *nods and straightens up, returning to the present.* CHARLIE *puts the papers back into his dispatch case and closes it.*]

DA: I never carried on the like of that.

CHARLIE: How?

DA: Astray in the head. Thinking it was old God's time and you were herself's da.

CHARLIE: Oh, didn't you!

DA: And you not a bit like him. Begod, I don't wonder at you putting me into the poorhouse.

CHARLIE [*getting annoyed again*]: You useless old man.

[*The gate squeaks.*]

DA: Sure it must have gev you a laugh, anyway.

[CHARLIE *is too angry to speak. He picks up his overcoat.*
DA *moves to assist him.*
DRUMM *appears outside the house carrying a briefcase. He is now 70, still erect.*]

Are you off, so? Well, God send you good weather, son. Tell them I was asking for them.

[DRUMM *knocks at the front door.*]

That must be another Mass card. Do you know, I have enough of them to play whist with.

[*As* CHARLIE *goes to the door*]

Did you see the flowers on me coffin? ... shaggin' weeds, the half of them. [*He sits.*

CHARLIE *opens the door.*]

CHARLIE [*surprised*]: Mr Drumm ...

DRUMM: I'm glad I caught you. Might I have a word?

CHARLIE: Of course ... come in.

[*They go into the kitchen.*]

DA: Oh, old Drumm is not the worst of them.

DRUMM: It's been many years. Will you agree to shake hands? ... it's a bad day for grievances.

[*They do so.*]

There, that's done ... I'm obliged. Mind, I won't say it's generous of you: *I* was the wounded party.

CHARLIE: It was a long time ago.

DRUMM [*good-humoured*]: Don't play word-games with me, my

friend. Time doesn't mitigate an injury; it only helps one to overlook it. [*Indicating a chair*] May I?

CHARLIE: Please.

DRUMM [*sitting*]: Years ago I made a choice. I could have indiscriminate friendships or I could have standards. I chose standards. It's my own misfortune that so few people have come up to them.

CHARLIE: Including me.

DRUMM: You tried. You had your work cut out.

CHARLIE: I had.

DRUMM [*being fair*]: I daresay I was difficult.

CHARLIE: Impossible.

DRUMM [*bridling*]: And you've become impudent.

CHARLIE [*unruffled*]: Yes.

DRUMM: A beggar on horseback.

CHARLIE: It's better than walking.

DA: There was a young fella went to confession. 'Father,' says he, 'I rode a girl from Cork.' 'Yerra, boy,' says the priest, 'sure 'twas better than walking.'

[CHARLIE'*s face twitches.* DRUMM *glares at him.*]

CHARLIE: I hope you're well.

DRUMM: Your hopes are unfounded.

CHARLIE: Oh?

DA: Didn't I tell you he was sick? Sure he has a face on him like a boiled —

CHARLIE [*hastily*]: It's hard to believe. You look well.

[DRUMM *chuckles to himself as if at a private joke. He leans confidentially towards* CHARLIE.]

DRUMM: I have this ... tummy trouble. I told a certain person — I don't know why, out of mischief, it isn't like me — I told him cancer was suspected. Quite untrue. Of course he told others, and since then my popularity has soared. I said to one man: 'I know you for a rogue and a blackguard.' Was he offended? 'You're right,' he said; 'come and have a drink.' [*With defiant pleasure*] I did.

CHARLIE: There'll be ructions when you don't die.

DRUMM: There will.

CHARLIE: False pretences.

DRUMM: Pity about them.

CHARLIE: Still ...

DRUMM: They shun a man because he's intelligent, but get maudlin over a few supposedly malignant body-cells. I'm as bad. Ten years ago I wouldn't have given one of them the time of day, still less have taken pleasure in their approbation.

CHARLIE: Do you?

DRUMM: People like them, like the old man – your foster-father – they thank God for a fine day and stay diplomatically silent when it rains. They deride whatever is beyond them with a laugh, a platitude and a spit. They say: 'How could he be a dental surgeon? – his father was warned by the police for molesting women.'

DA: Who would that be? Old Martin Conheedy used to tamper with women. Is his son a dentist now?

DRUMM [*answering* CHARLIE*'s question*]: They ... amuse me.

DA [*derisive*]: Who'd trust that fella to pull a tooth?

DRUMM [*picking up his briefcase*]: When the old man was in hospital he sent word that he wanted to see me.

CHARLIE: My father?

DRUMM: Who lived here.

CHARLIE [*persisting*]: My father.

DRUMM [*letting it pass*]: He asked my advice. I told him that not being related by blood you would have no natural claim on his estate.

CHARLIE: What estate? He had nothing.

DRUMM: At his request I wrote out a will for him then and there. He signed it and I had it witnessed. [*He takes an envelope and hands it to* CHARLIE.] It'll stand up with the best of them.

CHARLIE: But he had bugger-all.

DRUMM: There was also the matter of an heirloom which he gave into my keeping.

CHARLIE: Heirloom?

[DRUMM *dips into his briefcase and takes out a familiar-looking brown-paper parcel.*]

DA [*jovially*]: There now's a surprise for you.

CHARLIE [*staring at the parcel*]: No ...

DA [*crowing*]: You won't guess what's in that!

DRUMM: He said it was valuable, so I asked my bank manager to keep it in his vault.

CHARLIE [*under stress*]: *That* was in a bank vault?

DRUMM: I can see that the value was also sentimental. [*Rising*] Well, I'm glad to have discharged my trust.

CHARLIE: Thank you. [*Looking at the parcel*] His estate.

DRUMM: Oh, no. Whatever that is, it has nothing to do with what's in the will. And I'd be careful with that envelope. There's money involved!

CHARLIE: Money?

DRUMM: He mentioned the sum of a hundred and thirty-five pounds, with more to come.

CHARLIE: He never had that much in his life.

DRUMM: He thought otherwise.

CHARLIE: He was raving. I *know*. All he had was his pension and the cheques I sent him for − [*He breaks off and looks around at* DA.]

DA [*strategically*]: That dog from next door is in the garden. Hoosh ... hoosh, you bastard.

[CHARLIE *watches him murderously as he beats a retreat into the scullery*.]

DRUMM [*waiting for* CHARLIE *to finish*]: Yes?

CHARLIE: I was wrong. I've remembered where it came from.

DRUMM: The money?

CHARLIE: Yes.

DRUMM: I imagined it was hard-earned.

CHARLIE [*grimly*]: It was.

DRUMM [*sternly*]: Now, my friend, no caterwauling. To whom else could he leave it? I once called him an ignorant man. I still do. And yet he may have been better off. Everything I once thought I knew for certain I have seen inverted, revised, disproved, or discredited. Shall I tell you something? In seventy years the one surviving fragment of my knowledge, the only indisputable poor particle of certainty in my entire life, is that in a public house lavatory incoming traffic has the right of way. [*Acidly*] It isn't much to take with one, is it?

CHARLIE [*smiling*]: Well, now *I* know something.

DRUMM: I have always avoided him and his kind, and yet in the end we fetch up against the self-same door. I find that aggravating. [*Moving towards the door*] The old couple, had they children of their own?

CHARLIE: I was told once there were several. All still-born.

DRUMM: He didn't even create life – at least I have the edge on him there.

CHARLIE: How are the two Rhode Island Reds?

DRUMM: Moulting. [*He offers his hand.*] It was pleasant to see you. I enjoyed it. Goodbye.

CHARLIE: Mr Drumm, he never took anything from me, he wouldn't let me help him, what I offered him he kept and wouldn't use. Why?

DRUMM: Don't you know?

CHARLIE: Do *you*?

DRUMM: The Irish national disease.

CHARLIE: Bad manners?

DRUMM: Worse, no manners. [*He holds out his hand, inspecting the sky for rain, then goes.*

CHARLIE *closes the door, returns to the kitchen.*]

CHARLIE: Where are you? [*Yelling*] Come ... in ... here!

[DA *comes in.*]

DA: Do you want a cup of tea?

CHARLIE: You old shite. You wouldn't even use the money.

DA: I did.

CHARLIE: How?

DA: Wasn't it something to leave you?

CHARLIE: I'll never forgive you for this.

DA [*not worried*]: Ah, you will.

CHARLIE: Since I was born. 'Here's sixpence for the chairoplanes, a shilling for the pictures, a new suit for the job. Here's a life.' When did I ever get a chance to pay it back, to get out from under, to be quit of you? You wouldn't come to us in London; you'd rather be the brave old warrior, soldiering on.

DA: And wasn't I?

CHARLIE: While I was the ingrate. The only currency you'd take, you knew I wouldn't pay. Well, I've news for you, mate. You had your chance. The debt is cancelled, welshed on. [*Tapping his head*]

I'm turfing you out. Of here. See that? [*He tears the black armband from his overcoat and drops it in the range.*] And this? [*He holds up the parcel containing the spectacle frames.*]

DA: You wouldn't. Not at all.

CHARLIE: Wouldn't I? You think not? [*He bends and crushes the frames through the paper with increasing violence.*]

DA: Ah, son ...

CHARLIE: San Francisco earthquake!

DA: You'd want to mind your hand with them –

CHARLIE [*cutting his finger*]: Shit.

DA: I told you you'd cut yourself.

[CHARLIE *gives him a malevolent look and very deliberately shoves the parcel into the range. He sucks his hand.*]

CHARLIE: Now wouldn't I?

DA: Is it deep? That's the kind of cut 'ud give you lockjaw. I'd mind that.

CHARLIE: Gone ... and you with it.

DA: Yis. [*Taking out a dirty handkerchief*] Here, tie this around it.

CHARLIE: Get away from me. Ignorant man, ignorant life!

DA: What are you talking about, or do you know what you're talking about? Sure I enjoyed meself. And in the wind-up I didn't die with the arse out of me trousers like the rest of them – I left money!

CHARLIE: *My* money.

DA: Jasus, didn't you get it back? And looka ... if I wouldn't go to England with you before, sure I'll make it up to you. I will now.

CHARLIE: You what? Like hell you will.

DA: Sure you can't get rid of a bad thing.

CHARLIE: Can't I? You watch me. You watch!

[*He picks up his case, walks out of the house and closes the front door. He locks the door and hurls the key from him. A sigh of relief. He turns to go, to find DA has walked out through the fourth wall.*]

DA: Are we off, so? It's starting to rain. The angels must be peein' again.

CHARLIE: Don't you dare follow me. You're dead ... get off.

DA: Sure Noah's flood was only a shower. [*Following him*] Left ...
   left ... I had a good job and I left, right, left!
CHARLIE: Hump off. Get away. Shoo. I don't want you.
   [*He goes to the upper level.*
   DA *follows, lagging behind.*]
DA: Go on, go on. I'll keep up with you.
   [CHARLIE *stops at the top level.*]
CHARLIE: Leave me alone.
   [CHARLIE *slowly walks down as* DA *follows, singing.*]
DA [*singing*]:
   'Oh, says your oul' one to my oul' one:
   "Will you come to the Waxy Dargle?"
   And says my oul' one to your oul' one:
   "Sure I haven't got a farthin'."'

[*Curtain*]

A LIFE

IN MEMORIAM: JOHN T. MULLIGAN

This play was first produced at the Abbey Theatre, Dublin, for the Dublin Theatre Festival, on 4 October 1979, with the following cast:

DRUMM	CYRIL CUSACK
DOLLY	DAPHNE CARROLL
MARY	MAUREEN TOAL
MIBS	DEARBHLA MOLLOY
DESMOND	GARRETT KEOGH
LAR	STEPHEN BRENNAN
KEARNS	PHILLIP O'FLYNN
DOROTHY	INGRID CRAIGIE

CHARACTERS

DRUMM   DESMOND

DOLLY   LAR

MARY   KEARNS

MIBS   DOROTHY

The play is set in a house and a park in a small town just south of Dublin.

ACT ONE

Darkness. Then lights come up on a stone bandstand at stage centre. It is octagonal in shape, and although the roof is long gone the supporting pillars of curved Victorian iron remain. A short flight of stone steps leads down to stage level. The stage areas to left and right of the bandstand are in darkness.

DRUMM *is standing on the bandstand. He is wearing a fawn-coloured raincoat. He refreshes his memory by glancing at his notes, then puts them away. He addresses an unseen audience.*

DRUMM: To conclude. I have chosen to terminate today's walk in this park which is remarkable for its views of sea and mountains, such as may have inspired Bernard Shaw's observation that whereas Ireland's men are temporal, her hills are eternal. Any child familiar with the rudiments of geology could have told him otherwise, but then even Shaw was not immune to his countrymen's passion for inexactitude. These few acres have more than a scenic claim on our attention. This hillside is all that remains of what was called the Commons of Dalkey. Where the town – I speak in the Catholic sense: the Protestants call it a village – where it now stands there was once only gorseland and furze, moorland and wretched cabins. The coming of the railway in 1834 turned the wilderness into a place of habitation for the well-to-do, who were closely followed by tradespeople and members of the middle classes who knew their place and on that account lost no time in leaving it. The town evolved, grew and procreated, as our presence in it bears witness. Its population is four thousand, seven hundred, which figure can by simple division be broken down into nearly six hundred persons per public house. It was known to antiquity as the Town of the Seven Castles, of which the surviving two are vermin-infested, one being in ruins and the other the town hall. [*A thin smile,*

which disappears when there is no response to his joke.] The climate
is temperate, the birthrate relentless and the mortal – [*He hesitates.*]
... the mortality rate is consistent with the national average. I see
that some of you become restive. [*He looks at his watch.*] And,
coincidentally, the licensing laws are about to be in our favour. I
thank you for your attention. The next of the conducted walks so
ingeniously entitled 'Dalkey Discovered' will take place four weeks
from today, on Sunday, June 16th. Your guide will be Mrs Rachel
Fogarty. Good day.

> [*There is a thin spatter of applause, which suggest that his audience
> has been a thin one. He watches them leave, then takes a tube of Milk
> of Magnesia tablets from his pocket and puts one in his mouth. He sits
> on the steps of the bandstand and takes out a packet of Sweet Afton.
> With the cigarette halfway to his lips, he sits absolutely still as if a
> realization had suddenly come to him. A woman appears. She is his
> wife,* DOLLY, *aged 60.*]

DOLLY [*approaching*]: Woo-ee! Dezzie!

> [DRUMM's *only reaction is to complete the business of lighting his
> cigarette.*]

I came to meet you.

DRUMM [*not pleased*]: Did you?

DOLLY: I climbed over the very tip-top and down the rocks. Amn't
I great? [*Catching her breath*] Whoo ... It's so steep, I thought to
myself, God send I don't burst into a run and can't stop.

DRUMM: It would have enlivened my lecture.

DOLLY: I saw you from the top, talking sixteen to the dozen, only
I couldn't hear and I didn't want to come down and make you
nervous, so I waited. Was it a nice walk, what way did you go,
what did you say to them?

DRUMM: You are the only woman I know who can talk while
breathless.

DOLLY: I was dying to hear. Were they thrilled to bits?

DRUMM: They managed not to disintegrate. I spoke well. I think I
did. It's unimportant.

> [DOLLY *has a natural gaiety, under which is a terror of his dis-
> pleasure. She seizes at any opportunity of staying in his good graces.*]

DOLLY: Do you hear him! Where'd you walk them to?

DRUMM: To here.

DOLLY: You're mean. No, tell us.

DRUMM [*with a sigh, as if to say 'If I must'*]: Along the Metals by the old Atmospheric Railway, around the hill, along the Green Road to the broken cross and from there to the old semaphore station, which, thanks to my sense of smell, I kept them from entering. Then to Torca Cottage, and here by way of the Cat's Ladder and the Ramparts.

DOLLY: Such a distance.

DRUMM [*with satisfaction*]: I think I may say that I lost one or two of them en route.

DOLLY: And you made a lovely speech.

DRUMM: Not a speech: I gave a talk.

DOLLY: And it's not everyone they ask. They're most particular.
     [*He looks at her coldly.*]
And if they didn't ask you itself, a pity about them. What are they, only from the town.

DRUMM: Why did you come here?

DOLLY: To meet you.

DRUMM: I'm aware of that. I asked why.

DOLLY: I got tired of the four walls for company. [*Aware that he is looking at her*] The sun was splitting the trees out. You told me where you'd be finishing up, and I said why don't I give myself an outing and the pair of us can walk home.

DRUMM: So you went crawling through the gorse like a decrepit sheep.
     [*She has no ready answer. Pause.*]

DOLLY: You put me in mind of an old statue.

DRUMM: What?

DOLLY: When I was coming down. You were sitting with the cigarette halfway to your mouth and not a jig out of you. No more life than an old statue.

DRUMM: I was admiring the view.

DOLLY: No, you weren't. Like a statue by that French artist.

DRUMM: Not artist. Sculptor.

DOLLY: Mm, by him ... what's-his-name.

DRUMM [*deliberately*]: Renoir.

DOLLY: Mm. [*A pause*] And I'm not a sheep, Dezzie.

DRUMM: Quite so.

DOLLY: Or decrepit, either.

DRUMM: To be sure.

DOLLY: I know it's only your way and you mean nothing by it, but other people don't know that, and it's not very –

DRUMM: Could we have done?

DOLLY: ... very gentlemanly.

[*He looks at the view as if she were not there.*]

Are you not going to tell me what Ben said?

DRUMM: Who?

DOLLY: Ben Mulhall. I know you were in with him because I met Maddie Dowling in the chapel yard and she said she saw you coming out of his front gate.

DRUMM: So that's why.

DOLLY: Why what?

[*He does not answer: it is as if a reply would be beneath contempt.*]

I thought maybe he'd had news for you.

DRUMM [*affirmative*]: Mm.

DOLLY: Had he?

DRUMM: We met in the street. I asked him if he had had the results of the X-rays. He took me into his surgery: I think that being in it reassures him that he's a doctor. He gave me one of those looks of his, redolent of the cemetery, and said that I should buy day returns from now on instead of season tickets.

DOLLY: Oh, Dezzie ...

DRUMM [*annoyed*]: He was being fatuous. Do you think he'd make jokes in the face of having his practice diminished by another patient? After he had used up his small reservoir of wit he condescended to get to the point. My own diagnosis was correct: I have a duodenal ulcer. He is to give me a diet sheet and a prescription, and he said that I am to watch myself. I told him that my name was Drumm, not Narcissus. [*As she looks at him blankly*] Of course it was lost on him, too.

DOLLY: You won't have to go into – I mean, to be –

DRUMM: Certainly not. Only a fool donates his body to science *before* death. Mulhall said that I am to drink milk instead of tea

or coffee. Then senility overcame him and he began to babble about
my giving up whiskey as well. An ulcer: one lives with it, but at
least one lives.

[DOLLY *turns her head away and searches in her bag for a hand-*
kerchief.]

Now what?

DOLLY: Nothing.

DRUMM: Not tears.

DOLLY: I'm grand.

DRUMM: Are you so disappointed?

DOLLY: Over what? [*Taking his meaning, reproachfully*] I'm relieved.

DRUMM: Oh, yes?

DOLLY: That's a terrible thing to –

DRUMM: Lower your voice.

DOLLY: Making out I was disapp—

DRUMM: This is a public place. You are incapable of recognizing a
joke when you hear it.

DOLLY: It wasn't a –

[*He silences her with a look.*]

I was worried sick.

DRUMM: I didn't notice.

DOLLY: I wasn't going to let on to you, was I? But let's face it,
Dezzie, we're not youngsters, and when you get to be our age –

DRUMM: Don't bracket our ages.

DOLLY: It's just the sort of thing that happens when you think at long
last you're grand and clear and have the chance to enjoy life. Do
you know what I said? I said: Ah no, God, not now, not when
he'll be finished with the office in August and we can have our
holiday and a rest and get the little car and –

[*She stops, dismayed that she has said more than she ought.*
Pause. He waits until she tries to disentangle herself.]

I mean –

DRUMM: What little car?

DOLLY: If you owned up to it, you were as worried as I was.

DRUMM: You said a car.

DOLLY: When? [*As he draws in his breath; deprecatingly*] A small one.

DRUMM: Do you mean a motor car?

DOLLY: They're all the go.

DRUMM: All the . . . ?

[*She giggles nervously at the accidental pun.*]

DOLLY: Amn't I a panic.

DRUMM: What new foolishness is this?

DOLLY: We could afford it. You'll have your lump sum. [*Weakly*] It'd be nice.

DRUMM: How long has this been fermenting inside that brain of yours? A car. To be driven by whom, may I ask?

DOLLY: You could go for lessons.

DRUMM: You think so?

DOLLY: An ulcer wouldn't hinder you.

DRUMM: I daresay.

DOLLY: The Moroneys bought themselves one, and he gets black-outs.

DRUMM: And have you yet decided where we'll go in it, in this small car?

DOLLY: For . . . drives.

DRUMM [*without intonation*]: Drives.

DOLLY: And we could visit people. Friends.

DRUMM: Such as whom?

DOLLY [*vaguely*]: You know.

DRUMM: Friends, you said. Who?

DOLLY: New friends.

[*He decides that he has heard enough. He brushes down his coat and buttons it.*]

Don't be cross, Dezzie. I thought it'd be an interest for you.

DRUMM: I'm not at all cross, and it is of no interest either to me or for me. You take too much on yourself. Without consulting me, you sit weaving your little webs, letting your imagination run riot. And then, when I speak to you with the voice of reason, you come crashing to earth. You do yourself no kindness at all. Look here: don't you think there are enough fools and blackguards walking about on two legs without my having to contend with those in motor cars as well? Driving lessons, indeed.

DOLLY: If you don't want to learn, maybe I could.

DRUMM [*not unkindly*]: Have sense. The entire population would take to the fields. [*He looks at his watch.*] A quarter to. Go, now: off home with you.

DOLLY: I thought the pair of us could –

DRUMM: ... walk home. You said. I have a call to make.

DOLLY: Where?

[*He gives her one of his looks, as if she should know better by now than to pry.*]

I mean, I put the leg of lamb on for two o'clock. You won't be late?

DRUMM: Have I ever been late?

DOLLY: No, Dezzie.

DRUMM: No, never. Off you go, then.

DOLLY: Well, don't be –

[*She checks herself and sets off. He watches until she is out of sight, then goes towards the area at stage right, perhaps disappearing from view for a moment.*

Lights come up at stage right on the living room of a small red-bricked Edwardian house of the kind with a pocket-handkerchief garden in front. The room is neat and homely. It is newly decorated, and some of the furniture – perhaps the three-piece suite – is new as well. There is a television set and an electric fire with imitation logs.

MARY KEARNS *comes in. She is of an age with* DOLLY. *She is followed by* DRUMM.]

MARY: What is it they say? The dead arose and appeared to many. Come in.

DRUMM: If you're sure I'm welcome.

MARY: That's the last thing I'm sure of.

[*He stops in his tracks, affronted.*]

[*confused*] I dunno whether you are or not.

DRUMM: If you'd prefer I hadn't called ...

MARY: I'll tell you that when I hear what brought you. [*Looking at him*] The same old face on you. A body daren't look crossways at you.

DRUMM: You're in an aggressive mood.

MARY: I'm surprised, do you mind?

DRUMM [*reasonably*]: I daresay it would be surprising if you weren't. Perhaps this isn't convenient.

MARY: Ah, don't be such a dry stick.

DRUMM: I could call another time.

MARY: Aye, in another six years. Will you take that raincoat off you and sit. Wrapped up like an old mummy in the month of May.

DRUMM: A prudent man waits until June.

MARY: And one day you ought to go demented and buy yourself a new one. Give it me.

DRUMM [*removing his coat*]: Is he in?

MARY: Is who in?

DRUMM: Your husband.

MARY: In or out, he has a name.

DRUMM: Yes. Is he here?

[*She snatches the coat and bunches up her fist in exasperation, shoving it up to his face.*]

MARY: I'll do it yet, you see if I don't. He's at the – [*Taking care to mention the name*] Lar is at Finnegan's, having his pint.

DRUMM [*smiling sceptically*]: Pint, singular.

[*She does not deign to answer, but puts his coat away. We notice for the first time that she limps slightly.*]

Are you well?

MARY: The way you see me.

DRUMM: Fully recovered, I meant. The accident.

MARY: You're behind the times. I'm over that this long while.

DRUMM: I was concerned.

MARY: I know: I got your letter. I was suprised there wasn't a 'Mise, le meas' at the end of it. [*Regretting this*] And you sent Dolly to see me. It was nice of you.

DRUMM [*reasonably*]: You'd been injured.

MARY: I do often say to Lar, I was such a good patient they put a barometer inside my leg for a present. It gives me the weather forecast.

DRUMM: The limp is hardly noticeable. Does it trouble you?

MARY: Only when people mention it.

DRUMM: You look very well indeed. Hardly a day older.

MARY: Since when? Yesterday?

DRUMM: I mean, since we –

MARY: You go past me every day in the town. I might as well be a midge in the air or a pane of glass a body'd look through. If you see me in time, you go across the street, and if you don't you put that face on you as if there was a dead dog in the road. Making a show of yourself and of me as well.

DRUMM: We weren't on speaking terms.

MARY: And don't I know it!

DRUMM: I am not a hypocrite. I will not affect a pretence of goodwill simply for the benefit of every prying cornerboy and twitching lace curtain in the street.

MARY: A nod wouldn't have killed you.

DRUMM: You'd prefer me to be dishonest?

MARY: Be whatever you like. You're a bitter old pill, and you always will be.

DRUMM [*smiling tolerantly*]: I have never yet met the member of your sex who didn't prefer common abuse to common sense.

MARY: Did you come in here to vex me?

DRUMM: No, I did not, and your point is well taken. Whatever bitterness has been between us is in the past.

MARY [*ominously*]: It's where?

DRUMM: I thought it was time we were friends again.

MARY: Is that what brung you?

DRUMM [*gently*]: Brought me.

MARY: Brought you.

DRUMM: At our age, there aren't so many days left that one can afford to squander them in quarrels.

MARY: Life's too short.

DRUMM: Exactly.

MARY: That's the bee in your bonnet, is it? And so you walk in here, calm as you like after six years, expecting the welcome mat and to be offered rashers and eggs.

[*He makes no reply.*]

Do you want a cup of tea?

DRUMM: No, thank you.

MARY: There's a drop of whiskey.

DRUMM [*considering*]: Ah. Well, in that case I won't give offence, as they say, with a refusal.

[*She goes to the sideboard.*]

The merest tincture. It'll sharpen the appetite. Dolly is doing us a leg of lamb.

MARY: How is she?

DRUMM: Unchanged.

MARY: This is a sudden notion of yours.

DRUMM: Pardon me?

MARY: To make up.

DRUMM: I had some news this morning to do with health. Good news. [*As she glances at him*] I wasn't ill, but there was the possibility. A cloud threatening the autumn day.

MARY: And it's gone now?

DRUMM: A passing shower.

MARY: So you feel full of yourself.

DRUMM: That, too, perhaps. But it brought it home to me that one's time is finite. If instead of cracking his execrable jokes Ben Mulhall had offered me that whiskey and if his eyes had avoided mine –

MARY: What was it that ailed you?

DRUMM: Tummy trouble. And if these antennae and these [*He gestures towards his eyes and ears.*] had detected a verdict of another kind, well, I would have lived to reg— [*He amends, smiling*] I would have regretted those six years.

MARY: Will you pour this? I never know how much. [*She gives him the bottle and a glass.*] Six years? Did you ever add up all the time we haven't been talking since I knew you? How many years out of the forty? You're an Irish summer of a man: sunny skies one day and rain the next. For a week or maybe a month you'd be the height of company: you'd make a cat laugh; next thing, there's a face on you like a plateful of mortal sins and you're off out that door as if there was a curtain rod stuck up you. You can get on with no one: a cup of cold water would disagree with you.

DRUMM: You say that, but in your heart you know that I am the most reasonable man in this town.

MARY: Drink your drink.

DRUMM: As well as being a person of principle.

MARY: Oh, I know that: no need to tell me. You won't be ten
minutes in heaven before you're not talking to God. [*In wry despair*]
I dunno what to do with you.

DRUMM [*raising his glass*]: To both of us.

MARY: Until the next time.

DRUMM: No, no: I promise. I will never again allow you to provoke
me.

[*He drinks. She opens her mouth to make an angry retort, then gives
him up as hopeless.*]

An Irishman's claret: no finer drink.

MARY: You haven't noticed my room.

DRUMM: Haven't I? [*Looking about him*] Oh, yes.

MARY: We did it up with the compensation.

DRUMM: It has taste.

MARY: And got the few new bits of furniture.

DRUMM: I approve.

MARY: High time, says you.

DRUMM: I don't say. I felt always at home here

MARY: It was too dark. The old people, them that's dead and
gone, they went in for that: no sunlight, everything morose and
dusty. I thought we'd get into the fashion.

DRUMM: You did.

MARY: We never set foot in here except for Christmas and funerals.
That was the style in them days: one room for living in and
another that was a museum for cracked cups. The Room, we called
it. 'Who's that at the door?' 'Father Creedon.' 'Bring him into the
Room.'

DRUMM [*smiling*]: Yes.

MARY: I made a clearance. It's queer. The furniture was easy got
rid of: out the door and that was that. But the smell of beeswax
and the lavender bags my mother filled the house with: nothing'll
budge that, it'll bury all of us. Still, we use the room now, by
me song we do. And I had the kitchen done up as well. Do you
remember how it was?

DRUMM: I know how it was.

MARY: See if you recognize it. Come on.

[*They start out of the room.*]

Do you remember the old range and the dresser and the one tap over the sink?

DRUMM [*humouring her*]: Not all gone?

MARY [*pleased with herself*]: You'll see. In you go.

[*During this, they cross into the area at the left, passing the foot of the steps as if walking across a hallway. As they enter this area lights come up. We are looking at the kitchen of forty years ago, with the dresser, the range and the cold-water earthenware sink as mentioned by* MARY.

At the kitchen table are MIBS *and* DESMOND, *who watches as she reads silently from a book, her lips moving. There are exercise books and pen and ink.*

DRUMM *looks at the young* MIBS *as* MARY *talks artlessly about the room as it is now.*]

What do you think of it? Mr Comerford put in the kitchen unit and the shelves, but they had a fierce job with the new sink and the hot-and-cold, and as for the washing machine, don't talk to me. Anyhow, with that done I thought I might as well be the divil for style and break the bank altogether, so I got the new table and chairs.

DRUMM [*only half paying attention, looking at* MIBS]: You've done wonders.

MARY: At our age, what harm in a bit of comfort?

DRUMM: None.

MARY: If we don't spoil ourselves, no one else will. [*Prompting him*] So what do you think?

[DRUMM, *standing behind* MIBS, *touches her hair.*]

MIBS: Stop that.

DESMOND: Sorry.

MARY: Do you like it?

DRUMM: I'm sorry. It shines. What's that odious new word, that jargon they're so fond of? Functional. It functions.

MARY [*flatly*]: I see.

DRUMM: I meant that the word was odious, not the room.

MARY [*coldly*]: Yes, I know.

DRUMM: Once it was for living in, now you cook in it and wash clothes. It suits its purpose. Formica surfaces, a refrigerator, yellow cupboards —

MARY [*almost snapping*]: They're primrose.

DRUMM: Are they? [*With false enthusiasm*] So they are.

MARY: I'm sure you're interested.

DRUMM: Mary, you must never ask a man to give you an opinion of a kitchen. Dolly now would be over the moon about it.

MARY: Dolly has taste. You left your drink. [*Still mildly affronted, she leads the way back to the living room.*]

DRUMM: It's become a new house. What it cost you, I —

MIBS [*pushing her book aside*]: I can't make head or tail of it.

[DRUMM, *on the point of leaving, looks back at her.*]

DESMOND: It's simple.

MIBS: To them with brains.

DESMOND: Show me.

[DRUMM *follows* MARY *into the living room.*]

MIBS: This bit. [*Reading*] 'My friends, we will not go again ...'

DESMOND: '... or ape an ancient rage,

Or stretch the folly of our youth to be the shame of age.'

MIBS: What's it mean?

DESMOND: 'Ape an ancient rage.' The writer — Chesterton — what he's saying is that it's only natural for young people to be wild and passionate. [*Almost blushing*] Angry, that is. And no one minds foolishness, because it's too soon yet for them to be wise.

MIBS: But *you* are.

DESMOND: No. I'm intelligent: there's a difference. But an elderly person who behaves as if he were still young: that's ... well, it's not nice to see.

MIBS: That's what this means?

DESMOND: Mm.

MIBS: Pity he didn't say so, then. No it's me: I'm thick.

DESMOND: Never.

MIBS: Behind the door when the brains were handed out. Is that why you don't see old people kissing and stuff?

DESMOND: Well, what Chesterton was —

MIBS: I mean, is it because they don't like to be seen doing it, or because they're old and don't feel like doing it?

DESMOND [*embarrassed*]: Well, a mixture, I'd say.

MIBS: Imagine being kissed by someone who's all wrinkled and gubby. [*She thinks about it and shudders.*] Eeagh!

DESMOND [*picking up the book*]: The next line –

MIBS: And anyway, kissing is one thing, but whether they want to or not, they can't ... you know.

DESMOND: What?

MIBS: Do anything. They're not able.

[*He conceals his discomfiture by staring into the book.*]

At least the man isn't. The woman doesn't have to do a hand's turn: she has it easy. [*She giggles.*] It's a tough old station for fellows, isn't it? You start off in life by not being able to, and you end up by not being able to. It's a panic. [*Noticing him*] You're going red.

DESMOND: No such thing.

MIBS: Y'are so, you're on fire. [*Teasing him*] Answer this and answer true: will you love me when I'm old and grey?

DESMOND: Yes. Yes, I will.

[*He replies so gravely and with such directness that it is her turn to be taken off-balance.*]

MIBS [*deciding to make light of it*]: Is that a fact?

DESMOND: I've said so.

MIBS: Honest to God, like? No, tell us.

[*He is silent, not knowing how to rise to her tone.*]

You'd want to watch out I might believe you. [*Affectionately*] Chancer. You are: you're a fierce chancer, you know that?

DESMOND [*returning to his book*]: We ought to get on with this. [*He reads*] 'My friend, we will not go again or ape an ancient rage ...'

MIBS: Ah, quit it. My brains are in bits.

DESMOND: We're nearly done. Four more lines.

MIBS: Let me off them.

DESMOND: Two minutes.

MIBS: You will: you can't refuse me. [*She makes to put the book to one side.*]

DESMOND: Don't do that.

MIBS: I'll give you a kiss.

DESMOND: No.

MIBS: What?

DESMOND: I said no.

MIBS: And that's the fellow that lets on he loves me.

DESMOND: I don't buy affection, thank you.

MIBS [*mimicking him*]: 'I don't buy affection, thank you.' God, talk about a dry old stick. Do you know what they call you in the town? Do you know their nickname for you?

DESMOND: Because you can't have your own way –

MIBS: Mammy Cough-Bottle. It suits you.

DESMOND: 'Or stretch the folly of our youth to be the shame of age …

But walk with clearer eyes and ears this path that wandereth,

And see undrugg'd in evening light the decent inn of death.'

MIBS: Mammy Cough-Bottle.

DESMOND: Chesterton saw death as a country inn.

MIBS: Did he.

DESMOND: A place of shelter.

MIBS: Wasn't he great.

DESMOND: He employs a metaphor.

MIBS: What night's her night off?

[*He slams the book down with just enough force to make her jump in spite of herself. A moment's pause.*]

Don't do a sulk.

DESMOND: You'll fail that exam.

MIBS: There's a blue moon out: we agree at last!

DESMOND: And you could pass it.

MIBS: No bother. Like winking.

DESMOND: You have a good mind. Fine, quick –

MIBS: And demented. You've driven me distracted. I get up in the morning and there's a looking glass in the door of the wardrobe, and I look in it and there's this person staring back at me. But it's not the person you see. God knows what *she* looks like.

DESMOND: You make difficulties.

MIBS: Yourself and bloody Chesterton: I'm unfortunate with the pair of yous.

DESMOND: He's easy.

MIBS: I'm sure. For them that had a schoolmaster for a da, yeah.

DESMOND: That has nothing to do with it.

MIBS: Not much, not half. He beat it into you. Lar Kearns told me.

DESMOND: That ignoramus.

MIBS: He says –

DESMOND [*jealous*]: When did you see him?

MIBS: He says you were never let out after tea. You were kept in, and your da would take a cane and flay the legs off you. He says the roars of you –

DESMOND: He's a liar.

MIBS: The whole town knew it. Your da used to crease you.

DESMOND: I never roared: *that's* a lie.

MIBS: My da gave me the strap once.

DESMOND: When?

MIBS: I came home at all hours: missed the last tram and had to foot it out. I was sixteen. I walked in the door and he was weak from worrying. He asked if anyone had laid a finger on me, and when I told him no he murdered me.

DESMOND: My father ... [*He hesitates.*]

MIBS: What?

DESMOND: It was in case the other boys might think I was his favourite. He wanted to show them how fair he was.

MIBS: Well?

DESMOND: So he'd pretend I was day–dreaming or whispering or copying answers. 'Drumm, get out here.'

MIBS [*fascinated*]: Leave off.

DESMOND: And always on the legs, never the hands, because he wanted to be sure I could do homework.

MIBS: My da would have gone to the school.

DESMOND: I lacked that advantage.

[MIBS *gives a small giggle. She is listening intently.*]

He gave me extra subjects, you see. Three hours each evening, and he'd examine me next morning, before school. He wanted me to win scholarships. A teacher's son, he said, a boy with brains, ought to be ashamed to be paid for. If my work was poor, if it was slipshod, he'd take the cane out and lift my chin up with the tip of it. He'd say: 'I want you to know why I'm doing this. Let the others, the duds, the idlers, let them work in tramyards or on the roads or draw the dole. Let them live in public houses when they have money and on street corners when they have none. But not you, by Christ, no!' ... excuse me. 'An education, that's what puts the world inside of you. And in time to come you'll cry salt tears of gratitude for this, for I'm the only man you'll ever call your master.' He used a thin cane, the sort we nicknamed a whistler. [*He smiles.*] I was the envy of the class because I was the first boy to be in long trousers. Do you know, he's dead these nine years.

MIBS: He was killed, wasn't he?

DESMOND: Mm.

MIBS: In the tunnel.

DESMOND: Yes.

MIBS: Were you sad?

DESMOND: The first thought I had was: no cane tomorrow.

MIBS [*insisting: sentimental*]: Ah. And then you were sad.

DESMOND: I think I was. I was fifteen, and I wanted the moon and couldn't have it. I wanted my father alive and myself an orphan.

MIBS [*grinning*]: Chancer.

DESMOND: Truly.

MIBS: Still, you got on, thanks to him.

DESMOND: How, got on?

MIBS: If he hadn't been so hard on you, you wouldn't be made for life today.

DESMOND [*amused*]: Is that what I am?

MIBS: My da says so. He says the civil service is a bobby's job. He says you'll be a great catch.

DESMOND [*not displeased*]: I'm sure.

MIBS: Some day.

DESMOND: He said that?

MIBS [*airily*]: For someone.

DESMOND: Nonsense.

MIBS: Whoever she is. [*Then*] Of course, the way my da drops a hint, if it fell on your head it'd kill you.

DESMOND [*fishing*]: What hint? What about?

MIBS [*mimicking again*]: 'What hint? What about?' You're so innocent you'll skip Purgatory, won't you? Anyway, I'm not going to get married, not to anyone, and least of all to you, so you needn't ask me.

DESMOND: I won't.

MIBS: You bugger. No, you're too milk-and-watery for me: there's a nun inside of you.

DESMOND: A what?

MIBS: There is.

DESMOND [apparently amused]: Really?

MIBS: Mm.

DESMOND: A nun.

MIBS: A Carmelite.

[The fixed smile on his face begins to fall apart.]

Well, it's time you were told.

DESMOND: I daresay it is. [He makes a show of looking at his watch.] Good heavens, speaking of time –

MIBS: Now you're in a wax.

DESMOND: Not at all.

MIBS: You're raging.

DESMOND: Nothing of the sort. Only I think I ought to be –

MIBS: Take a joke.

DESMOND: I do: honestly.

MIBS: Then where are you going?

DESMOND: Home to the convent.

MIBS [moving to intercept him]: Ah, you messer, come back. Yes, you will, do as you're bid. Now sit.

DESMOND: I have to go.

MIBS: Don't tell lies: sit. Now listen. Why do you pick on me to persecute? We're night and day, chalk and cheese: I'm not your sort. So why?

[He looks dumbly at her.]

What's the fatal attraction?

DESMOND: You're a . . .

MIBS: Go on.

DESMOND: . . . very fine type of person.

MIBS [gently mocking]: Would you say?

DESMOND: Mind, I'm not a fool. The first time I saw you in the town I said to myself: she's human, she'll have faults like anyone else. And it's true. I mean, you fritter your time away on such rubbish. You moon over the latest crooner on the wireless and whatever the most slobbery song is. Your head is full of film stars with their divorces and carryings on. You have a mind like a mayfly. You don't read. That's one thing I can't understand: whenever I open a book it's the start of a journey. And you talk to cornerboys like Lar Kearns – do you know he goes into Larkin's? Well, it's no wonder you've picked up the habit of talking about people's ... bodies and such. Honestly!

MIBS [*straight-faced*]: But I'm a fine type of person.

DESMOND: Oh, yes.

MIBS: And the pair of us are a match, you'd say?

DESMOND: That's what I'm telling you.

[*She bunches up her fist and puts it to his chin as* MARY *did with* DRUMM *in the preceding scene.*]

MIBS: I'll do it yet. You see if I don't.

DESMOND: Do what?

MIBS: I'll – [*She is seized by an uncontrollable urge to laugh. She splutters and turns away from him.*] Oh, go home.

DESMOND: And that's another little fault of yours: you fly into moods for no reason.

MIBS: Will you buzz off?

DESMOND: Before I go –

MIBS: Goodbye.

DESMOND: Please. If you'll allow me, it'll make the whole evening seem worthwhile.

MIBS: Will it?

DESMOND: Let me.

MIBS: Well, don't take all night about it.

[*She closes her eyes and waits for the kiss.*
Instead, and without looking at her, he sits at the table and picks up the book of verse.]

DESMOND: The last two lines: one minute, I promise you.

MIBS [*outraged*]: Oh, for God's sake.

DESMOND: 'For there is good news yet to hear and fine things to be seen,

Before we go to Paradise by way of –'
   [*There are three loud knocks at the door opening on the back yard.*]
MIBS [*jumping*]: What's that?
   [*A low, eerie moaning is heard.*]
Oh, Sacred Heart, what is it?
   [*The door opens slightly.*]
Go 'way. Desmond, save me, don't let it come in.
   [LAR KEARNS *sticks his head in.*]
LAR: How are you, Mibs? I bet that shook you, what?
MIBS: It's you. [*Pleased to see him*] You bugger, you: I'm not worth
   me salt. [*To* DESMOND] It's Lar.
DESMOND [*coldly*]: Is it?
LAR [*noticing him*]: Ah, bejay, will you looka who's here.
   [*As he crosses to greet* DESMOND, *lights dim on the kitchen and
   come up quickly on the living room, where* KEARNS *has
   entered and, in a kind of mirror image, is crossing to* DRUMM.]
KEARNS: It's the Cough Bottle himself. The dead arose and
   appeared, what?
MARY: That's what *I* said.
KEARNS: Me old flower, put it there.
   [DRUMM *allows his hand to be shaken.*
   KEARNS *is his contemporary: a feckless, good-humoured man,
   physically gone to seed.*]
Well, it's high time you came to see us. We missed you. Are
   you in form?
DRUMM: I'm told so.
KEARNS [*looking from one of them to the other*]: And the hatchet's
   buried, what? The pipe of peace is lit, yes?
DRUMM [*querulously to* MARY]: He takes me for a Mohican.
KEARNS: And the war-drums is silent. Drums ... Drumm, that's
   a good one. Boom-boom. [*To* MARY] Did you offer him a
   jar?
MARY: Certainly I offered him a –
DRUMM: I don't want another one.
KEARNS: Yes, you do. Where's his glass?
DRUMM: My dear man, will you realize that there are people
   in the world who, unlike yourself, mean what they say?

KEARNS: Sure I know: you meet all sorts. [*He busies himself pouring drinks.*]

MARY [*signalling to* DRUMM]: Take it, to please him. [*To* KEARNS] And don't you go pouring for yourself.

KEARNS: Only the one.

MARY: No.

KEARNS: So's the occasion won't go by unmarked.

MARY: I 'clare to God, if the cat died he'd drink to the repose of its soul.

KEARNS: Stop growling.

MARY: He's been in Finnegan's since half-twelve. Well, it won't be the first time his dinner had to be thrun out.

KEARNS [*handing* DRUMM *a drink*]: You see what I put up with? It's the price of me for spoiling her.

MARY [*mock-anguish*]: God forgive him.

KEARNS: I ought to have borrowed a page from your book. Dolly soon found out who the boss was. You used the whip from the first fence on, and now she's afraid to look crossways at you.

DRUMM: Is that meant to be funny?

KEARNS: That's where I slipped up: too much of a softy. Is it what?

DRUMM: That remark is untrue and impertinent. Dolly has never been afraid of me.

KEARNS [*grinning*]: He's a terror.

DRUMM: Certainly not with cause. She's timid by nature, highly-strung, I grant you that. But to imply that I bully her –

MARY: Lar is joking.

DRUMM: Is he? I think not. And I'm sorry, but I do take exception. I despise tyrants, domestic or otherwise.

MARY: Sure we know. [*Glaring at* KEARNS] Trust you.

KEARNS: Trust me to what? Where's the harm in telling a man he wears the trousers? [*To* DRUMM] You're as prickly as bedamned: it's like talking to a gorse bush. Listen ... good health. Delighted to see you. [*He swallows most of his own drink with evident enjoyment.*]

MARY: That's him. A glass in his hand and not a care in the

world. You're talking to us again after six years and he's not even inquisitive enough to ask why.

KEARNS: What's there to ask? He's here and he's welcome. [*To* DRUMM] You'll stay and have a bite of dinner with us.

MARY: No, he will not. Dolly has his own ready for him.

KEARNS: Good oul' Dolly. How is she? Is she tip-top?

DRUMM: She went over the summit some time ago. [*Relenting*] She's well.

KEARNS: And how's the pen-pushing?

DRUMM: If by that you mean work, I retire in August.

MARY: You never.

KEARNS: The oul' pension at long last, what?

MARY [*incredulous*]: No, it's years away.

DRUMM: August 5th.

KEARNS: Not to mention the spondulicks into your fist.

DRUMM: It's called a gratuity.

KEARNS: Begod, but some fellows are rightly steeped, what? That's one of the disadvantages of being unemployed. There's no retirement age.

DRUMM [*ignoring him, to* MARY]: Ten more weeks.

MARY: It's true, it's true. The minutes crawl; it's the years that run.

KEARNS: Answer me this, though.

[*He prods* DRUMM *with his finger and thrusts his face forward so that they are nose to nose.*]

Here's the question. Where does the time go?

DRUMM [*snapping*]: What?

KEARNS: The time. Tell us.

DRUMM: Much of it goes in listening to banalities.

KEARNS: Oh, yeah?

DRUMM: Uttered by buffoons.

KEARNS: You're right: too bloody true. [*He reaches for the bottle.*]

MARY: So what'll you do?

DRUMM: Do?

MARY: With your time. I suppose you have it all cut and dried as usual.

DRUMM: I did my sums the other day. I discovered that I have been eight times around the world. Two hundred and ten thousand miles. Unfortunately, it was as a passenger on the Dalkey to Westland Row Train. Dolly says that now is our chance to visit Stella and her husband in Toronto.

MARY: You ought to.

DRUMM: She can go. I doubt if Canada and myself would see eye to eye.

KEARNS: Did it offend you?

DRUMM: Those who have been there tell me it wants for character. I get the impression of the great outdoors and next to nothing indoors.

MARY: You'll see Stella and the children.

DRUMM: She has four now.

MARY: I heard.

DRUMM: They were with us last summer. You may have seen the boys in the town: they looked like pygmy lumberjacks. As for Stella, she's always been a rather colourless girl. Too docile: like her sister, like Una. Perhaps Canada and she were destined for each other. I've come to think of her as a kind of walking Ontario.

MARY [reproachful]: Desmond.

DRUMM: No, I'll stay here.

MARY: You're not natural.

DRUMM: I beg to differ. I'm fond of both my children, but that fondness doesn't blind me to the fact that through some perverse biological quirk they favour their mother. I realized it in Una's case on the day of her confirmation. I am reliably told that when she was asked if she renounced the devil and his works and pomps, she blushed and said: 'I don't mind.' As for Stella, I ask her how she is; she tells me, and thereafter our conversation consists of a torrent of two words every half-hour. Hardly worth crossing the Atlantic for.

MARY: But you'll let Dolly go?

DRUMM: It'll be a holiday for her. And perhaps the change of air will blow some of the bees out of that bonnet of hers. She wants a motor car.

MARY: The style of her.

DRUMM: She gets worse with age.

MARY: How?

DRUMM: A car.

MARY: Buy it for her.

DRUMM: You're as bad as she is.

MARY: Don't be so mean.

DRUMM: It's a whim. She lives two hundred yards from a bus stop. She has no need of a car.

KEARNS: Ah, but there's places a bus can't take you.

DRUMM: What? [*As previously, this is almost a bark of hostility.*]

KEARNS: Halfway up Booterstown Avenue.

DRUMM: What about it?

KEARNS: You can't get there be the bus.

DRUMM: Well?

KEARNS: A motor car's your only man.

DRUMM: What have I to do with Booterstown Avenue?

KEARNS: You can get the Stillorgan bus that passes the top of it, or you can take a Number Eight or a Seven-A to the other end. But for any place in between the two you have to hoof it.

DRUMM: Hoof it where?

KEARNS: I'm telling you. Up Booterstown Avenue.

DRUMM: Are you mad?

KEARNS: To call on people.

DRUMM: I don't know anyone on Booterstown Avenue.

KEARNS: I'm not surprised.

[DRUMM *stares at him in fury, then turns to* MARY.]

DRUMM: Of course, what's behind this is, she wants to queen it in front of the neighbours ...

KEARNS: You'd walk your feet off to the knees.

DRUMM: ... and thinks that I'm going to be her unpaid chauffeur.

KEARNS: We're getting a car.

DRUMM: *You* are?

KEARNS: I was thinking of a Vauxhall.

MARY [*smiling*]: Don't mind him.

KEARNS: You won't laugh when I drive up in it. [*To* DRUMM] I'm putting in for a job as a rep. Car supplied.

MARY [*winking at* DRUMM]: I'm sure you'll get it.

KEARNS: You wait.

MARY: At your age.

KEARNS: Me age is me trump card. An employer knows he can trust a man with snow on his thatch, a man that'll do a day's work and not go chasing bits of stuff. And I know the ins and outs of commodities. Didn't I travel for six months for Swinnertons' in kitchen implements?

DRUMM: You did? When?

MARY: He means the potato peelers.

KEARNS: A toppin' little gadget.

DRUMM: You hawked them, door to door.

KEARNS: I travelled, I was on the go. You're so hot with words: was I moving or wasn't I? I was my own worst enemy on that job. I could have swung the lead: instead, I saturated half the county. No one left to sell them to. Dolly bought one.

DRUMM: I know: it broke.

KEARNS: The time herself got the compensation, we coulda had a car then, only she wanted the house done up. I said to her: 'You're the one that got the going over: you spend the money.'

MARY: He did: it's true.

KEARNS: 'Buy whatever you like with it, even if it's a kept man.'

MARY: He said that, too.

KEARNS: I mean, fair's fair. She got a fierce old knock. 'Right,' says I, 'do the house up. I won't touch a ha'penny.'

DRUMM: I'm impressed.

MARY: He's not the worst of them.

DRUMM: I'm bound to say I wouldn't have given you that much credit. I apologize.

KEARNS: Ah, dry up.

DRUMM: No, no: I lack charity.

KEARNS: I won't forget that night in a hurry. I thought she was dead.

DRUMM: You saw the accident?

KEARNS: Did I see it!

MARY: It's over and done with.

KEARNS: Begod, I saw it.

MARY: Now that'll do.

KEARNS [*heartily*]: Who do you think ran over her?

DRUMM: What?

KEARNS: You don't know?

MARY [*uneasily*]: Desmond doesn't want to –

KEARNS: Give you a laugh. Sister of mine that lives the far side of Athboy, off in the bloody wilds – her second youngest is getting married, and of course guess who's invited. 'We'll go in style,' says I to your one here, 'or not at all.' So I get the lend of Joe Duggan's car: the Mini. Slip him a few quid: the job is right. Well, we have a good day of it: the Mass, the breakfast and the few harmless jars, and at the end of the story back we come: not a feather out of us. Grand. So I pull up outside Joe's house and your woman gets out to open the gate for me, so's I can reverse in, like.

MARY: I go behind the car –

KEARNS: Will you let me tell it.

MARY: It wasn't his fault.

[DRUMM *is motionless, waiting for* KEARNS *to finish.*]

KEARNS: The clutch pedal is so worn, me foot slips off it. Well, the car gives an almighty buck-jump backwards, and next thing she's pinned against the pillar of the gate.

MARY: Joe Duggan had no business lending that car to people.

KEARNS: Mercy of God she wasn't killed.

DRUMM: Yes, it was.

KEARNS: Still, it could happen to a bishop.

DRUMM: I'm sure: if he was drunk at the time.

KEARNS: Ah, now . . .

MARY: Lar wasn't –

DRUMM: You maim the woman for life, and then you have the gall, the impudence to put on airs because you magnanimously allow her to spend her own money as she chooses.

MARY: You weren't there. You don't know what happened.

DRUMM: I know this much: that if he were ever at a wedding and came home sober, there would be a prima facie case for an annulment. [*To* KEARNS] As long as I've known you you've been a millstone around her neck: soft, easy and worthless, an idler whose idea of hard work was having to stoop to pick up his dole money. I thought that trying to cripple her spirit would be enough for you, but apparently not: you wanted to break her body as well. I'm not surprised the boy left home.

[*A pause.* KEARNS *stares at* DRUMM, *then the moment passes. He laughs, shaking his head.*]

KEARNS: God, Dezzie, you're a queer harp. [*To* MARY] I'll go and give me hands a rub.

MARY: Are you all right?

KEARNS: Oh, a shocker. [*He goes out.*]

DRUMM: You see? No answer.

MARY: If you please, I want you to go.

DRUMM: You're upset. I'm not surprised.

MARY: You haven't changed and you never will. More fool me for thinking you could.

DRUMM: Are you saying you're vexed? With me?

MARY: I have a dinner to get.

DRUMM: Because I tell the truth?

MARY [*angrily*]: You and your truth, I'm sick of yous. Take it home with you. Pour it over your leg of lamb. Bring it to bed with you and warm your feet on it.

DRUMM: Old age hasn't made you less contrary.

[*She faces away from, waiting for him to leave.*]

Very well. I'll leave you for a day or so.

MARY: I don't want you back here.

DRUMM: Nonsense. [*His smile disappears as he realizes that she means it.*] Or perhaps it isn't. [*Affronted*] As you wish.

[*He puts his coat on, watching as he does so for a sign that she may relent. Her face is tight with anger.*]

You know this is foolishness.

MARY: I won't have Lar talked to like that, by you or anyone.

DRUMM: I don't see the crime in saying what every inhabitant of this town over the age of reason knows to be true. He is weak, shiftless and irresponsible. It's hardly a secret.

MARY [*wearily*]: Will you go away.

DRUMM: I really don't understand you. [*He goes to the door and stops.*] Would it change matters if —

MARY: No.

DRUMM: ... if I were to tell you —

MARY: I said no.

DRUMM: I don't thank you for this. You force it upon me. If I'm forbidden the house it'll be on your conscience, and I'll not have that on mine. I don't thank you at all. Ben Mulhall gives me less than six months to live. Now am I to go?

[*The lights fade slowly. As if in counterpoint, music is heard: a vocal of* 'You Can't Stop Me from Dreaming'.

The lights come up in the kitchen. LAR *is winding up a portable gramophone, while* DESMOND *is at the table resenting his presence.*]

LAR: It's real hi-di-hi stuff, wha'?

DESMOND: Pardon me?

LAR: Hi-de-hi, ho-de-ho, like.

DESMOND: I didn't know you were a linguist.

LAR: Yeah, Fred Astaire the second.

[MIBS *comes in. She has been getting ready to go for a walk.*]

MIBS: Who put that thing on?

DESMOND [*virtuously*]: I didn't.

MIBS [*turning the gramophone off*]: Lar Kearns, do you not know what day it is? If me ma and da walked in they'd skin me.

LAR: Wha'?

MIBS: Can you not be like Desmond and sit quiet till I've me coat on? Messer. [*She goes out.*]

LAR: Holy Thursdays is brutal.

DESMOND: Is they?

LAR: All the picture houses shut and no hops. Tomorrow's worse: it's Good Friday.

DESMOND: Never.

LAR: Oh, yeah: it's the day after.

[DESMOND *looks at him quizzically.*]

After Holy Thursday, like.

DESMOND: Ah.

LAR: Peculiar day, Good Friday: give you the hump. Me and the lads, we go down to the Lady's Well and play ponner for ha'pennies. It's sorta like stayin' out of the way till it's over. J'ever notice how if you say a curse on a Good Friday it doesn't sound right?

DESMOND: Amazing.

LAR: True as God. Try it.

DESMOND: I must.

LAR: You don't go to hops?

[DESMOND *shakes his head.*]

Y'ought to. It's how you get off your mark. I do always get up for the slow waltz: you know: when there's only the coloured lights goin' all over the place, like in the pictures when there's a jail break. Last Sunday in Dun Laoghaire town hall, the Missouri Waltz, I got a great old lie in. Massive.

DESMOND: I'm sure it was.

LAR: A nurse. I couldn't see her home on account of she was on a bike, but I got a promise for Easter Monday. Don't tell Mibs.

DESMOND: Mary? Why not?

LAR: Spoil me chances.

[DESMOND *looks at him with hostility.*]

No flies on Jembo. No names, no p— Wha's up?

DESMOND: In your pocket.

LAR: Where?

DESMOND: Is that a pencil?

LAR: Yeah.

DESMOND: I thought it was. Where'd you find it?

LAR: I didn't find it. It's mine.

DESMOND: Yours? [*With an air of one solving a mystery*] Ah, I see. You draw, do you?

LAR: No, it's for – [*He realizes that he is being insulted. Easily*] Ah, that's good, that's quick, I like that. Sure I'm not a scholar, Dezzie: I never let on to be. [*He takes out the pencil.*] Do you know what this is for? I help me cousin Mattie that has the fishin' boat: I count the catch for him. That and tickin' off winners. Couldn't even write a Christmas card to save me life. [*Still pleasantly*] Mind, if I could, at least there's people I could send them to.

[MIBS *returns. She has her coat on.*]

MIBS: Maybe I ought to wait for them. Do you think?

LAR: What time did they go out at?

MIBS: Eight.

LAR: Sure doing the Seven Churches'll take till all hours. [*He hands her the pencil.*] Here, write them a note.

[*She tears a page from one of the exercise books on the table.*]

MIBS: Desmond says he has to be off home.

LAR [*pleased*]: Can you not come with us? Aw.

DESMOND: I don't *have* to be anywhere.

[LAR *signals to him not to stay.* DESMOND *pointedly ignores him.*]

It's a good idea. A breath of fresh air. [*To* LAR, *as if not taking his point*] Yes?

MIBS [*scribbling*]: 'Gone ... for ... a stroll.'

DESMOND: Two 'l's.

MIBS: There, short and sweet. So where'll we go?

DESMOND [*a jibe at* LAR]: Good heavens, need you ask? To a 'hop'.

MIBS: The very thing. Where ... the Metropole? No, the Gresham for style, seeing as I have me fur coat on.

LAR: Why don't we?

MIBS: What?

LAR: Go to a hop. You think we can't? [*He snaps shut the catches on the portable gramophone and carries it towards the door.*] Come on ... I'll show yous.

MIBS: Will you stop acting the –

[*He starts out, perhaps by way of the living room where* DRUMM *and* MARY *are, and where the lights now come up.*]

Lar, you're not to take that out of the house. It's me ma's ... she'll reef me.

LAR [*calling back*]: Sorrento Park.

MIBS: No, bring it back. Lar!

[*She follows him out.*

DESMOND *picks up his coat and is unaware for the moment that she has gone.*]

DESMOND: I told you he was a cornerboy, but of course you knew better. Now you can –

[*He hurries out after her.*

During the following, lights come up on the bandstand. LAR *appears and sets up the gramophone on the balustrade. He takes a record out of the storage space in the lid, puts it on the turntable and begins to wind up the gramophone.*]

DRUMM: Nice news for a Sunday morning.

MARY: I think you're drawing the longbow.

DRUMM: Do I ever?

MARY: Ben Mulhall never said that to you.

DRUMM: He hummed and hawed, of course. I told him to waste his own time if he wished, but not mine, that I wanted none of his verbal placebos.

MARY [*insistent*]: He never said it straight out.

DRUMM: I told him, I said to him: 'Look here, my friend, I was at the altar this morning, but one more word, one syllable of prevarication from you, and I shall unhesitatingly hurl myself into a state of mortal sin and you into eternity.' That changed his tune for him. [*He chuckles.*]

MARY: May God forgive you.

DRUMM: Eh?

MARY: What are you laughing at?

DRUMM [*a small bemused gesture*]: I suppose at what I can.

MARY: Coming here to frighten a body. I don't believe any of it.

DRUMM: You will.

MARY: I know you too well. You're a cod.

DRUMM: More, I would say, of a mackerel.

[*She gives him an angry look.*]

The ... um, specialist recommends what he calls an exploratory operation.

MARY: Well, then!

DRUMM: Impudence. I've been a civil servant for long enough to recognize as such the instincts of a customs official. I am not a suitcase to be stared into and ransacked.

MARY: If it cured you –

DRUMM: What I have, as Ben Mulhall admitted when I managed to hack down the bush he was beating about, is in here [*He touches his abdomen.*] and it's terminal. More jargon from America. I keep expecting to arrive at a celestial Dublin Airport.

[*In the bandstand.* LAR *mimes a compère speaking into a microphone.*]

LAR: And now, ladies and gentlemen, the last dance before the raffle will be a Gents' Excuse-me.

DRUMM: It will go against me later, but if I could have just a drop more of ...

[*He indicates his empty glass: it is as if he feared his composure might desert him.*

As MARY *goes to fetch the whiskey bottle,* MIBS *and* DESMOND *arrive at the bandstand.* LAR *starts the gramophone. The lighting is from a street lamp. It is an evening in early April:* MIBS *and* DESMOND *are warmly dressed;* LAR *wears a jacket and is tieless.*]

LAR [*to* MIBS]: Now isn't there a hop? Come on.

MIBS: Turn it off.

LAR [*to* DESMOND]: Hey, it's the tune, the one I told you. Do you remember?

DESMOND: No.

LAR: Yes, you do. The Miss –

MIBS: It's Holy Week. Do you want us to be read off the altar?

LAR: Who's to hear? They're all at the devotions. [*He dances on his own.*] All the Holy Marys. Hey ...

[*This, as* DESMOND *gets to the gramophone and puts the brake on. A moan from the record as it slows down.*]

Feck off, that's not yours.

DESMOND: Is it yours?

[*A moment of confrontation.* DESMOND *is between* LAR *and the gramophone.* LAR *is too easy-going to want to fight.*]

LAR: Be a sport.

MIBS: Leave it off, or I'm going home. You loony, trying to get us a bad name.

LAR: It's all right for yous. Yous have coats, I'm freezin'.

[MIBS *sits on the steps.*

DESMOND *makes haste to sit beside her.*

LAR *blows on his hands and comes down to sit on the other side.*]

Dead losses the pair of you. Move over in the bed.

[MIBS *moves, obliging* DESMOND *to shift up also, so that he is almost off the edge of the steps.*

LAR *lights a cigarette.*

In the living room, MARY *pours water into* DRUMM's *whiskey. He makes a sign when he has had enough.*]

MARY: He oughtn't to have told you.

DRUMM: Ben Mulhall?

MARY: He had no right.

DRUMM [*with some satisfaction*]: In my case, I think he knew his man. But look here: not a word to Dolly.

MARY: Ah, now ...

  [*He puts a finger to his lips.*]

  She'll have to know.

DRUMM: Not yet.

MARY: She's entitled.

DRUMM: I made up a story for her, days ago, just in case. A duodenal ulcer.

MARY: Desmond, why?

DRUMM: Peace of mind.

MARY: You're a nice man.

DRUMM: Not *her* peace of mind, for heaven's sake. My own.

MARY [*blankly*]: I see.

DRUMM: I did it well. I even invented some cut-and-thrust between Mulhall and me, with myself putting a flea in his ear, just to make it convincing. I should have been a novelist.

MARY: It's wrong for me to know and not her.

DRUMM: You forced my hand. Anyway, you're an exceptional woman: you have sense. Dolly is excitable and foolish: she'd make anyone's death a misery. Can't you see her? Beating a path between the chemist's and the church. And at home, the drugs and medicines set out in fearful symmetry like new ornaments. First, the cushions plumped; later on, the pillows. Sympathy and beef tea. She'll tell me hourly on the hour how vastly improved I look. She'll go about on tiptoe until me head splits. Her tenderness will saturate me like damp rot.

MARY: Nice talk. You don't know how well off you – [*She stops, remembering.*]

DRUMM: Don't I.

MARY: She's devoted to you.

DRUMM: Yes!

MARY: Thinks you're the be-all and the end-all.

DRUMM: I'm not disputing her affection, but I will not be at its mercy. Until I have to.

MARY: You don't deserve her.

DRUMM: The time I had pneumonia, she joked as if it were a head cold. Smiles and warm words, but the eyes of a child at the world's end. I don't want that again.

MARY [*understanding this*]: I know.

DRUMM: You'll appreciate now why I won't go to Canada. I daren't. You know how I've always had a passion for language. The pleasure of minting a sentence that's my own: not borrowed or shopworn. Yet now I have to stoop to the banality of saying of a place that I wouldn't be seen dead in it.

[*He gives a fastidious shudder.*

MARY *looks at him, not knowing what to say.*]

In time, I suppose Dolly will send to Toronto for Stella and to Rathfarnham for Una. They'll have me helpless at – [*He breaks off.*] No . . . please.

MARY: What?

DRUMM: That's the look I don't want to see on Dolly's face.

MARY: Pity about you.

DRUMM: You're upset.

MARY: I can't come over it.

DRUMM: I agree. It's a damned imposition.

MARY [*rallying*]: Well, I don't care what Ben Mulhall says, or what you say. If you turn your face to the wall, I won't.

DRUMM [*smiling*]: What will you do? Pray?

MARY: Jeer away: no one minds you. I have a great leg of St Jude.

DRUMM: Ah, yes: hopeless cases.

MARY: He might surprise you.

DRUMM: Talk away to him: I can't hinder you. It's odd: I've been a Government employee for forty years, and this will be the first time I've used pull.

MARY: You cod, you.

DRUMM: In the Department, when a man retires there's a presentation. The hat is passed. They give him a nest of tables or a set of Waterford. In August it'll be my turn, but I doubt if I'll put a strain on their pockets. I've indulged in unnatural practices with my subordinates, such as obliging them to do a day's work. But whatever it is, if it were only a fountain pen from Woolworth's, I mean to have it.

MARY: Sure won't you?

DRUMM: They won't be let off. I'll last that long. [*He looks at the ceiling.*] Our friend upstairs . . .

MARY: Do you mean Lar?

DRUMM: Will he come down?

MARY: What you said to him, he took it to heart. You mightn't think so, but he did: I know him.

DRUMM [*his thoughts elsewhere*]: I'm sure.

MARY: Will I tell him you didn't mean it?

DRUMM: Mary . . .

MARY: Ah, I will.

DRUMM [*there is an intensity in his voice which stops her*]: I need to know what I amount to. Debit or credit, that much I am owed. If the account is to be closed, so be it: I demand an audit. Or show me the figures: I can add and subtract: I'll do my own books. A man has rights: if he is solvent, tell him. [*He realizes that* MARY *has not grasped his meaning. More calmly*] I have a most impressive title now: Keeper of Records. My enemies grow cunning. It takes a rare kind of peasant villainy to inflict injury and promotion with the same stroke of the pen. I have been a thorn in too many sides, and now I've been given a room to myself where I can antagonize the four walls and abuse the dust. In the strongroom there are files: so many, you could grow old counting them. Each one has a person's name and a number, and if I were God and breathed on them they'd become lives. I seem to have access to everyone's file but my own.

[*She has been watching him rather than listening; sensing rather than understanding.*]

Yes, you may tell him I didn't mean it: then I must go. And Dolly is not to be told.

DOROTHY: You can look as innocent as you like. I'm nobody's fool.

[MARY *goes out of the living room.*

In the bandstand area, DOROTHY *has appeared. She wears a home-knitted Tam-o'-Shanter, with a woollen scarf and gloves to match. She is carrying two library books.*]

You can swear black is white, but I know what I heard.

MIBS [*to* LAR]: There, didn't I tell you? Me da'll find out and burst me.

DOROTHY: What was it?

MIBS: It's our gramophone from home. He brung it.

DESMOND: Brought it.

MIBS: Do you know Desmond Drumm? And Lar ... Laurence
  Kearns.

LAR: Howayah.

MIBS: This is a friend of mine: Dorothy Dignam.

DESMOND: How d'you do?

  [DOROTHY *is so flustered that she looks steadfastly away from him.*]

DOROTHY [*breathlessly, the first word a snub*]: Hello, no, honest and
  truly, such a fright I got, music in the pitch dark on a Holy
  Thursday, all I could think of was the Agony in the Garden. I
  thought I'd drop down dead, and then I said to myself, that's the
  tune that goes ''Way down in Missouri where you hear this
  melody', a funny old ghost that'd be.

  [*She gives a small, shrill laugh by way of providing a full stop.*

  DESMOND *looks at her stonily.*]

MIBS: You won't split on us?

DOROTHY: For what?

MIBS: Because –

LAR: No fear of her. Here, squeeze in. Dezzie's doin' gooseberry.

MIBS: Mm, sit with us.

DOROTHY: I said I'd be home after the library ...

LAR: Where's your rush? Dezzie, good lad, be a gent.

DOROTHY [*looking at* DESMOND]: If I'm disturbing anyone ...

  [MIBS *nudges* DESMOND, *who gets to his feet reluctantly to give
  her his place.*]

MIBS: You aren't. For a minute ... [*She pats the space beside her.*]

DOROTHY [*to* DESMOND, *shortly*]: Thanks.

LAR: That's the dart: nothin' like an even number.

DOROTHY: I won't stay.

MIBS [*to* DESMOND]: Dolly goes to the Tech in Dun Laoghaire.

DESMOND: Who does? Oh?

MIBS: She's blue-mouldy with brains ... aren't you? She was the
  head of our class in the Loreto.

DOROTHY: Don't tell stories.

MIBS: You were.

DOROTHY: I was second.

MIBS: Well!

LAR: Begod, there's no doubt. Someone is well-matched, wha'?

DESMOND [*venomously*]: And someone else isn't.

LAR: Steeped, so y'are.

MIBS: Desmond lives with his aunt on Nerano Road. I'm sure you know him to see.

DOROTHY [*lying*]: I don't think so.

MIBS: He's around the corner. Yes, you do.

DESMOND [*suddenly amiable*]: Why should she? I'm sure Dorothy doesn't walk about staring at people. You go to Dun Laoghaire Tech, do you?

DOROTHY: Yes.

DESMOND: Woodwork?

[*She makes to rise.* MIBS *holds her by the arm.*]

MIBS: Don't be so smart. Dolly does ... what?

DOROTHY: It's called Commerce.

LAR: Hey, tell yous a joke. There's this fella and this mott, and they go out to Baldonnell ... you know, to the –

MIBS [*indicating* DOROTHY]: Now be careful.

LAR: No, it's clean: honest. They go out to the aerodrome, like. And they see this aeroplane landin' –

DOROTHY [*to* DESMOND]: For your information, it's typing, short-hand, book-keeping and senior English.

LAR: Ah, Jasus, listen.

MIBS: Don't take the sacred name.

LAR: Sorry. They take this feckin' aeroplane –

MIBS: Lar!

LAR: They see this ... oul' aeroplane comin' done. And your woman, the mott, she says to your man: 'Is that a mail plane?' And he says: 'No, them's the landin' wheels.'

[*There is silence for a moment. Then* MIBS *gives a snort and punches* LAR. *She averts her head so that* DOROTHY *cannot see her laugh.*]

DESMOND: Oh, for God's sake.

LAR: Good, wha'?

DESMOND: Yes, for a street corner I suppose it's –

DOROTHY: Excuse me, do you mind? [*To* LAR] And then what?

LAR: Hoh?

DOROTHY: After the landing wheels.

LAR: No, you don't get it. Your man, the fella ... he thought that *she* thought the wheels was –

[*In panic and to create a diversion,* DESMOND *snatches the library books from* DOROTHY.]

DESMOND: These look interesting. What are they?

DOROTHY: Well, honestly.

LAR: ... that she thought they were –

[MIBS *puts a hand over his mouth.*]

DOROTHY: Such manners.

DESMOND: This one's a waste of time: trash; but this isn't bad. You'll enjoy it.

DOROTHY [*coldly*]: You don't say.

DESMOND: It's not one of his best, mind. Have you read 'Goodbye to All that'?

MIBS [*suddenly*]: Dolly Drumm.

DESMOND: What?

MIBS: I just remembered. It's a sort of game Dolly used to play.

DOROTHY: Mary, you're not to.

MIBS: When we were at school, like. Honestly. Whenever she'd meet a fellow, anyone, she'd put her name along with his.

DOROTHY: No, you're mean.

MIBS: To see how it would sound.

DOROTHY: It was for a joke.

MIBS: Trying it out, like.

DOROTHY: I was not.

MIBS: Dolly Drumm. God, that's the worst yet. Brutal.

[DOROTHY *looks at the ground in embarrassment.* DESMOND *is aloof, unamused.*

LAR, *restless, goes into the bandstand.*]

LAR [*laughing, to* DESMOND]: That's your hash cooked for you.

DOROTHY [*without looking up; a whisper*]: Stop it.

LAR: Hey ...

[*As they look around, he begins to sing, conducting as he does so.*]

'Goodbye Dolly, I must leave you,

Goodbye, Dolly, I must go ...'

[MIBS *at once joins in, motioning to him to keep his voice down.*

DRUMM, *in the living room, looks around, as if suspecting mockery.*
After a few lines, DOROTHY, *too, joins in, happy that the joke is over.*
Towards the end, DRUMM *begins to beat the time with his finger and*
hums the tune audibly.

Then MIBS *overrides the others:*]

MIBS [*loudly*]: '... Goodbye, Dolly ... Drumm!'

[*She laughs and hugs* DOROTHY, *whose feelings are again hurt.*
DRUMM *and* DESMOND *are both looking at her resentfully.*
Her laughter as it tails off overlaps the entrance of KEARNS *and*
MARY.]

I'm a horror.

MARY [*indicating* DRUMM]: There he is now.

KEARNS: Dezzie, are you off? Sure put it there.

DRUMM: I was rude to you. It was uncalled-for.

KEARNS: What rude? When?

DRUMM: Mind, I hold to the substance of what I said, but this is
your house and I was unmannerly.

KEARNS: Will you go 'long outa that. You weren't.

DRUMM: I insulted you.

KEARNS: Not at all.

DRUMM: Are you stupid? I say I did.

MARY: Now, Desmond.

DRUMM: And I ought not to have mentioned the lad.

KEARNS: Who?

DRUMM: The boy. Young Sean.

KEARNS [*flatly*]: Sure you didn't.

[DRUMM *turns away in exasperation.*]

MARY: Now that will do. After tea, Desmond and Dolly
will be coming over for an hour or so. [*To* DESMOND] Yes, you
will.

KEARNS: And why the hell wouldn't they?

DRUMM: I'd like that. Thank you.

KEARNS: All together again like Brown's cows, wha'? Sure, Dezzie,
do you know what I'm goin' to tell you? In this town ... look
at all the great characters we had. And you never seen such a
clearance. They're all gone, except for the pair of us. You and me:
that's as true as I'm standin'. Gone with the poor oul' trams. Sonny

Doyle and Darley the landlord, and your own da in his time, God
be good to him ...

MARY: Will you let the man go to his dinner?

KEARNS: ... an', an' Fanny Cash, an' Slippers we thought was the
German spy. [*He clamps an affectionate hand on* DRUMM'S *shoulder,
his face at too-close range.*] Meself an' yourself, the last of the good
stuff. Sure they'll never bate the Irish out of Ireland.

DRUMM [*freeing himself*]: Who else would have us? [*He puts on his
raincoat. To* MARY] About Dolly. I'll give her this much: she's
loyal. Our long silence, yours and mine: she had no part in it. So
if she stopped coming here –

KEARNS [*amused*]: If she did what?

MARY [*a warning*]: Hold your tongue.

DRUMM: ... That was my doing, not hers. You mustn't be cross
with her.

MARY: With Dolly? Ah, get sense.

  [*She sees him to the door.*]

DRUMM: Do you remember once, when you thought of taking a
secretarial course?

MARY: When *you* thought.

DRUMM: I tried to teach you a poem.

MARY: And I'm sure I learnt it!

DRUMM: 'My friends, we will not go again or ape an ancient rage,
Or stretch the folly of our youth to be the shame of age.'
No.

MARY: What about it?

DRUMM: 'But walk with clearer eyes and ears the path that
wandereth,
And see undrugg'd in evening light the decent inn of death.'
[*Gently*] It isn't a decent inn, Mary. When you get up close, it's a
kip.

  [*He goes out.*

  *If possible, he should remain in sight; at any rate, there should be no
  impression given of an 'exit'.*

  In the bandstand, LAR *is going through the other records in the
  lid of the gramophone. Stealthily, he puts one on.*

  DESMOND *is standing, perhaps still looking at one of the books.*

MIBS *and* DOROTHY *are still seated together.*

DRUMM *is seen walking to the rear of the bandstand.*]

KEARNS [*picking up his Sunday paper*]: Sure poor oul' Dezzie.

DOROTHY [*to* DESMOND]: I did see you in the town.

DESMOND: Pardon me.

KEARNS: I always had a great leg of him.

DOROTHY: Mary knows I did. And I knew your name and where you lived and that you were in the civil service.

DESMOND [*indifferent*]: Really.

DOROTHY: I don't know why I pretended I didn't, because I was brought up to be straight with people. So I apologize for telling lies, and if I can please have my books back I'll go home.

MIBS: Stay.

DOROTHY: No, Mary. I think I've been disappointed enough in people for one night. If you don't mind . . .

[*She holds out her hands, waiting for* DESMOND *to return the books. He is about to do so when there is a blare of music from the gramophone. It is a dance tune of the late 1930s.*]

MIBS: Lar Kearns, you wretch. You turn that off.

LAR: You do it.

MIBS: Watch me.

[*She goes into the bandstand.* LAR *is between her and the gramophone. He grabs her, forcing her to dance.*]

You messer, will you . . . will you let me go. Lar, you'll get me into trouble.

LAR: I know, but we'll have a dance first.

DESMOND: Kearns, you stop that.

[MIBS, *yielding, begins to dance with* LAR. *Encouraged, he holds her close.* DESMOND *looks on, consumed with jealousy.*]

LAR: That's the girl.

MIBS: I'm going to be murdered.

LAR: Hey, Cough Bottle, how about this for a lie-in, wha'?

DESMOND: Kearns! [*He goes into the bandstand and makes for the gramophone.*]

MIBS [*laughing*]: God, if someone sees us . . .

[DESMOND *stops the gramophone.*

DRUMM *is now visible at the far side of the bandstand.*]

LAR: Ah, will you put it back on.

DESMOND: You were told to stop.

LAR: Quit actin' the maggot. Fair do's now: give Dolly a dance, come on. [*He takes a step forward.*]

DESMOND: I warned you. [*He takes the record from the turntable.*]

LAR: Sure, you did.

DESMOND: I mean it.

LAR: Look, don't be such a –

> [DESMOND *deliberately smashes the record.*
> MIBS *screams.*
> For a moment,* DESMOND *is appalled by his own action, then, as* LAR *moves forward, he attempts to take the other records from the lid.*
> LAR *grabs him and throws him easily to one side.*]

DESMOND: You guttersnipe.

> [*He rushes at* LAR, *who holds him off effortlessly.* DESMOND *strikes out at him, but every intended blow falls short.*]

LAR: Easy, now. What the hell is the –

DESMOND [*flailing*]: Damn cornerboy . . . you leave her alone . . . you lout, you blackguard, I'll kill you.

> [LAR *grins at the ease with which he keeps him at bay.* DESMOND *is close to tears.*]

DOROTHY: Mary, Stop them.

MIBS: Yes, Desmond . . . Lar, will you stop it.

> [DRUMM *enters the bandstand. He shoulders his way between* DESMOND *and* LAR, *causing them to fall apart. He looks at them, his eyes filled with his own pain and anger.*]

DRUMM: Be damned to the lot of you.

> [*He goes off. They stare after him.*]

[*Curtain*]

ACT TWO

DESMOND *is in the bandstand, alone. He consults his notes, then puts them away as* DRUMM *did at the start of Act One. As an orator, he lacks assurance; this is merely a rehearsal, but his voice quavers from nerves.*

DESMOND: To conclude. As from December next this country shall at ... or is it 'will'? ... *will* at last cease to be merely a Free State and instead take its place as a free land. In place of – [*To himself*] You're rushing it: wait for applause. In place of a Governor-General, we will have a ... no, blast it: we shall, *shall* have a President. My respectable ... [*Almost moaning*] respect*ed* opponents have said ... [*Under his breath*] God, make them say it! ... that now is our opportunity to cut ourselves finally free of all that is English.

    [DOROTHY *enters the bandstand behind him and listens, unnoticed.*]
Mr Chairman, I cannot understand people who hold grudges, who sulk, who cling to old wrongs and injuries. If it is in their nature, it is not in mine. I say that we should retain all that is best of the old to take with us into the new Golden Age, into the – and those of you who have been to the Picture House in Dun Laoghaire this week will grasp my meaning – into the beckoning Shangri La of which Mr De Valera is the two-hundred-year-old High Lama.

    [*He laughs, pleased at his own wit.*]
DOROTHY: They'll boo you for that bit.
DESMOND [*embarrassed*]: Good evening. I was –
DOROTHY: ... Practising. I heard.
DESMOND: There's to be a –
DOROTHY: ... Debate, at the Harold Boys' School. I know.
DESMOND [*annoyed*]: Excuse me, but do you happen to live here?
DOROTHY: Pardon me?

133

DESMOND: I mean *here*. In the bushes somewhere or under a flat rock. [*As she stares at him*] I wondered.

DOROTHY: Honestly and truly, for a young man your age you're the most dreadful crosspatch.

DESMOND [*dismissive*]: Amn't I.

DOROTHY: And for your information, the reason I'm here – and excuse me for mentioning that people talking to themselves is the first sign of madness – what brought me is to say that Mary can't go with you.

DESMOND: Do you mean to the debate?

DOROTHY: She said not to wait for her and all the best.

DESMOND: Why? It was –

> [*He breaks off as* DRUMM *and* DOLLY *appear. They cross towards the living-room area.* DRUMM *notices* DESMOND *and* DOROTHY, *who wait until he and* DOLLY *have passed.*]

DOLLY [*lagging behind, breathless*]: She spent a fortune on having the house done up, paid out every penny she got from the accident. Did she show you her kitchen? The cupboards and the new washing machine and the –

> [DRUMM *stops suddenly so that she all but collides with him.*]

DRUMM: How do you know?

DOLLY: What? [*A small, nervous laugh*] I heard in the town.

> [DRUMM *continues off, letting her pass him.*]

DESMOND: Why can't she?

DOROTHY: What?

DESMOND: Come with me.

DOROTHY [*the same nervous mannerism as* DOLLY'*s*]: A toothache.

DESMOND: Since when?

DOROTHY [*embellishing*]: I think it must be an abscess. She tried oil of cloves, and now her father is taking her to Mr Corbet.

DESMOND: Who?

DOROTHY: To have it pulled.

DESMOND [*dismayed*]: But I wanted her to ... [*He leaves the sentence unfinished. He will not show himself as vulnerable in front of her.*]

DOROTHY: He pulled one of mine once. See? [*She draws back the corner of her mouth to show him.*]

DESMOND: Damn.

DOROTHY [*pointing*]: Arrh?

DESMOND: Yes.

DOROTHY: Her father is dragging her there. I know she'd miles rather go and listen to you and suffer.

[*He looks at her as if suspecting a gibe. Her face is ingenuous.*]

Really, she's as cross as two sticks. I mean, who wouldn't be? She said to me: 'He'll be there, standing his ground against T.D.s and professors out of colleges and such. The whole town will see him except me.'

DESMOND: She won't miss much.

DOROTHY: Do you hear him! Anyway, she said all the best.

DESMOND: It's my first time, you know.

DOROTHY: Go on. After this, you won't talk to us.

DESMOND: Far too grand, yes.

DOROTHY: You might be. Wait till you see tomorrow's papers: you'll be a stone's throw from famous. Do you know what my father says? 'Young Desmond Drumm? . . . oh, he's a born genius.'

DESMOND: Yes, I'm much liked by fathers.

DOROTHY: From this out, there'll be no stopping you. And Mary is going to be very sorry, you'll see. [*As he looks at her*] I mean, even sorrier.

DESMOND: Was that a story?

DOROTHY: What?

DESMOND: About a toothache.

DOROTHY: No!

DESMOND: Because –

DOROTHY: Excuse me, I'm not in the custom of telling –

DESMOND: Because if she'd prefer to go some place less boring . . . I mean she's free to, she needn't lie about it. I'm not her keeper: God forbid. [*Unable to keep the question back*] I suppose she went out with him.

DOROTHY: Who?

DESMOND: 'Who'!

DOROTHY: Do you mean Lar Kearns? You're wrong.

DESMOND: I'm sure.

DOROTHY: Well, you are wrong. Because he's going to the debate.

DESMOND [*appalled*]: He's what?

DOROTHY: With a crowd from the town. To cheer you.

DESMOND: Oh, my God.

DOROTHY: Isn't it nice of him? So there.

DESMOND: What time is it? [*He pulls out his notes, sits on the balustrade and pores over them in an agony of stage-fright.*]

DOROTHY: I thought I might go as well.

[*He is memorizing, eyes closed, lips moving.*]

If nobody minded.

KEARNS [*to* DOLLY]: Sure you're welcome.

[DRUMM *and* DOLLY *have appeared in the living room, ushered in by* MARY. *It is very much a Sunday evening occasion: sandwiches and a cake are on the sideboard. In the bandstand,* DOROTHY *lingers, watching* DESMOND.]

DOLLY: Hello, Lar. How are you?

KEARNS: Gettin' younger, the same as yourself. But sure you've been giving us the go-by for so long I wouldn't know a bit of you. Donkey's years, wha'? [*He gives her an overdone wink of complicity.*]

DOLLY [*nervously*]: Oh, now.

MARY [*a warning*]: Will you take Desmond's coat off him and not leave the man standing.

KEARNS: Who's this? Another stranger, begod. Haven't clapped eyes on him since dunno when.

DRUMM: Good evening.

KEARNS: Ha-ha, quick as a flash. Give us that.

[*He takes* DRUMM'S *coat. From* MARY *and* DOLLY *there is a fusillade of small talk.*

DRUMM, *who loathes whatever he considers banal, looks on in disgusted fascination.*]

MARY: Isn't the weather glorious?

DOLLY: Beautiful.

MARY: I'm sure the crowds of the world are out.

DOLLY: The town is black.

MARY: Such a day. I did half me wash.

DOLLY: Go 'way.

MARY: And hung it up. Dry in no time.

DOLLY: Aren't you great.

MARY: 'It's a Sunday,' I said. 'It's a sin. I don't care.'

DOLLY: These days, no one minds.

MARY: But if it was twenty years ago . . .

DOLLY: Oh, then! Oh, yes!

MARY: One stocking on a line on a Sunday . . .

DOLLY: Don't I know.

MARY: And Father Creedon 'ud be at that door.

DOLLY: Giving out to you.

MARY: He was a terror.

DOLLY [*fondly*]: Ah, Father Creedon.

DRUMM [*who can stand no more*]: Oh, good God.

DOLLY: No, it's great drying weather. [*To* DRUMM] What, pet?

DRUMM: Will you have done with this damned table-tennis and look at your surroundings?

DOLLY: Where? [*She looks about her vaguely. It has slipped her mind that she is supposed not to have seen the room lately.*]

MARY [*prompting*]: At me new room.

DOLLY: What? [*Then*] Oh. Oh, it's beautiful. Look at it, Dezzie, it's exquisite.

DRUMM: Really.

DOLLY [*babbling*]: I wouldn't know it. That's new and that's new and the wallpaper is –

MARY: Before we sit, come and look at my kitchen. Lar, give Desmond whatever he's having. Be useful.

[*She urges* DOLLY *out of the room. As they cross towards the kitchen,* MARY *begins to laugh helplessly.*]

DRUMM: That woman becomes more of a fool each day.

[DOLLY, *although she has been shaken by her narrow escape, catches* MARY's *mood and laughs, too.*
DRUMM *turns his head suspiciously.*
As MARY *switches on the kitchen light, we see that* MIBS *is at the table, weeping. She dabs at her eyes with a handkerchief.* MARY *sits near her and wipes her own eyes.*]

DOLLY: It's not comical; it isn't.

MARY: You aren't safe to be let out on your own.

DOLLY: When he came home and said you'd invited us, I thought: I must remember now to act surprised at the house and go 'ooh' and 'ah' and all the rest of it. And it went clear out of my head.

MARY [*laughing again*]: 'That's new', says you, 'and that's new and that's new . . .'

DOLLY: Stop it, I got a fright.

MARY: If he could see you having your Friday cup of coffee.

DOLLY [*frightened*]: Will you hush.

[KEARNS *has produced an unopened half bottle of whiskey and a six-pack of stout.*]

KEARNS: I have me orders from the Commandant: no hard stuff. So you get dug into this. [*He opens the whiskey.*]

DRUMM [*testily*]: A cup of tea would have sufficed.

KEARNS: You'll get that as well. No one goes out of here sayin' they weren't asked if they had a mouth on them.

DRUMM: You're an ostentatious man.

KEARNS [*proudly*]: I am, begod.

DRUMM [*half to himself*]: And a hopeless one.

KEARNS: No, I prefer the drop of stout. The occasional ball of malt is harmless, but at my age, when there's a bit of mileage on the oul' clock, a man ought to go easy.

DRUMM: What about *my* age?

KEARNS: You're different, Dezzie. You have acid in you. 'S a fact: it's in the canals, I studied it. You could drink Jameson's distillery dry, and you might get half shot; but the element in the whiskey that does damage to the human liver would be nullified by the acid your system is glutted with.

DRUMM: Balderdash.

KEARNS: Laugh, I don't mind. You wouldn't be the first one to make a mock of science. The body doesn't manufacture acid for a hobby, you know.

DRUMM [*calling*]: Dolly . . .

[DOLLY, *who does not hear, is in the kitchen talking with* MARY.]

KEARNS: Still, a man's a right to mind himself. Did you hear that poor oul' Nick Tynan was brought to the chapel yesterday?

DRUMM: Who?

KEARNS: Out of Begnet's Villas. You knew him.

DRUMM: Yes. His boy, his foster-son, was with me for a time: in my Section, that is.

KEARNS: A great oul' warrior.

DRUMM [*aggressive*]: A what?

KEARNS: A character. There'll be a big turn-out at that funeral.

DRUMM: I'm sure.

KEARNS: The chapel was packed.

DRUMM: I'd expect no less. He worked hard and lived decently, and by now he'll have given his mind back to the Almighty in the same unused condition as he received it. Yes, I knew him. A man of no malice and less merit. Lord have mercy.

KEARNS: All the same, Dezzie, he was a –

DRUMM: A character, yes. It's a word used to describe any ignoramus or bigot over sixty. You'll have a most impressive funeral yourself one of these days.

KEARNS [*pleased*]: Who, me?

DRUMM: Given the existing criteria for large attendances, I've no doubt of it. Mass cards and floral tributes. Your coffin will be invisible under the wreaths of intertwined platitudes.

KEARNS [*he looks at* DRUMM *for a moment; then, almost blushing*]: How much do you want to borra?

DRUMM: Mine, I think, will be a more modest affair. The chief mourners are likely to be a small weeping group of unsplit infinitives.

KEARNS: Not at all. Aren't you one of our own?

DRUMM: Am I? [*He drops the subject, almost with contempt.*] Tynan's son, the boy he adopted: I took a special interest in him.

KEARNS: A brainy lad.

DRUMM: Dangerously fond of saying 'yes'. He needed starch in his backbone. I watched over him, took no nonsense, told him that as long as he worked for me he would pull his socks up! In the end, of course, he was a disappointment.

[KEARNS *makes to top up his drink.*]

[*covering his glass*] Leave it. I wondered afterwards why I'd bothered with him. I'm not a masochist. I don't ask to have kindnesses flung back at me, or for that matter to become an office joke. 'I hear that Drumm has been let down again.' How stupidly we deceive ourselves. It was because of Sean.

[KEARNS'*s watery eyes become uneasy. He makes a lumbering attempt to avoid the subject.*]

KEARNS: I hear young Tynan is over for the –

DRUMM: He left here just about then. I suppose I missed him and made a friend of the other boy.

KEARNS: ... for his da's funeral.

DRUMM: Do you hear from him? From Sean.

KEARNS: Herself does.

DRUMM: Don't you?

KEARNS: Sure he knows I read the letters. Christmas and Easter ... he never starves us for news.

DRUMM: Is he well?

KEARNS: Tip-top, he says himself. He's teachin', you know, in a school in ... uh, it's near London. Can't get me tongue around the name. Slow, is that it?

DRUMM: Do you mean Slough?

KEARNS: Slough! You done that for him ... got him interested in books an' stuff. [*Grinning*] A bloody schoolteacher, wha'?

DRUMM: Bravo.

KEARNS: Was he married when you were here last?

DRUMM: Newly married, yes.

KEARNS: Him and her, there was what you might call a separation. I dunno the ins and outs of it. Sure over there is not like here. It's all choppin' and changin': everything on again, off again, like a vest in the autumn.

DRUMM: He had no right to go, not as he did.

KEARNS: Ah, well.

DRUMM: Ah, well what?

KEARNS: That's the way o' the world.

DRUMM: Will you stop mouthing banalities? He had a life here: his people. I'd have thought better of him: it showed a want of feeling.

KEARNS: Sean and me never hit it off. Chalk an' cheese.

DRUMM [*reluctant to seem to care*]: Does he ask for me?

KEARNS: Hoh?

DRUMM: In his letters.

KEARNS: Oh, I'm sure he does.

DRUMM: Well, does he or doesn't he?

KEARNS: Yis. Oh, catch him forgettin'. 'How's ... uh, Uncle Dezzie?'

[DRUMM *glares at him, not convinced.*]

There was a time I thought of makin' the trip, droppin' in to see him. But sure my travellin' days is over.

DRUMM: Your what? My dear man, I've been further around a chamber pot in search of the handle than you've travelled in your entire life.

[DRUMM *hears* DOLLY *and* MARY *moving back from the kitchen.*]

DOLLY: ... He was great. he told them all about the Cat's Ladder and where Shaw lived and Sorrento Park and I don't know what else.

MARY: This morning, you say? How well he kept it to himself.

[*As they leave the kitchen,* MARY *shuts the door behind them.*

MIBS *runs to it and speaks through it.*]

MIBS: Daddy? Can I come out? Can I please come out and talk to you and Mammy?

[*Getting no answer, she returns and sits at the table.*

DOLLY *and* MARY *enter the living room.*]

MARY: I hear you've been speechifyin'.

KEARNS: Who?

MARY: Walking the legs off half the town and telling them what happened in old God's time.

DRUMM: There were two dozen people, and it wasn't a speech: it was a ... talk.

DOLLY: Don't mind him: he was great.

DRUMM: You weren't there.

DOLLY: I saw you.

DRUMM: Now she reads lips.

DOLLY: Everyone's talking about it.

DRUMM: Who is? Name one.

MARY: That'll do. Behave yourself.

KEARNS: I remember Dezzie one time makin' a toppin' speech. Below in the Harold Boys', and that wasn't today nor yesterday.

DOLLY: Don't I know? I was there.

KEARNS: You were in me boot. You were at home in your pram.

[*A shrill laugh from* DOLLY.

In the bandstand, DESMOND *rises, ready to face his ordeal.* MARY, *who has brought a teapot with her from the kitchen, sets about distributing the cake-plates.*]

MARY: And I was in me go-car. Shift your feet. Dolly, will you sit?

DOLLY: Do you hear him, Dezzie? In my pram!

KEARNS: It was so packed, we were sittin' on the window-sills. I don't forget that night.

DOROTHY: Is it the time?

[DESMOND *nods. Panic has set in.*]

Well, all the very best.

DESMOND [*dry-mouthed*]: Thank you.

DOROTHY: You've no call to be nervous. Just don't think what a great night it is for you. Pretend it isn't.

DESMOND: Mm.

DOROTHY: And I know it's none of my business, but honestly and truly I'd leave out that bit about Mr De Valera, because it's only trying to be smart.

[DESMOND, *too nervous to heed her, begins to move off.*]

Do you want me to walk with you? If you'd sooner go by yourself, it's a free country. One thing I was taught and I've always kept to is, never go where you're not –

[*She realizes that he is moving out of earshot. She follows him off: a walk that longs to be a run.*

Through this, MARY *has been pouring tea and now offers milk and sugar.*]

KEARNS: Boys, oh boys, you gev them a great talk that night.

DRUMM: Did I?

KEARNS: You damn well did. I can still hear them clappin' and cheerin' you.

DRUMM: You heard more than I did.

MARY: Excuse me. Two spoons for you, Dolly?

DOLLY: Thanks.

DRUMM: You have a good memory.

MARY: How? [*A small embarrassed laugh*] Like an elephant. And for yourself it's . . .

DRUMM [*he waits a moment, calling the bluff; then*]: None.

MARY [*affecting to remember*]: None.

KEARNS: Acid!

DOLLY: Dezzie says he might write a book now. About the town.

KEARNS: A book?

MARY: You'd never.

DRUMM: Dolly takes the ... whim for the deed. I said that *someone* should –

KEARNS: No better man. Y'ought to put me in it.

DOLLY: No, it's about the olden times. History. Dezzie knows every stick and stone in the town, don't you, pet? And he has all the bits out of the papers and the old maps, albums of them in the loft, and the reams of stuff his father left.

DRUMM [*to* MARY *and* KEARNS]: Fuel for a bonfire.

DOLLY [*smiling*]: Oh, I'm sure.

DRUMM: There are as many books in the world as there are fools. I don't intend to augment the ranks of either.

DOLLY: But you must do it.

DRUMM: Must?

DOLLY: You said you would.

DRUMM: It was a daydream.

DOLLY: Well, I don't see why you won't. You have all the time you want now.

> [*A pause.* MARY *fetches the sandwiches and the cake.* DOLLY *looks at* DRUMM, *waiting for his response.*]

The first proper history, you said. You were over the moon: yes, you were. It was all you ever talked of. [*Bitterly*] It's only because you know how pleased I'd be. A book with your name on it. If I said it was foolish or a waste of time, then you'd write it to spite me.

MARY [*offering the food*]: Dolly ...

DOLLY: Wouldn't you? [*To* MARY, *attempting to act the role of the guest*] Oh, now, such trouble, aren't you awful?

MARY: What trouble? A bit of sweet cake. Desmond ...

> [DRUMM *takes a sandwich.*]

KEARNS: Eat away. When we haven't it, we'll do without. Do you know, Dezzie, the mornin' after that evenin' the talk in the town was that you might end up runnin' the country.

DRUMM: Running from it, I think.

KEARNS: No, 'clare to God: the whole shebang. Dolly, was he great or was he not?

DOLLY [*still hurt*]: I dunno.

DRUMM: I do.

KEARNS: You were massive. I remember.

DRUMM: Through a Guinness glass darkly.

KEARNS: Wha'?

DRUMM: Delude yourself by all means: not me. Oh yes, you were there, perched on a window-sill, and by the door I saw the gentlemen of leisure who haunted the betting shop and Gilbey's corner. And when my turn came to speak, there was what disguised itself as a cheer. I imagine it was the kind of noise the Romans made when the first Christian entered the arena. I heard you shouting: 'Good old ... Mammy Cough-Bottle.'

KEARNS: For a joke.

DRUMM [*sincerely*]: I know it was. I cleared my throat, and at once half the room turned consumptive. I began to speak. Someone yelled: 'Can't hear you.' That was the signal for a barrage of meaningless, inane catch-phrases: the sort that are thrown as boys throw stones at a broken wall, to see which one brings it down. Did my mother know I was out? Who swallowed the dictionary? Did I wash my neck lately? Would I work for a farmer?

KEARNS: Not at all: you're dreamin'.

DRUMM: It was like a dream at the time: a bad one. My nerve went. I gabbled. I heard my voice become shrill, like a girl's. Whenever I used a word with more than two syllables, they hooted. I skipped to the end, I fled to it ... to a facetious – I suppose a juvenile – quip about De Valera. They applauded that.

KEARNS: Amn't I sayin'?

DRUMM: Yes, they clapped: slowly. May I? [*He offers his cup for more tea.*] Our chairman was the then parish priest. When he obtained order, he said: 'And now that we've all had our bit of fun ...'

KEARNS [*laughing, meaning* DRUMM]: A fierce man for drawin' the longbow.

MARY: Desmond, will you get sense? Any place you go, you'll find a pack o'jeers. More fool you to mind them.

DRUMM: Once it was over and I'd sat down, I didn't mind them in the least. I even saw the humour of it.

[DESMOND *runs on, in flight from the humiliation of his speech. He stops by the bandstand. He is shaking. In a wave of nausea he grasps one of the iron pillars and begins to retch.*]

I was calm, quite unperturbed. You see, I understood. It was a punishment. I had broken the eleventh commandment. I had tried to be different, to be the clever boy, the ... [*A look at* DOLLY] born genius. Well, they were not impressed.

DOLLY [*suddenly*]: I cried.

DRUMM: What?

DOLLY: That evening.

DOROTHY [*calling, off*]: Desmond ...

DRUMM: Did you? I was amused. I had discovered for the first time that being clever was like having a disfigured hand — to be tolerated as long as you kept it decently hidden.

DOROTHY [*off*]: Desmond, is that you?

[DESMOND *runs quickly towards the kitchen area.*

DOROTHY *appears and follows him.*]

DRUMM: I actually believed that if I spoke well and carried the argument they would admire me. I wanted it. I longed to be ... [*He looks at* KEARNS.] one of our own. Dear God, what a contemptible ambition: to please the implacable. Well, I never gave them a second chance: I had that small triumph. [*He smiles at* MARY.] Your tea is as good as it ever was.

[DESMOND *comes into the kitchen.* MIBS *looks at him sullenly.*]

MIBS: Who let *you* in?

DESMOND: Your father. He said ... well, he seems to be in a bad humour.

MIBS [*toneless*]: That so?

DESMOND: Grumpy, I thought. You'd think he was the one with the toothache. [*He gets no answering smile.*] That friend of yours – Dolly Dignam – gave me your message. I was sorry you couldn't come.

MIBS: When? Oh, to the thingummy.

DESMOND: It was too crowded: I doubt if you'd have enjoyed it. And there was a rough element: it wasn't quite the occasion they'd hoped for.

MIBS: How was your speech?

DESMOND: Well, I clowned, so they laughed a lot. I mean, if they weren't going to take it seriously, why should I? The history professor from Trinity, he got a rough time of it. Still, for the experience –

MIBS: I'm in awful bloody trouble.

DESMOND: . . . I daresay it was worth it.

MIBS: I said, I'm in –

DESMOND: I know: I heard you. What kind of trouble?

MIBS: Don't ask me.

DESMOND: Is it . . . pyorrhoea?

MIBS: No, it's – Is it what?

DESMOND: She said your father was taking you to the dentist.

MIBS: It was to Father Creedon. [*As he stares at her*] Are you thick? He took me to see old Credo on account of a letter Lar Kearns writ me.

DESMOND: Wrote you. [*Almost laughing*] Lar Kearns?

MIBS: The first letter he ever writ in his flamin' life, and he sends it to me and me da opens it.

DESMOND: It must have been . . . worth reading.

MIBS: You shoulda heard old Credo. [*A florid, booming voice*] 'Oh, yass, yass, this is what happens in the house that neglects that grand and glorious Irish custom of the family rosary.' Me da was buckin'.

DESMOND: I don't see why.

MIBS [*sourly*]: Do you not!

DESMOND: If Kearns's level of prose is anything like his level of conversation, I can imagine the kind of letter it was. That isn't your fault.

MIBS [*not answering*]: Do you want tea?

DRUMM: If you're making it.

MIBS: Might as well. I'm to stay here till I'm called. Put the cups out. [*She sets about making tea.*]

DESMOND: Why'd your father open the letter?

MIBS: Because I never get any. 'Specially ones with 'S.W.A.L.K.' on one side and 'S.A.G.' on the other. The rotten messer didn't even seal it: he tucked the flap in and put a ha'penny stamp on it.

DESMOND: What did it say?

MIBS: Stuff.

DESMOND: Such as?

MIBS: Things.

DESMOND: Keep it a secret, then.

MIBS: Such a fuss. I went out with a girl I know to Killiney. There was a hop on in the White Cottage, that place on the strand. Lar was at it. He asked me up and bought me a cornet, and at the interval we got two pass-outs and went up on the bank of the railway.

DESMOND: You and he.

MIBS: God, don't you start.

DESMOND: Well?

MIBS: Well nothing. Mind your own business. Anyway, this morning this letter comes. Writ with a pencil, smelling of mackerel, and all slushy and romantic. [*With an embarrassed laugh*] Saying he loved me. I mean, Lar Kearns: would you credit it?

[DESMOND *is silent.*]

And God, doesn't he put in the lot about him and me on the bank of the railway. You'd think I wasn't there and had to be told: it was like the Grand National on the wireless. He even went and put in extra bits: he must have got them out of some book. When I think of me da reading it: all about me creamy breasts. Two 'e's' in 'creamy' and 'b-r-e-s-t', 'breasts'.

DESMOND: Father Creedon must have enjoyed it.

MIBS: Desmond, he was awful, he ate me. I mean, you'd think we'd done something desperate.

DESMOND: I wouldn't know: I wasn't there.

[*The thought of* DESMOND *being present causes her to giggle.*]

Not that I'd want to be.

MIBS [*on the defensive*]: We had a coort.

DESMOND: Is that what it's called?

MIBS: Well, blast your nerve.

DESMOND [*feigning amusement*]: A coort!

MIBS: A bit of messin'. I didn't go all the way with him.

DESMOND: Ah-ha.

MIBS: No, I did not.

DESMOND: Wasn't it dark enough?

MIBS: If you want to know, I nearly did. It was the closest I ever came. Only I wouldn't let him. I wouldn't let anyone.

[*He is unmollified.*

She glares at him, fetches the tea-tray and slams it down.]

MIBS: Because I haven't the nerve. Here.

DESMOND: I don't want your tea.

MIBS: It's bloody made. [*She sloshes tea into his cup.*] Me da went down to the harbour to see him ... to see Lar, I mean, and give out to him. [*She puts one spoonful of sugar into his cup.*] How many?

DESMOND: None.

MIBS: Don't stir it. He says he wants to marry me. [*This is what she has been leading up to. She affects to give her attention to putting milk and sugar into her own tea.*] I dunno how he came out with it. I bet you me da waved the letter at him and began rantin' and ravin'. And of course you know Lar. If you said you were starvin' he'd tell you seaweed was bread and butter. Whatever he thinks you want to hear, that's what he'll say to you, so I suppose he told me da he'd marry me.

DESMOND: In the letter he said he loved you.

MIBS [*derisive*]: E-eh.

DESMOND: Well, didn't he?

MIBS: Yeah, because he got a red-hot coort ... don't mind him. So now what am I to do?

DESMOND: Marry him.

MIBS: Ah, for God's sake.

DESMOND: Why not?

MIBS: Old jealous-boots.

DESMOND: Who?

MIBS: He hasn't even a proper job. Give over.

DESMOND: Jobs aren't important. I think you should marry him because I think you're his sort.

MIBS: Yeah, the perfect – [*Her smile dies away as the insult goes home.*]

DESMOND: And you won't need a railway bank then, will you, or to be afraid of going all the way with him.

MIBS: Ah, Desmond –

DRUMM: No, you could do worse. I doubt if you'll do better. And you'll be much more your own self at his level than at ... anyone else's.

[*She realizes that he is determined to tear down their relationship past all chance of repair.*]

MIBS: Sure. Go on, now: go home.

DESMOND: Mm, it's all hours. I'm sure you'll have a happy life. You'll make a nice home for him, perhaps in one of those cottages in the Alley Lane. He needs someone like you: you can help him count his dole money.

MIBS [*waiting for him to go*]: Yeah, thanks.

DESMOND: Because –

MIBS: I said, go. You done what you wanted: you said what can't be took back.

DESMOND: Taken back. [*He is unable to leave ill enough alone. He wants to draw blood, needs to be certain that her hurt equals his own.*] I'm very stupid. I mistook you for someone with self-respect. It was my fault. I thought that at least your ambitions went higher than Lar Kearns.

MIBS: Do you mean you?

DESMOND: I was wrong.

MIBS: Yes ... you do. Well at least Lar is a bit of gas. I can laugh with him. He's glad of me the way I am. I don't need to have a scaffolding put around me brain before I'm fit to be seen with him. He can give a body a coort and a kiss, and they know it's a person, not bones and cold skin. You think you're so great. Just because you get up and make a speech and they slap you on the back and cheer you, you act like you were someone. Well, you're not. They laugh at you. You have a smell of yourself and you're no one. Honestly, you're not all there, you know that? The whole town knows about the Drumms. Ask them. Go and ask. You're as cracked as your oul' fella was. I'm not surprised he went and – [*She breaks off.*]

DESMOND: That he what?

MIBS: Go on home.

DESMOND: Yes.

[*As he turns to go, the lights fade in the kitchen and come up in the living room.* DRUMM *is in genial mood.*]

DRUMM: It was in that field across from what they called the rabbit wood.

MARY: The back meadow.

DOLLY: There are bungalows now.

MARY: Oh, but then it was the meadow.

DOLLY: Oh, then!

DRUMM: We were walking, the four of us.

KEARNS: Was I there?

DRUMM: My dear man, was Hamlet in Denmark? This, mind you, was in the far-off days when young people wore shabby clothes from poverty rather than affectation. There were still fields to walk in: it was before the country became one vast builder's yard.

MARY: Tell the story.

DRUMM: There were the four of us . . .

DOLLY: The times we had.

DRUMM: And on the path alongside the wood we found a baby bird.

MARY: He's romancin'.

DRUMM: It had fallen from its nest. And he [*indicating* KEARNS] picked it up.

KEARNS: God bless your memory.

DRUMM: And there in a hedgerow he saw a nest filled with baby birds. So he took this . . . foundling and very tenderly put it in with them.

DOLLY: Ah.

MARY: Well, I'll say this much for him: that's Lar. Now that's him to a 't'.

KEARNS: Yis, that'd be me.

DRUMM [*to* MARY]: I agree with you. It sums him up. Because I went back a week later, and all the other birds had gone. [*To* KEARNS] But yours was still there. Plump and thriving, and no wonder. It was a cuckoo.

MARY: No.

DOLLY: Lar, you didn't.

KEARNS: He's drunk: don't mind him.

MARY: A cuckoo. Oh, that's him, that's the price of him.

[DRUMM *laughs.* DOLLY *joins in.*]

DRUMM: That man ... put a predator into a –

KEARNS: Yis, more power. Laugh away, make me out a gobshite.

MARY [*reprimanding him*]: Lar.

KEARNS: Take his part, why don't you?

DRUMM: It did happen.

KEARNS: When?

DRUMM: That Sunday.

KEARNS [*suddenly violent*]: In me hump it happened.

MARY: Now, boys, boys ...

KEARNS: You think I wouldn't recognize a coo-coo? With my experience? Who was it owned Mary Mine?

DRUMM [*mystified, looking at* MARY]: Mary M—

MARY: Not me: his pigeon.

KEARNS: Dezzie, we're all goin' downhill. 'S a fact. And in your case the cells of the brain is handin' in its cards.

DRUMM: Drivel.

KEARNS: Take this evenin'. What did happen, you can't remember, and what didn't happen you have off be heart.

MARY: Can't you take a joke?

DRUMM [*to* MARY]: You miss the point.

MARY: No matter: leave it. Dolly, more tea ...

DRUMM: This afternoon, I took it into my head to go over some old accounts. [*The remark is intended for* MARY.] A few figures to be totted up, interest paid, a balance struck.

MARY: Doing sums in this weather.

DRUMM: I sat in the garden. I dragged the deckchair around with me, to keep out of the shadow.

DOLLY: It's still the month of May. Out of the sun it's bitter.

   [DRUMM *looks at her.*]

Sorry, love.

KEARNS: The news first, Dolly, then the weather.

   [*He laughs.* DOLLY, *smiling, puts a finger to her lips.*]

Ah, God. Say what you like, I'm a great character.

MARY [*to* DRUMM, *prompting*]: And then what?

DRUMM: It's no matter.

MARY: Yes, it is. You thought of that day and the four of us.

DRUMM: That unimportant walk we had. From forty years ago:

why? What value had it? So I went back to my accounts, and I remembered another time: when a priest came to my aunt's house. I'd been sent to live with her: it was the day of the inquest. He told me to be a brave boy and never turn from God, and he asked a strange question. Had my father written me a letter? I said no: never. I had lived with him in the master's house: why should he write to me? That priest with the pink hand that shook mine: today I remembered him and understood what he'd been after. It was for evidence of suicide ... the business of burial in consecrated ground.

KEARNS: Suicide? Who?

MARY: Priest and all, the cheek of him.

DOLLY: Aren't people dreadful?

DRUMM: Why?

MARY: Why? Being killed like your father was is one thing, but to take the poor man's character ...

DRUMM: How?

KEARNS: I remember him: a decent skin. He taught me.

DRUMM: Now *that's* taking his character. [*To* MARY] And if the poor man, as you call him, did die by accident, it was by the same law of probability as being run down by the Dun Laoghaire mailboat halfway up the Volga.

MARY: Desmond, you have no nature in you.

DOLLY: Honestly and truly, some people have nothing better to do than spread stories.

KEARNS: It was a mishap. He was short-cuttin' it through the tunnel.

DRUMM: That was the coroner's finding.

KEARNS: Down the bank at the Ramparts, through the dark along the railway line and up the bank again. I done it meself.

DRUMM: Boys do it, yes.

KEARNS: Oh, a dangerous pastime.

DRUMM: At school I was informed with some glee that he had put his head on the track.

MARY: You're not to say that.

DRUMM: The town says it.

MARY: When? I never heard it.

KEARNS: No, nor I.

DRUMM [*to* MARY]: I thought you did.

[*Almost certainly,* MARY *has forgotten their old quarrel, but she senses an accusation.*]

MARY: You were wrong, then. And your song and dance about it has Dolly upset.

DRUMM [*to* DOLLY]: Are you? Why?

DOLLY: It was the thought of a soul going to hell.

DRUMM: My father?

DOLLY: It's what the Church says. A mortal sin.

DRUMM: I know what the Church says. That the creator of heaven and earth is a bungler who burns his mistakes. Tommy-rot. God made him, let God put up with him. At least He knew him: I never did. Whatever was breakable in him, he kept under lock and key, away from vandals. Sooner a shuttered house than a plundered one. You were welcome to what was left, what passed for all there was of him ... the bones and cold skin. If he ever tried to speak to me, or to anyone, it was in that tunnel. And damn them: they called it an accident, so he said nothing. [*To* MARY] I'd say that was taking his character.

[*A pause. He looks at his watch, then, with a social smile*] Well, now.

DOLLY [*taking her cue*]: It was gorgeous.

MARY: Where are you harin' off to?

KEARNS: They're not goin'. [*To* DRUMM] Will you sit?

DRUMM: Tomorrow is Monday. I'm not on a perpetual holiday, like some. [*Not unkindly*] Do you know, this man's continued survival without ever lifting a finger makes the mystery of the Holy Trinity look like a card trick.

DOLLY [*laughing*]: Poor Lar.

KEARNS: You'll have a tincture.

DRUMM: I will not.

KEARNS: To see yous up the hill. I've two jars left for meself, and if yous go home on me she'll have them locked up before you're on Sorrento Road. You will.

MARY: Humour him.

DRUMM: One, and that's all. [*To* DOLLY] Yes?

DOLLY: I'm enjoying myself. And you are, too: don't pretend. Dezzie got great news this morning.

KEARNS: That a fact?

DRUMM [*muted*]: Dolly ...

DOLLY [*winking at* MARY]: It's a secret.

KEARNS [*getting the drinks*]: Ah, but Dezzie, the changes in this town. If your da, God be good to him, cem back again, he wouldn't know a bit of it.

DRUMM: I'm sure.

KEARNS: He would not. If you told him the oul' steam trains was gone, he wouldn't believe you.

[*They stare at him. He realizes his gaffe and makes a bumbling attempt to cover up.*]

An' ... the poor oul' trams, wha'? Yis. An' ... an' the fizz-bags the chiselurs could buy for a ha'penny. An' did j'ever go out in the Sound and look at the nuns on the rocks below the Loreto, with the striped bathin' togs down to their ankles?

DRUMM: You've drained life's cup to the full, haven't you?

MARY [*smiling*]: Trust him! [*To* KEARNS, *privately, she presents a bunched fist for his indiscretion about the trains.*]

KEARNS: Yis. An' do you 'member Cussin's shop? With the yoke for slicin' the rashers. I'd stand for hours and look at that thing goin' round. It was better than the pictures.

MARY: Give the man his drink.

KEARNS: True as God. Zz ... zzz ...

DOLLY: Did it have a happy ending?

[*She almost blushes at her own daring.* DRUMM *is surprised, almost admiring.*]

DRUMM: Well, now.

KEARNS: Did it have what?

MARY: Was Laurel and Hardy in it?

[*There is a faint yelp from* DOLLY. KEARNS *ignores her.*]

KEARNS: And, Dezzie, I'll tell you what else I remember. Girls, will yous listen. A bit o' shush. No, this is as true as God. [*Impressively*] An' it was the best thing that ever happened to me.

[DOLLY *mutters inaudibly.*]

DRUMM: I can't hear you.

DOLLY: 'Gone with the Wind' was on the bacon slicer.

[*Her laughter goes out of control.* MARY *joins in.*]

DRUMM: Dear God.

MARY: Desmond, will you stop her?

DRUMM: Dolly, that will do. I said, it's quite enough. [*His voice trembles. He leans his head on one hand.*]

KEARNS [*still trying*]: No, as true as you're sitting. In the whole o' me life, the best thing that ever — Well, if yous are all goin' to make a shaggin' hee-haw of it —

MARY: We're listening.

[*A whimper from* DOLLY. DRUMM *nudges her and, unwilling to trust himself to speak, signals to* KEARNS *to continue.*]

KEARNS: There was nothing like it before nor since.

MARY: This'll be good.

DRUMM: You might get a compliment.

MARY: Not before it's time.

KEARN: I'll tell yous . . .

MARY: Do.

KEARNS: It was the day Workman won the National.

MARY: Thanks very much.

DOLLY [*a handkerchief to her mouth*]: Mmm . . .

KEARNS: Yous can laugh. It was the time herself and me were as poor as Job's ass. Nothin' comin' in only the few shillin's assistance, and your one here expectin'. Weren't you? You were expectin' Sean.

MARY [*a hint of reserve*]: I might have been.

KEARNS: No one remembers nothin' tonight. Yes, you were, and your da was six months dead, so he couldn't help us. Yis, hard times. Herself had a path worn between here and the pawn office. Everythin' you could wrap up in a parcel, so's it wouldn't shame you. The watch her da left her: thirty years on the trams. An' there was this sweepstake up in Larkin's-that-was, a draw on the National. I won a couple o' bob that day playin' pitch-an'-toss, so I said to meself: 'I'll risk the lot.' An' didn't I draw a horse, and wasn't it Workman.

DRUMM: Highly appropriate.

KEARNS: You're right. Well, I wasn't worth me salt till the day o' the —

[DOLLY, *as a result of* DRUMM's *remark, holds back another fit of laughter and gets to her feet.*]

MARY: Dolly, are you all right?

DOLLY: Grand. I'll just use your upstairs. Excuse me.

DRUMM [*mischievously, as she passes*]: Disgraceful woman.

[*She slaps at his shoulder and hurries out. In the passageway, she releases her laughter in one gasp. She leans against the wall, recovering. During what follows, she goes out of sight: presumably upstairs.*]

KEARNS: It must be Dolly's night for laughin'. Yis, now where was I . . . ?

DRUMM: Presumably the horse won.

KEARNS: Dezzie, it walked it. Fifty quid put into me fist, and I mean fifty quid then, not now. We were landed.

DRUMM: I'd say so.

KEARNS: Steeped. We were in the clear. Everythin' back from the pawn – may I drop down dead, I had to borry a handcart – and the pram and the stuff for the baby bought and paid for. Dezzie . . .

DRUMM: What?

KEARNS: It was the hand o' God.

DRUMM: Was it?

KEARNS: I said to meself the day the lad was born: 'He didn't see us stuck, and I'll never doubt Him be worryin' again.'

DRUMM: A promise you kept.

KEARNS: I never reneged.

DRUMM: God will provide.

KEARNS: Leave it to Him.

DRUMM: And He watches over you?

MARY: Over all of us.

KEARNS: Them that has faith in Him.

DRUMM: Ah, yes. Don't dig the garden: pray for an earthquake.

KEARNS: Jeer away.

DRUMM: Faith? If either of us, you or I, had a scrap of it, we'd be in a monastery living on black bread and doing atonement. What we have is hope. We call it faith.

KEARNS: Rubbidge.

DRUMM: Mind, I'll concede that as a race we have more to believe in than others. Christians elsewhere worship three Divine Persons:

God the Father, God the Son and God the Holy Ghost. We have
added a fourth one: God the Jockey.

KEARNS: You won't act the hard root when your time comes.

MARY: Now, Lar ...

KEARNS: Then what'll you do?

DRUMM: Envy you your certainty.

KEARNS [crowing]: Ah! You've had it too soft, Dezzie. No goin'
short, nothin' to pray for. A grand cushy job with a collar an' tie
on it, an' a pension in the wind-up.

MARY: Don't row with the man.

KEARNS: What rowin'? Sure more power to him. I'm only sayin'
that poor people like ourselves, them that has it hard, we're more
in with God, like, than the rest of them.

DRUMM: He's one of your own.

KEARNS [delighted]: Now you have it. [Grabbing DRUMM's glass]
Gimme that.

DRUMM: I won't.

KEARNS [masterful]: I say you will.

DRUMM: A cushy job, you called it. Perhaps it is. But a man who
carves penny whistles at least knows his own worth: I don't know
mine. I spend a third of my life in a hot-house of intrigue and
skulduggery which would make the court of the Borgias seem
like a whist drive, and I do work of doubtful value for a
government of doubtful morality. Cogito ergo sum. I am a cog,
therefore I am.

KEARNS: Still, isn't it money for jam?

DRUMM: Quite.

KEARNS: And you're on the home stretch now, with the pension at
the winnin' post.

DRUMM: If God doesn't get there first.

KEARNS: Not forgettin' the lump sum.

DRUMM: True.

KEARNS: Paid for, don't forget, by yours truly.

MARY: By who?

KEARNS: Income tax. I don't begrudge it to you. Only it's time
you stopped takin' life so serious. Y'ought to pop off some place:
folly the sun. An' give Dolly a bit of a break. That's a great girl.

MARY: He's right there.

KEARNS: A topper.

DRUMM: Yes.

KEARNS: 'Yes,' says he. Say it an' mean it.

DRUMM: You seem to think at this late stage in her life she needs references.

KEARNS: I'm sayin' you got the right girl, the same as meself did. Only you were slow in findin' out, on account of you had a soft spot for this one.

MARY: Now no blatherin'.

KEARNS: I don't miss much.

MARY [*embarrassed*]: I'll guzzle him.

KEARNS: What harm's in sayin' it? We're all past that sort o' jack-actin', wha'? The blood is gone cool.

MARY: In a minute it won't be the only thing.

KEARNS: No, own up to it, I wiped your eye. And sign's on it you got Dolly and she's a credit to you.

DRUMM: I'm sure.

KEARNS: *Be* sure.

DRUMM [*becoming nettled*]: Yes, now could we have done?

KEARNS: A smasher, so she is.

DRUMM: My dear man, don't tell me about it: tell Dolly.

KEARNS: I did tell her.

DRUMM: Well, then.

KEARNS: Many's the time.

DRUMM: Well done.

KEARNS: More times than you told her.

DRUMM: No doubt.

KEARNS: In this room you're sittin' in.

MARY [*anxiously*]: Lar . . .

KEARNS: Last Friday.

[*A pause.* DRUMM *is quite still.*]

No. No, it was the time I met her up the town. Yis, that was when I told her.

[DRUMM *looks at him with contempt.*]

MARY: That tongue of yours: it ought to be cut out of you.

KEARNS: Wha's up?

MARY: You'd talk if it killed you. A mouth. A mouth, that's what you are, no good for an'thin' else.

KEARNS: I met her up the town –

MARY: Shut that gob of yours. Shut it. [*To* DRUMM] She came in for a cup of coffee. She'd do her shoppin' and buy the few things for the week, and she'd come in and I'd put the kettle on. No harm in that.

[DRUMM *is silent.*]

Ten minutes the one day in the week. She has her neighbours: who else has she? Do you expect her to live like a statue? I said to her: 'Tell him, why can't you?' She said: 'I'm afraid to.'

[DRUMM *does not react. A faint cough as* DOLLY *comes into view outside.*]

[*Hearing her*] Now let it lie. You will.

[DOLLY *comes in.*]

DOLLY: Honestly and truly, I'm weak from laughing. Look at me: I'm a sight for the crows.

[DRUMM *looks towards her.*]

You're very quiet. Is something up? [*Touching her hair*] Is it me?

[*The lights cross-fade with those in the kitchen.*

DESMOND *is standing facing* MIBS *and* LAR. *He is holding a package.* LAR *is wearing a new off-the-peg blue serge suit.*]

DESMOND: I'm sorry. I came to leave a message. Your father said I was to come in.

LAR: Cough Bottle, the hard man: I wouldn't know a bit of you. Hey, c'm'ere an' tell us. [*Modelling the suit*] Is this the berries or isn't it?

DESMOND: Pardon me?

LAR: The suit. I was tryin' it on for Mibs.

DESMOND: Very smart.

LAR: It's new. You're supposed to say 'Well wear'.

DESMOND: Well wear.

LAR: Might as well go to me doom in style, wha'? Fifty-two an' a tanner ... five bob a week.

MIBS: Don't tell everyone our business. [*To* DESMOND, *coldly*] Did you want something?

DESMOND: I was at the Sodality Mass yesterday. I heard the banns being read out ...

MIBS [*flatly*]: Did you?

DESMOND: It was the first I knew of it.

LAR [*revelling in his moment*]: Wasn't it lovely? ... makin' a show of a man, readin' his name out from altar. Dezzie, she landed me. Talk about a conger-eel: you never seen the fight I put up, an' just when I was away an' clear with the hook in me mouth, she stuck the gaff into me.

MIBS: Dry up.

LAR: The banns called, the new suit bought and the chapel booked. Here, look at the Made-in-Shanghai. [*Taking hold of* MIBS's *left hand*] Show him.

[*She pulls her hand away.*]

The diamond cem out of a watch.

DESMOND: Anyway, I thought I'd offer my congratulations.

MIBS: Thanks.

LAR: Me oul' comrade, put it there.

DESMOND [*offering the package*]: This isn't very much. Just to ... mark the occasion.

LAR: Ah, for the love-a! [*Feeling the shape*] It's a book.

DESMOND: Nearly as bad. But with every good wish.

LAR: Can we open it?

DESMOND: Well, it's not for Christmas. [*Less abrasively*] Of course. [*To* MIBS] When is the ... uh?

MIBS: The 2nd.

DESMOND: Ah.

LAR: Did you hear tell her da put me to work? 'S a fact. He found me a spiffin' job. I'm in it for life.

DESMOND: Oh, yes?

LAR: I'm on the trams.

DESMOND: Good for you. As a conductor?

LAR [*shaking his head*]: I'm above in the yard. Not so much on them as under them. Sure isn't it a start? Hold on: I have it.

[*He has undone the wrapping and finds an attractively-framed Van Gogh print. It is a still-life: 'Yellow Chair with Pipe'. We have already seen this reproduction: it is hanging in the living room.*]

[*To* MIBS] It's a pitcher.

DESMOND: Not the original, I'm afraid. It's by Van Gogh, a Dutch artist. I've always been fond of it.

LAR: Mibs, have a dekko.

[*She moves reluctantly to inspect it.*]

DESMOND: Wherever it is you'll be living, I thought you might find a place for it.

LAR: Mibs's oul' lad: he says we can bunk here.

DESMOND: I see.

LAR: Until we find a place. Dezzie, about the weddin'. The spondulicks is a bit short, so there'll only be her parents an' me ma, an' Harry Young, that's standin' up for me.

DESMOND: I understand.

LAR: I mean, don't expect a card in the post with gold writin' on it. You have me?

DESMOND [*heartily*]: Yes!

LAR: You're sure now?

MIBS [*suddenly*]: It's only an old chair.

DESMOND: That's all.

MIBS: A bit of wood standing there: it's nothing. And yet it's like as if whoever done it ... put himself inside of it. [*She smiles at* DESMOND, *delighted by her discovery.*]

LAR: Give us a gawk. Hey, it's crooked. I wouldn't sit on that yoke. [*Remembering his manners*] It's nice an' bright, but. Great in a room.

[*It is the difference between the two reactions that provokes* DESMOND *into the following.*]

DESMOND: Mary, if I might talk to you ...

MIBS: Talk away.

DESMOND: No ... uh ... [*He indicates* LAR.]

MIBS: If you mean where he can't hear us, no, you can't.

DESMOND [*to* LAR]: You don't mind.

MIBS: Yes, he does. [*To* LAR] Stay where you are. [*To* DESMOND] I know what you want to say, and I'll save you the trouble. 'Marry Lar,' you told me, 'you're his sort.' And you were right.

DESMOND: No.

LAR: Decent man. Won't forget it to you.

MIBS: Yes, you were. You used to say to me: 'Think for yourself.'

Many's a time you said it. 'Put this on one side and that on the other and look at them.' And it's what I done. [*Amending*] What I did. And I knew that with Lar there'd be a bit of me left over. Not with you: you'd want the lot. The bit of me that's not yours at all: that likes to go to a do or a hop and sing songs on the road home. Or talk too loud and say 'Shag it' and be what you call common. You'd take it all: there'd be nothing left for Lar, not even the bit of harmless likin'. You don't know where half-way is. Lar does: he's glad of what you can give him. He won't begrudge you the bit of me that's yours. [*With a grin*] Even though you'll turn your nose up at it.

[*A pause.* LAR *has been listening with an amiable, uncomprehending smile.* DESMOND, *knowing his cause is lost, wants to back out with at least his pride intact.*]

DESMOND: I don't take leavings.

MIBS: Hard lines, then.

DESMOND: Yes ... well, you know best. [*Formally*] I'm obliged to you for the courtesy of a –

MIBS: Oh, balls.

DESMOND [*ignoring this*]: And forgive the intrusion. I wanted to wish you both all ... [*Unable to resist the inflection*] possible happiness.

LAR: Look, sit down.

MIBS: Let him alone.

LAR: Well, listen ... you're to drop in on us, do you hear? No makin' strange.

MIBS: And thanks for the picture.

DESMOND: Oh ... there's a card with it. The very best, then.

MIBS: Yeah. 'Bye, now.

[*He goes.* LAR *follows him to the door.*]

LAR [*calling*]: Now if you don't drop in you'll be back o' the neck: I mean it. Hey ... and don't pick up any good things.

[*He comes back into the room.* MIBS *is searching the wrapping paper and finds a greetings card.*]

I think the Cough Bottle's gettin' a bit queer in himself, do you not? Too much oul' readin' an' stuff. [*He looks at the picture.*] Hey, was I polite to him?

MIBS: You were great. Change out of that suit.

LAR: 'Cause I wouldn't like to hurt his feelin's. Whoever sold him that yoke rooked him.

[MIBS *is reading, half-audibly.*]

What's on it?

MIBS: 'For there is good news yet to hear and fine things to be seen, Before we go to Paradise by way of Ken ... sal Green.'

LAR: Wha's it mean?

MIBS: Nothing. It doesn't mean anything. Except that he'd make me finish that bloody lesson if it killed him.

[*The lights cross-fade with those in the living area.*

DOLLY *is tense and silent.* MARY *is trying to keep up the pretence that the evening is on the same relaxed level as previously.*]

MARY [*referring to* KEARNS]: One day he was off out mowin' her grass, and the next he was puttin' a washer on her tap, and the day after that her drains needed mendin' ...

KEARNS [*protesting*]: Now you're makin' a yarn of it.

MARY: 'A poor widow,' says me man here, 'with no one to do her a hand's turn.' Oh aye, I thought to myself that's how it starts. Josie Murnaghan on the Barrack Road ... Josie McDonald that was. [*To* DOLLY] You know her.

[DOLLY *shakes her head.*]

Ah, you do. Well, 'clare to God, I was at the state where I was examinin' his coat for hairs.

KEARNS: Yis, at my age.

MARY: The older they are, the worse they are. Next thing, he says her wall needs whitewashin'. 'It's a big job,' says he. 'I know,' says I, 'I've seen her.' And then, doesn't this woman, a total stranger, come to the door, and a little boy with her, and he roarin'. Him ... [*Meaning* KEARNS] it turns out he's after burstin' the child's chestnut. He was never next or near Josie Murnaghan: he was off playin' ... [*To* KEARNS] What?

KEARNS: Conkers.

MARY: Conkers ... with the little chiselurs off the road.

DOLLY [*faintly; a glance at* DRUMM]: Goodness.

MARY: When he ought to be sayin' his prayers.

DOLLY: Oh, now.

MARY: A right go-be-the-wall. But sure there wasn't a family yet where there weren't secrets.

KEARNS: She thought I was –

MARY [*silencing him; to* DRUMM]: Do you hear me?

DRUMM: Perfectly.

MARY: So will you come out of your sulks.

DRUMM [*not harshly*]: Now don't interfere.

MARY: You can blame it on me. I met her in McLoughlin's one day, and I said: 'Come back to the house.' She didn't want to. I made her.

DRUMM: At gunpoint.

MARY: What?

DRUMM: You abducted her.

MARY: No, I didn't need to. But Desmond, don't go gettin' sarky with me, not in here. This is my house you're sittin' in.

DRUMM: That can be rectified.

MARY: It can, yes, and off you go again. But for how long this time? [*It is a reminder. He looks at her resentfully.*]

MARY: That'd suit you. You could spend the rest of your life with your feelings hurt: being cool with one half o' the world and not talking to the other half.

DOLLY [*not wanting a scene*]: Don't . . .

KEARNS: I think we ought to be all grand and sociable and as happy as Larry. I wasn't christened be accident, you know.

MARY: Have sense. What did she do on you? Nothin'.

DRUMM: Whatever Dolly did or did not do, I don't wish to discuss it outside my own home.

KEARNS: Proper order.

MARY: You hold your tongue. [*To* DRUMM] Too true you don't. Because you know I'm well able for you and she isn't. She walks on tippy-toes around you. When you come home like a divil because someone has got on the wrong side of you, she has to put up with it. I don't.

DRUMM: I agree. And you won't have to. Dolly . . .

MARY: No. You'll go out of here when you tell that woman she done nothing wrong. Ah, Desmond: all this because she was still talking to me when you were black out with us.

DRUMM [*indignantly*]: No.

MARY: What, then?

DRUMM: Nothing of the sort. Dolly is free to make friends. Or to lose them, or keep them: it's her choice. I don't ask her to live in my pocket. I don't want it.

MARY: Then for the love an' honour –

DRUMM: Because of the deception. How do you think it feels to know that one has been listening to the same lie for five years?

DOLLY [*timidly; helpfully*]: Six.

[*He looks at her as if suspecting an attempt at humour. Then*]

DRUMM: Six.

MARY: I know, yes. And all the harm it did you!

DRUMM: It was behind my back. You knew and he knew. Probably half the town did as well.

MARY: Now we have it.

DRUMM: And laughed at me for a fool.

MARY: Oh, aye: the town. What'll the town say?

DRUMM: I don't give a damn what it says, but I will not stand arraigned before a judge and jury of gossip-mongers and idlers. They've had their day.

MARY: You told us. They made a mock of you because you were out of step with them, so you got your own back. You stopped walking. You were going to do the divil an' all: yes, you were, but no: you might get laughed at. You let on they're not worth passing the time of day with, but they rule you.

DOLLY: Mary, they do not.

DRUMM: Thank you, I can defend myself.

MARY: It's true, they bett you.

DRUMM: Beat me.

MARY: However you say it.

DRUMM: I do fear them, yes. I fear the ... good nature of their malice. But if I failed to accomplish the devil and all, as you call it, it wasn't because of the town: the town had nothing to do with it. It was because the devil and all wasn't in me. But I'll tell you what is. I've never lied to a man or about him, and I've never smiled into the face of a blackguard or been called an idler or a licker of boots or a hanger-on. I don't call that a total defeat. And if it makes you happy, the reason I was angry with Dolly is that I can no longer afford to be angry with her. I consider that ... an impertinence.

[MARY's *smile is hard as she turns to* DOLLY. *Inside her, probably to her own surprise, an old wound has been re-opened.*]

MARY [*to* DOLLY]: There, now. Isn't he good to you?

KEARNS: That's the dart: forgive an' forget. Sure who could be cross with Dolly? And Dezzie is not the worst o' them either.

MARY: Oh, he's a great man.

[DRUMM *catches the note of hostility. He looks at her, puzzled.*]

DOLLY: I'm glad Dezzie found out.

KEARNS: A fuss over nothin'.

DOLLY: Because I hate anything that's hole-and-corner. [*To* MARY] I do, I told you.

DRUMM: It's over and done with.

MARY [*to* DOLLY]: It is. Everything except the absolution and the three Hail Marys.

DRUMM [*to* DOLLY]: We must go. [*To* MARY] You're in a fighting mood.

MARY: Am I?

KEARNS [*to* MARY]: But be the holy, you're a fierce woman. Goin' for him bald-headed, wha'?

DRUMM: Mary herself says it: she's well able for me. [*To* DOLLY] Had you a coat?

KEARNS: Still, there's one thing that's askin' for a puck in the gob, an' that's to go interferin' between a man an' a wife. I thought he was goin' to draw out at you.

DRUMM: It was close. If today hadn't been Sunday ...!

[DOLLY *laughs.*]

KEARNS [*to* MARY]: There was a narra escape for you.

MARY: He interfered between *us*.

[*The suddenness of the accusation takes* DRUMM *off guard.*]

KEARNS [*unheeding*]: Oh, a comical card.

DRUMM: Do you mean me?

MARY: So exchange is no robbery.

DRUMM: Interfered between you? I never did.

KEARNS: Between *us*? Begod, he'd have his work cut out for him, so he would. What are you carryin' on about?

DRUMM: How did I? Well?

[*She retreats from the edge. Her manner becomes sullen, evasive.*]

MARY: Coming in here, telling us how great you are. Never told a lie in your life, never kow-towed to anyone, never done nothin'. A saint, so you are. And poor oul' Dolly, the row there was over a mangy cup of coffee in her hand the one day in the week.

DRUMM: I thought that was settled.

KEARNS: Don't mind her.

DRUMM: You said I interfered between the two of you.

KEARNS: Not at all. She's romancin'.

DRUMM: I'm asking her what she meant.

MARY: Nothing.

DOLLY: Dezzie, leave it. She's upset.

DRUMM [*gently*]: Mary? Are you going to tell me?

[*She shakes her head.*]

No need, then. Are we friends?

MARY [*almost in despair*]: Yes.

KEARNS: Certainly we're friends. Who the hell says different?

DRUMM: That's what matters. We'll see you soon.

[*He has taken* MARY'*s hand. She keeps a grip on his when he makes to leave.*]

MARY: This morning ... you said about what you were owed. I've no head for words ... credit and something.

DRUMM: Debit and credit.

MARY: To add up with.

DRUMM: To add and subtract.

MARY: I thought all day about it. At first I said No, then I said: 'It's what's due to him.' And that's why. Not to harm you ... I wouldn't, but you have the right. [*A pause*] You were good to Sean. No one could have –

KEARNS [*in alarm*]: Eh ... eh ...

MARY: ... could have done more for him. You paid for him at the Christian Brothers, you taught him, made a scholar of him ...

KEARNS [*blustering*]: Now I'm the boss here, and I say No.

MARY: You took him for walks with you. Yourself and Dolly and the girls, yous brung him with yous that time for a holiday. The day of his confirmation, it was you put the suit on his back. And we let you. We never stood between you and him, because it was take what you gev him or go without. Now I'm not sayin' you meant to do it –

KEARNS: I'm tellin' you you're not to.

MARY: I'm not sayin' that. But you turned him against Lar.

KEARNS [*muttering to* DRUMM *and* DOLLY]: Get out, get out.

DRUMM: I turned him against . . .?

MARY: Maybe without meaning to.

DRUMM: No, it's untrue. I never did.

KEARNS: Sure certainly it's –

DRUMM: Meaning to or not meaning to . . . I reject it.

MARY: His father was no good. He never did a tap of work. He was ignorant, he was useless. He smelt of porter.

KEARNS [*weakly*]: I told you. The lad an' me . . . ile an' water.

DRUMM: I never uttered one word . . .

MARY: No, I'll give you that, But you schooled him well. He seen you look at Lar and heard you talk to him, throwing a word to him the way you'd throw a bone to a dog. Sean couldn't stand to be in the same room as him. Do you wonder he got the idea into his head?

KEARNS: Now that will do.

DRUMM: Idea?

MARY: He said it to us. It was the evening he had the row with Lar and went off to England. It's why you've heard the last of him, because you have . . . you may bank on that. It was the exam he passed that summer and the great marks he got. I think that was what started him wondering . . . wondering where he got his brains from.

[DRUMM *and* MARY *look at each other.*]

KEARNS: Dezzie, listen . . .

MARY: Be quiet, now.

KEARNS: A bee in his bonnet.

MARY: Now you can do your adding up. Desmond, it wasn't to harm you.

DRUMM [*dazed*]: Very well: he was your son, I meddled, I took too much on myself; but it was to find him a place in the world, away from street corners. But to put that idea in his head, to work that kind of mischief ... no.

DOLLY: Dezzie wouldn't, Mary. It's not in him.

KEARNS: Sure don't we know, aren't we sayin'? Me oul' comrade, wha'?

DRUMM [*to* KEARNS]: And you. You've known why the boy went, and all these years you've let me be a guest in this house?

KEARNS: Why wouldn't I? Aren't we pals, tried an' true, the last of the oul' stock. Put it there!

DRUMM [*it is the nearest he has come to liking* KEARNS]: You really are an impossible man.

KEARNS: An' in the heel o' the hunt wasn't it tit for tat? I took your one here offa you. So you took the lad, and aren't we even?

[DRUMM *looks at him in shock. It is as if a blow had been struck.*]
Listen, you'll have a jar. There's a drop still in the –

[DRUMM *turns and goes out.* DOLLY *starts after him, sees his raincoat, picks it up and follows him.*

The lights dim on the living room and come up on the bandstand. DESMOND, MIBS, LAR *and* DOROTHY *are there. They watch as* DRUMM *comes into view. He stops, as if from exhaustion.*]

LAR: We'll scram off outa here to some place else. Are yous on?

DOROTHY: I know ... we'll go to the White Rock.

MIBS: That'll take us till all hours. I have a tea to get ready.

LAR: Tell yous what. We'll go up Higgins's Hill and round be the Back Meadow. I'll show yous a bird's nest. Hey, Cough Bottle ... mind the missus for me.

[LAR *takes* DOROTHY *by the hand.* MIBS *follows.*

DESMOND *looks at* DRUMM *and is the last to go.* DOLLY *appears.*]

DOLLY: Honestly and truly, going off without your coat. You're asking for it. Are you all right?

DRUMM: I walked too fast. Give me a moment.

DOLLY: Put this on.

DRUMM: Yes.

DOLLY: I mean now. [*She helps him into his coat.*] What Mary said, you're never taking it to heart? Such a thing for her to come out with.

DRUMM: Wasn't it!

DOLLY: And poor Lar ... you'd pity him.

DRUMM: One day ...

DOLLY: What, love?

DRUMM: I'll take a microscope and an axe. With the microscope I'll discover where his brain is, and then I'll sink the axe into it.

DOLLY: Will you stop ... no one minds you.

DRUMM: I know.

DOLLY: I think Mary has a jealous streak in her. The way she's forever trying to make out that you and she are so great. It's to show off in front of me.

DRUMM: Dolly ...

DOLLY: I mean, she missed her chance. You were the brainiest boy in the town, and now it's too late. Lord knows I'm fond of her, but it's her own fault. [*She sees that* DRUMM *is glaring at her.*] I'm listening, pet.

DRUMM: I've achieved nothing.

DOLLY: How?

DRUMM: Three hundred days a year for forty years ... I've spent twelve thousand days doing work I despise. Instead of friends, I've had standards, and woe betide those who failed to come up to them. Well, *I* failed. My contempt for the town, for the wink and the easy nod and the easier grin ... it was cowardice; Mary was right. What I called principles was vanity. What I called friendship was malice.

DOLLY: Will you go 'way. This is because Mary upset you.

DRUMM: Not much to boast of at the end of the day.

DOLLY: The end, how are you.

DRUMM: Well, is it?

DOLLY: You're in the glooms: I'm not going to answer you. And if it were true itself ...

DRUMM: Well?

DOLLY: And it isn't, not a blessed word of it. You have me as bad as yourself.

DRUMM: Go on. If it were true itself ...

DOLLY: I was going to say, if it was, it needn't be from now on. I mean, Dezzie, are we alive or aren't we? [*Pause*] Now don't stand here: come home. Look at the way the evenings are getting a stretch: there's still light in the sky.

DRUMM: I have a question.

DOLLY [*smiling*]: More silliness.

DRUMM: Supposing I were to offer you a choice between buying a motor car –

DOLLY [*excited*]: Dezzie!

DRUMM: Be quiet. Between that and my writing a book about this place. Which would you choose?

DOLLY [*after a pause*]: The motor car.

DRUMM [*a little sadly*]: Of course you would.

DOLLY: Because ... whatever I want, you do the opposite.

DRUMM: You are a most aggravating woman: you get more foolish every day. Go ... be off home with you. Make a start.

[*They set off.* DRUMM *holds out a hand, looking up, then opens his umbrella, a pall over his head, and goes off slowly.*]

[*Curtain*]

TIME WAS

THIS PLAY IS FOR PAULE

This play was first produced at the Abbey Theatre, Dublin, on 21 December 1976, with the following cast:

P.J.	GODFREY QUIGLEY
ELLIE	KATE FLYNN
JOHN	DESMOND PERRY
BEA	DEARBHLA MOLLOY
TISH	MAY CLUSKEY
HARRY	RAYMOND HARDIE
ARAB	LARRY MURPHY
TWO DECORATORS	JOHN MOLLOY
	MICHEÁL O HAONGHUSA

CHARACTERS

WHO: P.J.

ELLIE

JOHN

BEA

TISH

HARRY

ARAB

TWO DECORATORS

VOICE OF A NEWSCASTER

WHEN: A summer evening ... next August.

WHERE: Killiney, south of Dublin.

AUTHOR'S NOTE: Two points. For obvious reasons, the play is set
'next year'; so in future productions the year, which is given as 1977
throughout the text, should be advanced accordingly. Also, I have not
indicated the stage mechanics by which one member of the cast shall
appear instantly on stage and another as instantly disappear; this,
because the ingenuity of a director, with the possible collaboration
of an illusionist, is bound to be greater than mine.

ACT ONE

The living room reflects the delight of P.J. *and* ELLIE *on discovering, five years ago, that they could afford this kind of house. It has been furnished with one eye on comfort, the other on visitors. The room is large, modern and slightly selfconscious. The only faintly jarring note is the presence of a coloured tin-type of Laurel and Hardy, which is too cheap for the room. A glass door leads in from the hall, and there is an archway beyond which, unseen, are the dining area and kitchen. When the curtains at the rear are open the window will prove to be a bubble-type affair made of perspex, which provides a panoramic view. At audience range, however, images swim in it as in a distorting mirror.*

It is late Saturday night in the summer of next year. The lights are on and there is music from an 8-track player.

A car door slams, then the front door. P.J. *comes in, putting away his car keys. He is in his late 30s, easy-going. He has been out to dinner, is smartly dressed.*

P.J. [*in mock-horror, calling off*]: Oh, my God, Ellie, we've been ...
[*He realizes he cannot be heard. He goes to the player and removes the cartridge.*] Oh, my God, Ellie, we've been burgled!
[ELLIE *comes in. She is two or three years younger than* P.J. *For this evening, she has decided to 'go long'.*]
Look ... cleaned out, nothing left.
ELLIE: You don't catch me a second time, so stop trying.
P.J.: Thought I'd give you a start.
ELLIE: Every joke, you work it to death.
P.J.; ... Put the heart crossways.
ELLIE: Well, you didn't.
P.J.: Can't win 'em all. [*He sits.*]
ELLIE [*without malice*]: You're so boring. [*Then*] Ah, love.
P.J.: What?

179

ELLIE: The Meldrums are coming. Be useful.

[*He rises.*

The following is a pas-de-deux which has been performed a thousand times. P.J. *casually sets out glasses and liquor.* ELLIE *puts out coffee things; her movements are fast, wide-ranging: she swoops to plump a cushion, adjust a chair.*]

And I don't know why you find burglar jokes so hilarious.

P.J.: Now don't get steam up.

ELLIE: You may have a short memory. I don't.

P.J.: Everybody gets done once. It's like making your confirmation.

ELLIE: You go out to dinner with friends ...

P.J.: I know.

ELLIE: ... You come home ...

P.J.: Sure.

ELLIE: And you walk into a ...

P.J.: Shambles.

ELLIE [*not liking to be reminded that she has given this recital to the point where he knows it by heart*]: Well, that is what it was. A ...

P.J.: Shambles. I said it was.

ELLIE: A nice way to live, isn't it, when you have to leave the house lit up like a beacon. And music blaring. What was that rubbish?

P.J.: When? Oh, 'Moon over Miami'.

ELLIE: Yuck.

P.J. [*reeling if off*]: Betty Grable, Don Ameche, Robert Cummings ... good old nineteen-forty-one.

[*She glares at him and thumps a cushion into shape.*]

Originally made as 'Ladies in Love', Nineteen-thirty-six; then as 'Three Blind Mice', Nineteen-thirty-eight; finally remade in Nineteen-fifty-three as 'How to Marry a ...'

ELLIE: Will you shift yourself?

P.J. [*lilting*]: 'Moon over Miami, shine on my love tonight ...'

ELLIE: Gutter words written on our walls in lipstick, cushions ripped to pieces, footmarks everywhere.

P.J.: No, that was the police. In some respects the thieves were neat.

ELLIE: Neat?

P.J.: They used the scraper.

ELLIE: They took the scraper.

P.J. [*remembering*]: So they did. Still, we got some new conversation out of it. Kept us going for months.

ELLIE: You forgot to buy mixers.

P.J.: No, I didn't.

ELLIE: Show me.

P.J. [*displaying a six-pack*]: Smarty.

ELLIE [*not to be beaten*]: Wrong sort.

P.J.: Pardon?

ELLIE: I mean, what kind of jungle animals smash and tear whatever is no use to them?

P.J.: You told me to ...

ELLIE: People spend half of their lives gathering a few nice ...

P.J.: You said 'We need tonic'.

ELLIE [*quickly*]: I said 'bitter lemon' ... A few nice bits and pieces together to make a house liveable, and the other half sitting at home in case someone steals them.

P.J.: When *I* was a kid ...

ELLIE: Of course *you* make a joke of it.

P.J.: ... We never locked a door. No thieves.

ELLIE: But I'm the one who was on Valium for a month.

P.J.: And you can laugh at this if you like, but it's gospel. The weather *was better* then.

ELLIE: It was what?

P.J.: You could tell the seasons.

ELLIE: Who mentioned the weather?

P.J.: Summers were warm and the winters were ... [*Which reminds him*] We'll need ice.

ELLIE: You're not all there, do you know that? [*She goes into the kitchen.*]

P.J.: Laugh away, but it didn't piss rain in August. [*A small boy's look of cunning comes on his face. He switches on the television.*] Moonshots and supersonic aircraft ... they have the ionosphere in flitters.

[*A light shines on his face from the television screen. A* NEWS-CASTER'*s voice is heard.*]

NEWSCASTER: ... near Henley-on-Thames. Miss Arbogast returned home from choir practice at St Cuthbert's Church nearby, to discover that her sister had vanished without trace. On the premises she found two men who claimed to be chimney sweeps. One of these men she described as being of corpulent build and having a small moustache. His companion was thin, and both men were shabbily dressed and wore bowler hats. Miss Arbogast, who was later treated for shock, told the police that when she raised the alarm the men escaped through a window, and that the more heavily built of the two waved his necktie at her and said: 'Pardon us.'

P.J. [*calling*]: Ellie, there's been another one!

NEWSCASTER: Identikit pictures of both men are being issued. Meanwhile, police are at a loss to explain how the missing woman, who has for some years been bedridden, can have been removed from the premises.

[ELLIE *reappears.*]

ELLIE: Been another what?

P.J.: Disappearance.

ELLIE: Do we need that on?

NEWSCASTER: And that, apart from the weather nationwide, brings us to the end of programmes for this evening.

P.J. [*blankly*]: The end?

NEWSCASTER: Again, we apologize to viewers for the cancellation of our late-night movie, 'Beau Geste'.

P.J.: There's no film.

ELLIE: I don't believe it. One Saturday night ... [*Switching off the set*] ... when we can have friends in without you hunched over that damned box.

P.J. [*staring at the set*]: It's not fair.

ELLIE: Oh, grow up. We've seen 'Beau Geste' so often there's sand in the carpet.

P.J.: Well, I'm going to write in.

ELLIE [*wearily*]: Do.

P.J.: Women don't like 'Beau Geste'. It's about chivalry.

ELLIE: There's a car.

P.J.: Saw it when I was ten. We stopped throwing rocks at girls for a week.

[ELLIE *opens the curtains.*]

ELLIE: It's them. Now don't fill yourself with drink, you hear?

P.J.: You know, in those days . . .

ELLIE: Yes, dear. Films were better, summers were hotter and there weren't any burglars.

[*The door chimes are heard. She goes into the hall.*]

[*Musically*] Com-ing!

P.J.: *That's* what she sounds like . . . door-chimes. [*Going to the living room door*] Well, of course there were burglars. They wore cloth caps and gloves and went up drain pipes. And when you caught them they said: 'It's a fair cop, I'll come quietly.' Today it's: 'Out o' me way or I'll fuckin' kill ya.' [*Eyeing the television set*] You could have put something else on, couldn't you?

[*Voices from the hall.* ELLIE *comes in with* JOHN *and* BEA. JOHN *is very much the professional man; his sense of humour is not noticeable.* BEA *is a handsome woman with a hint of the predator. Like many sexy women, she hints at more brains than she has.*]

ELLIE: . . . Really, we'd given you up. Thought you had a puncture.

JOHN: Bea wanted to look in on the children.

ELLIE: Were they all right?

BEA: Roland was peevish.

JOHN: You'd be, too, if your name was Roland.

BEA: Monster.

JOHN [*beaming*]: Now, now, now.

BEA: Beast.

[JOHN *laughs.*]

Bless him, he's so easily pleased.

JOHN: Ha, ha . . . no, poor Roland was all agog to see that film you [P.J.] were so keen on. We make a point of letting him stay up late if there's violence on the box: it syphons off his aggressions. But it seems it's been cancelled.

ELLIE: We heard. Guess who's livid.

P.J.: Who is?

ELLIE: You are.

P.J.: I am not livid, I am peeved, don't ex . . .

BEA: What's on instead of it?

P.J.: Bugger all. They just . . .

ELLIE: Who cares! Serve the drinks.

P.J. [*crossing*]: . . . cancelled it.

JOHN: I knew they would.

P.J. [*derisive*]: Sure, you did!

JOHN: That is to say, I was warned to expect it.

P.J.: Warned?

[JOHN *smiles and puts a finger to his lips enigmatically.*]

BEA: John knows everything, don't you, sweetness?

P.J. [*writing him off*]: Spoofer.

JOHN: External Affairs has been on the hot line to Downing Street. Old movies are banned as from midnight.

P.J.: On TV?

JOHN: Everywhere.

P.J. [*stares at him; then loudly*]: Geroff!

ELLIE: Too bloody much to hope for.

[P.J. *is aware that* JOHN'*s attitude has not changed, as it would when a joke reaches its tag-line. The subject has not been dropped, we sense, but is in abeyance.*]

BEA: By the way, not fifty yards from here we met the devil.

ELLIE: Pardon?

JOHN: In person.

P.J.: Oh, yeah? John ... vodka and ... ?

JOHN: Tonic.

P.J.: Tonic! [*He sticks his thumbs in his ears and waggles his fingers at* ELLIE.]

ELLIE [*ignoring him*]: The devil?

BEA: Mm ... all in scarlet. Horns, forked tail and one of those thingummies.

JOHN: Trident.

BEA: He said he was looking for the ... Callaghans?

ELLIE: Oh, the Carnahans.

P.J.: There's a party on.

BEA: There had better be!

ELLIE: Fancy dress ... well, honestly. They're so common.

JOHN: Nouveau riche, you mean?

P.J.: No, no ... same as us. Nouveau middle-class.

ELLIE [*heated*]: At least *we* don't proclaim it from the treetops. [*To* BEA] They have a colour TV aerial on their roof. It's a ...

P.J. [*supplying the word*]: A dummy.

ELLIE: For showing off. They get it piped.

BEA [*a shriek of delight*]: You bitch, it's a lie.

ELLIE: Don't talk to me.

P.J.: Bea ... Dubonnet and white.

JOHN: Weren't you invited?

ELLIE: We hardly know them.

P.J. [*bringing* ELLIE *her drink*]: They live behind us. When we appear at our back doors simultaneously we exchange mimes. [*He demonstrates, saying 'hello ... how are you?' elaborately and in utter silence.*]

ELLIE: You're spilling it.

P.J.: It's the kind of neighbourhood where no one shouts. In fact, Ellie has to give herself a home perm before she puts out the dustbin. Pathetic.

ELLIE: What is?

P.J.: In my day ...

ELLIE [*under her breath*]: Oh, Christ ...

P.J.: My parents were on intimate terms with every person on our road.

BEA: All of them?

P.J.: Young and old.

BEA: What fun.

ELLIE [*to* P.J.]: And why? Because the kind of life your parents led, the next street was Outer Mongolia. Well, we're different, we have wheels, we can choose our friends. [*Pointing off*] And I don't fancy that lot. You can call me a snob, you can ...

P.J.: Snob.

ELLIE: I am not, and you know it. [*Retaliating*] Bore.

P.J.: Shrew.

ELLIE: Little man. Nobody.

P.J. [*to* JOHN]: You want to swap wives?

JOHN: Thanks, I'd rather not.

ELLIE [*feigning outrage, glaring at* JOHN]: No? The brazen cheek!

BEA [*stroking* JOHN]: Isn't he lovely?

JOHN: Meaning no offence to yours ...

ELLIE: He's refused me.

JOHN: ... but mine is the conqueror of forty.

BEA: My God, he's comparing me to a ...
   [JOHN *laughs, pleased with his joke.* BEA *looks at him darkly.*]
   ... a chestnut, I hope.
P.J.: Would you take Green Shield stamps?
JOHN: How many books?
P.J.: Three.
JOHN: Done [*He drinks.*] Cheers.
P.J.: Cheers.
ELLIE: And thank you again for the ...
P.J.: ... The dinner. Terrific.
JOHN [*a gesture*]: We'll get our revenge. Next time.
   [*A relaxed pause. They are sitting, in after-dinner mood.*]
BEA [*muttering: it is intended for* JOHN]: Bugger.
JOHN: So what's new since the Mirabeau?
P.J. [*laughs; then*]: Oh, there's been another disappearance.
JOHN: Yes?
P.J.: It was on the box. Some woman ... Henley-on-Thames.
BEA: How many does that make?
P.J.: Dunno ... I've lost count. In England, somewhere near the two hundred.
ELLIE: I wouldn't live there if you paid me.
JOHN: You don't need to. It's happening here.
BEA: Liar.
P.J.: Since when?
ELLIE [*a hint of unease*]: Don't mind him.
JOHN: What a pack of chauvinists. Do you really think we're the only country to be exempt? We've had seventy-six disappearances that I know of.
ELLIE [*in dismay*]: Oh, no.
P.J.: Do you mean it's been hushed up?
JOHN: Not deliberately. The head of the Government Information Bureau was one of the first to go. In his absence the Cabinet has spent the past week trying to prepare a statement. You know how it is: grammar isn't their strong point.
P.J.: Good God.
JOHN: The most notable disappearance to date has been the deputy for Leix-Offaly.

ELLIE: He never!

JOHN: He wasn't missed for five days. His wife thought he was in the Dail, and the Government were too delighted by his absence to look a gift horse in the mouth.

BEA: It's the I.R.A. It's got to be.

JOHN: Darling, one of the victims was a miner on a coal-face in South Africa. There are depths to which even the I.R.A. will not descend.

P.J.: But who's doing it?

JOHN: Whoever it is, they're efficient. Not once have they been caught in the act. No violence used, no bloodshed. And in nearly every case the victim is a nonentity.

BEA: Like the deputy for Leix-Offaly.

JOHN: Right.

P.J.: Aren't there any theories?

JOHN: Dozens. Fine Gael is convinced it's the Red Chinese, and Fianna Fail, being more intellectually mature, believe it's the Martians. The Hierarchy has been consulted, of course, and Bishop Lucey has given it as his considered opinion that God is removing sinners from the face of the earth.

BEA: That's a bit thin.

JOHN: Yes. Especially since there's been an unconfirmed report today that Bishop Lucey has gone, too.

P.J.: Which explodes his theory.

JOHN: Unless he's had some unsuspected excitements in his life, yes.

P.J.: And there's no pattern to it ... none?

JOHN: Well ...

ELLIE: Is there?

JOHN: They've run every available statistic on every person who's vanished, world-wide, through the computers. The victims have all had two factors in common.

P.J.: Go on.

JOHN: One: every person who's disappeared has been aged thirty or over.

BEA: Oh, good ... that lets me out.

[*The others look at her. Her smile goes lame.*]

P.J.: And the second?

JOHN: Every victim was ... [*He breaks off and looks at* P.J.]

P.J.: Was what? Tell us.

    [JOHN *shakes his head abruptly. It is as if he were rejecting an idea which had offended his intelligence.*]

    Why not?

JOHN: I think you know the nature of my unofficial incumbency.

BEA: He means his job.

P.J.: Sure. You're the looney doctor for the Dail.

JOHN: Thanks.

P.J.: You ship the dipsos off to be dried out.

JOHN: I prescribe treatment for the consequences of occupational stress. Well, today I was obliged to sign committal papers for one of our ministers.

P.J.: He went bonkers?

JOHN: If you persist in using psychiatric terminology, yes.

P.J.: From booze?

JOHN: Not at all. He attempted to kill himself and his family. Luckily, his idea of suffocating his two sons while they slept was a failure. They're both rugby internationals.

ELLIE: The poor man. But why?

JOHN: It seems that at Harvard University a professor of advanced physics has formed a theory about the disappearances. He bases it on the second factor I mentioned. You know what the Americans are like: they see a picture of a phallus and they think it's the symbol for a banana.

BEA: Silly people! [*She laughs in private amusement.*]

JOHN: Well, our minister got wind of this theory, and tonight he's in the private wing of St Pat's.

P.J.: And now you're going to tell it to *us*?

JOHN: No.

BEA: Yes, he is. Sweetness, you've got us, we're hooked. Now what drove the nice man crackers?

ELLIE: Is it terrible?

JOHN: It's ...

P.J.: Here it comes!

JOHN: ... piffle! [*In what for him is an outburst*] And I refuse to dignify rubbish by giving it utterance.

P.J. [*in amused surprise*]: Hey ...

JOHN: I am a rational being. I will not abuse my intelligence by repeating what I know to be drivel. For twenty years I have been a man of science and an agnostic, and I decline to make a mockery of the brains God has given me.

[*In his indignation he crosses himself. The others stare at him.*]

BEA: Well, now!

JOHN [*copping out*]: I'm an outsider, all I know is the ... tip of the iceberg. If you want answers, go to our overlords in Merrion Street. They're the credulous fools who've banned old films.

P.J.: You said that was a joke.

JOHN: *You* said it was a joke. By unilateral agreement, films more than ten years old have been outlawed in Europe and North America.

[*A moment's pause; then, like a mass exhalation*]

BEA: Fool!

P.J. [*laughing*]: You bugger!

ELLIE: Was it a joke?

P.J.: And we fell for it.

ELLIE [*relieved; reproachful*]: John!

P.J.: Spoofed the lot of us.

BEA: A joke after all these years ... who's a clever sweetness, then?

ELLIE: You wretch, I was shaking.

P.J.: It damned near worked. If he hadn't gone over the top about old films being ...

JOHN [*suddenly*]: Look here, you promised me a record.

P.J.: Eh?

JOHN: Who was it ... Fred Astaire?

P.J. [*still laughing*]: Early soundtracks. Why?

JOHN: Where is it?

P.J.: On order. There's been such a run on vintage stuff, the wholesalers can't cope. You'll get it.

JOHN: I won't. Old records are banned, too.

P.J.: He never gives up.

ELLIE [*to* JOHN]: Now leave off ... I'll murder you.

P.J.: Heart of a lion! Give me your glass.

JOHN: And there's more besides.

BEA: Darling, the music has stopped, don't go on dancing.

JOHN: They're turning half of Kerry into a concentration camp.

P.J.: And high time, too!

[*All laugh, except for* JOHN, *whose attitude is one of prim detachment.* P.J. *goes to freshen* JOHN'S *drink.*
Through the following we become aware of a sound fading in from outside: a hard, staccato, tapping noise.]

ELLIE: It shows you how gullible people are.

BEA: Anyone will believe anything if the words are long enough.

ELLIE: I know, but when he said that Bishop Lucey had ...

JOHN [*listening*]: What's that?

BEA: It's from outside.

ELLIE: But what is it?

BEA: Someone's out there.

[*She goes towards the window. As the noise continues,* P.J. *begins to whistle.*]

ELLIE: Shush up.

[P.J. *shakes his hand at her. He is whistling 'Top Hat, White Tie and Tails' in time with the tapping.*]

My God, he's right. Someone's dancing.

BEA [*at the window*]: I can't see.

ELLIE: On our terrace!

P.J.: He's not bad.

[*The tapping fades away.*]

ELLIE: The nerve. How dare they?

P.J.: Who?

ELLIE: 'Who? Who?' If they want to have a party, let them have it in their own house, not here. I'm going to phone up and tell them so.

P.J.: Leave it.

ELLIE: Honestly ... you treat them like neighbours, you don't as much as say hello to them from one week to the next, and this is your thanks!

[*She storms into the hall.* JOHN *takes his drink from* P.J.]

JOHN: Mind if I get some ice?

P.J.: Sorry ... Ellie forgot it.

JOHN: No, no, let me. I know the topography. [*He starts towards the kitchen, glass in hand.*]

BEA: Do you hear him? ... 'topography'. He'd call a po a functional ceramic.

[JOHN *smiles at her and disappears into the kitchen.*]
Sod.

P.J.: Me or him?

BEA: You heard him. Calling me a conqueror of forty.

P.J.: Bea, that's silly. Who cares what age you are?

BEA [*stiffly*]: He wasn't talking about my age.

P.J.: Oh.

BEA: Which isn't forty.

P.J.: I know that.

BEA: I mean, you slave for him, you lead the life of a nun, you never as much as look at another man ...

P.J.: Right.

BEA: And for what? Insinuations.

P.J.: It's tough.

BEA: Sly little digs.

P.J.: If he has no reason to ...

BEA: None, I swear it. God knows he hasn't: not once.

[*A small pause.* P.J. *has refilled her glass. He hands it to her, standing behind her chair. Then, severely*]

And you promised you'd ring me, and you never did.

P.J. [*looking nervously towards the hall*]: Ah. I've been a bit ...

BEA: ... busy. Yes, that's what they all say.

P.J.: Do they?

BEA: Of course if you forget what you said the night of the party ...

P.J. [*trying to remember*]: Fat chance.

BEA: Because I'm not exactly hard up, you know; I'm not desperate. And God forbid I should throw a person's words back at him, but you did make a certain intriguing remark, and I asked you then and there – I can still see your face swaying in front of me – I asked you if you meant it in full sobriety. And you said, your exact words: 'Certainly, I mean it; every man tells the truth after midnight.' [*In parentheses*] Is that true?

P.J.: No question.

BEA: I never knew. It's worth remembering.

P.J.: Don't spread it around.

BEA: But you *are* still interested?

P.J.: Keen as mustard. [*He is perspiring. He takes aim at the back of her head with an imaginary gun.*]

BEA: And you'll ring me ... you promise?

P.J.: First thing Monday. [*He sprays bullets into her. In the process, his hand accidentally bumps against her hair.*]

BEA: Super. If Roland answers, hang up ... No, don't fondle me, he'll come in. Sit where I can see you.

[*He fires off a coup de grâce and moves from behind her.*]

You're a funny man.

P.J.: Oh, yeah.

BEA: Those rubbishy old films you like, and your records.

P.J.: Rubbish ... that's what Ellie calls it.

BEA: Does she? ... no, I'm joking, some of them are *fabulous*. Far more interesting than him with his old archery and his squash.

P.J.: Does John do archery?

JOHN [*appearing*]: Twang. [*He comes towards them with a bowl of ice-cubes.*]

BEA [*without looking*]: Oh, it's the rogue of Sherwood Forest.

JOHN: I thought I'd make myself useful and empty your ice-trays.

BEA: It took you long enough.

JOHN: I was hoping it would. [*Before she can reply*] Do you want some? ... no? I'm told that the practice of putting ice in drinks was on the verge of catching on in Europe, and then the 'Titanic' sank. Do you believe that?

P.J. [*nervously*]: Old films ...

JOHN: Oh, yes?

P.J.: We were discussing them.

BEA [*not to be intimidated*]: Among other things.

JOHN: Years since we've seen a film. What was the last one, darling ... 'The Jazz Singer'?

BEA [*to P.J.*]: You see?

JOHN: No, unlike yourself, Bea and I have managed to escape the plague.

P.J.: Come again?

JOHN: This sickly infatuation with the past. It's spreading like the Black Death.

[ELLIE *returns, still angry.*]

P.J.: Why is it sickly?

JOHN: Because ...

ELLIE [*finding her glass*]: And they're the people he [P.J.] wants us to be friends with. [*She drinks.*]

BEA: What happened?

JOHN [*to* P.J.]: It's sickly because ...

ELLIE: She takes half an hour to come to the phone, then informs me that her guests have better things to do than dance on our terrace. Would you believe it, they're playing Strip Monopoly.

BEA: My God.

JOHN: There, you see: even Monopoly is coming back.

P.J.: And that's sick?

ELLIE: It is, with your clothes off.

JOHN: On or off.

P.J.: Balls.

JOHN: Last year, in seventy-six, this ... longing for the desirable past was a fad, a fashion. This year it's run riot. Half the factories and offices are closed down from absenteeism because everyone is at home reading reprints of 'The Hotspur' and 'The Magnet' and listening to Cole Heaver.

BEA: Cole Porter, dear.

JOHN: It's a nightmare. Last week in London I picked up a copy of 'Playboy' ... I get it for the book reviews.

P.J. [*laughing*]: Sure, you do.

BEA: It's not funny: he really does.

JOHN: I opened out the thing, the centrefold, and who is the 'Playmate of the Month'?

P.J.: Who?

JOHN [*to* BEA]: Tell him.

BEA: Barbara Stanwyck.

JOHN: Charming, yes?

P.J.: That's nice.

JOHN: It's pathetic.

P.J. [*becoming riled*]: Would you say?

ELLIE: I agree with John.

P.J.: Well, we're married: you could hardly agree with *me*.

ELLIE: Isn't he a jewel?

BEA [*brightly, unheeded*]: Why don't we play Monopoly?

JOHN: I hear it every day in my consulting rooms. 'Doctor, I can't cope, I want to get out, I want to go back. Life is hurting me, it's too real, make it stop.' Half of them grew up during a world war, yet they'll swear to you the past was better.

P.J.: *I* was.

JOHN: You think you were.

P.J. [*dogged*]: I was better.

JOHN [*the professional*]: An example.

P.J.: What?

JOHN: You were better ... tell us how.

P.J.: I was ... [*He stops.*]

ELLIE: He can't. He doesn't know.

JOHN: Speak up, we're listening.

ELLIE: Hasn't a clue.

JOHN: Come along ... out with it. [*He snaps his fingers.*]

BEA: Don't be so rude: he's not a patient.

JOHN: So much for the good old days.

P.J.: No, wait.

ELLIE: Forget it.

P.J.: I do know that business is bad. I know that last week I laid off one of my reps.

JOHN: So?

P.J.: It was easy, no sweat. I called him in, I told him it had been a joy, a privilege. I snowed him with grade-A bullshit, and by his face you'd think I'd promoted him.

JOHN: If it had to be done ...

P.J.: It shouldn't have been easy. That's what I mean: there was a time when it wouldn't have been. There was a ...

   [*A ship's siren is heard and the sudden alarmed squawking of seagulls.* JOHN *looks around, startled.*]

   It's from the bay, it's a fog-horn.

JOHN [*uncertain*]: Is it?

P.J.: There was a girl in our town, name of Tish. She was beautiful. She wore gold earrings, like hoops. She stood at the head of the mailboat pier and waited for sailors.

BEA: Oh, yes?

[JOHN *goes to the window*.]

P.J.: If they wouldn't talk to her she'd step back out of their way and say in what she thought was a posh voice: 'Oh ... pawr-don.'

ELLIE: I hope you never went with her.

P.J.: My income wouldn't have stretched that far: I was twelve. She'd stand there in the rain. I asked my father; he told me she was looking for news of a long-lost relative. Then someone explained to me what a prostitute was and that Tish was one of them.

JOHN: It's a moonlit night; there's no fog.

BEA: Be quiet.

P.J.: I was so in love with her, and when I found out what she did with men I ran to the mailboat pier. She was there. In a beret and the gold earrings. I punched her. I cried and said I hated her.

BEA: You hit her?

P.J.: With my fists. She was amazed. She tried to catch hold of me. I called her names and ran away.

BEA: And she was beautiful?

P.J.: A stunner.

JOHN: Did she have a heart of gold?

P.J.: Pardon?

JOHN: In stories about whores it's standard equipment.

P.J.: You think I'm spinning a yarn?

JOHN: I distrust the human memory.

P.J.: It happened.

JOHN [*shrugging, letting it pass*]: Is there a point to it?

P.J.: I'm trying to say that the distance between then and now is that last week I fired someone and couldn't have cared less.

JOHN: There's no comparison.

ELLIE: None.

P.J.: I thought: bugger him, I've troubles enough of my own. I mean, I won't say I drink too much, but if I died tomorrow three pubs would close out of respect. I have a house I can no longer afford to live in ...

ELLIE: Don't discuss our affairs.

P.J.: ... and a wife who wears a halo of disappointment as though somehow she's slept through Christmas.

ELLIE: That is not true.

P.J.: And blames me for not waking her.

ELLIE: You are a liar.

BEA: Now, children: no squabbling.

P.J.: We do not squabble, fight or have rows. We collect grudges. We're in an arms race, storing up warheads for the domestic Armageddon.

ELLIE: A saint couldn't live with him!

P.J.: And as for our fifteen-year-old pride and joy ...

ELLIE [turning on him]: Don't you dare.

P.J.: My beloved Emma ...

ELLIE: I said that will do.

P.J.: What a girl.

ELLIE: Just shut ... up.

BEA: Is she not well?

ELLIE: She's still with my sister. She's fine. Doesn't want to come home. [She darts a bitter look at P.J.]

JOHN: How splendid. [He looks at his watch.] Well, I think it's ...

ELLIE: Honestly, I could drown him. Every day I have this to put up with ... and he's getting worse.

P.J.: That's what I'm telling you.

ELLIE: What?

P.J.: I was better.

ELLIE: I disagree.

[P.J. cannot win. He takes a sip from his glass and stands facing the 'fourth' wall.]

JOHN [trying again]: It's really time we were ...

ELLIE: Stay. There's no rush.

BEA: We always get up early on Sundays. John likes to be sure we're missing Mass from principle and not laziness.

ELLIE: You've loads of time. Come on ...

[This, as she takes BEA's glass and goes to recharge it. A pause as JOHN comes to stand beside P.J.]

P.J.: Plenty of people sailing tonight.

JOHN: Aha?

P.J.: For Holyhead. The pier's crowded. Look at that mob.

[JOHN *instinctively looks out front, then stares at* P.J. ELLIE *turns.*]
Wow.

ELLIE: *What* pier is crowded?

P.J. [*starting to point*]: The ... [*Then, blankly*] I saw the mailboat pier.

ELLIE: You what?

P.J.: Out there. I saw it.

[BEA *begins to laugh, then stops as she realizes he is not joking.*]
And in broad daylight. The old mailboat ... not the new one.
It was the steamship, the old 'Princess Maude'. It was ...

JOHN: Let's not get excited.

ELLIE: He saw sweet damn all.

P.J. [*to* JOHN]: As clearly as if I was ...

ELLIE: It's an act. He wants to be noticed.

JOHN: If I may get a word in ...

ELLIE [*a note of panic*]: Because if it's not an act, if it's come to the
point where he's beginning to see things, well, that's the bloody
limit, it really is.

JOHN: We mustn't get overwrought.

ELLIE: Other people can hold their drink, they can get mouldy,
falling-around drunk in a civilized manner, but not him ... no,
he has to go ...

JOHN: If you will allow me ...

BEA [*to* ELLIE]: Leave it to John, dear.

JOHN [*approaching* P.J.]: Right. Now, then ...

BEA: He does know his job: I'll grant him that.

JOHN [*to* BEA]: Please ... may I?

BEA [*a whisper*]: He's marvellous.

JOHN: P.J., do you feel well?

[P.J. *shrugs.*]
And this isn't a leg-pull?

P.J.: No, I saw it. What the hell's wrong with me?

JOHN: No panic, now.

P.J.: I distinctly saw the ...

JOHN: This is not as rare a phenomenon as you might think. Tired-
ness can cause it, so can anxiety. Be calm, there's no cause for alarm.

BEA: Be calm? You stupid quack, how can he be calm if he's seeing mailboat piers that aren't there?

JOHN: I'm trying to explain. When the mind is ...

BEA: Calls himself a doctor! My God, if I saw something that wasn't there I'd ...

[*She gives a yelp of fright.* TISH *has suddenly appeared in the room. She is a tough and battered-looking streetwalker, born and bred to hard times. She is 40 and looks older. She is dressed in the fashion of the late 1940s, and has made an impoverished attempt to look seductive. She wears a beret, rakishly tilted over one ear, and gold hoop earrings. One stocking is laddered. Her face is thick with stale pancake make-up; her lipstick is an outsized cupid's bow; there are moons of rouge on her cheeks. She is standing, hand on hip, one knee jutting forward. She takes a drag from her cigarette, then notices where she is.*]

ELLIE [*at* BEA's *cry*]: What is it? What's the ...

[*She sees* TISH *and gasps with shock.* TISH *stares back at the group. A pause.*]

TISH: Sweet Jesus, where am I? What happened to me? What place am I in?

JOHN [*putting on his horn-rims*]: Good God.

P.J.: All I ask is, don't humour me. Is it real or is it me again?

TISH: Am I in a kip? [*To* JOHN] You ... you with the hair-oil, stop scratchin' yourself and answer me.

ELLIE: Who are you? How dare you walk into this house?

TISH: Beg your pardon?

JOHN: She seems confused. What are you doing here?

TISH: Beg your pardon?

JOHN: You've intruded into this lady's house. I think she's entitled to an explanation.

ELLIE: I shut that front door.

P.J.: You couldn't have.

ELLIE: I did. She broke in. Get the police.

JOHN: One moment. [*To* TISH] Are you an itinerant?

TISH: Beg your pardon?

BEA [*helpfully*]: He means one of the travelling people, dear.

TISH: Ask me arse.

BEA [*affronted*]: I see!

TISH: I never seen youse before. Who brung me here?

JOHN: That's for you to tell us.

TISH [*dazed*]: Dunno where I am. I musta got a bad pint ... I'm in the jigs. Me ma ... where's me ma? The legs is goin' from under me. [*Calling*] Mammy!

JOHN: I think she's ill.

BEA: I almost dropped dead. One moment there was no one there, and the next she was ...

JOHN: Never mind that. Get some spirits ... anything.

TISH [*feebly*]: I want me ma.

JOHN [*assisting her*]: Just sit and relax. I'm a doctor.

TISH: Queer place to wake up in. I musta fell outa me standin'. Is me face cut?

JOHN: Not at all. Truly.

TISH: Thanks bit o' God. If me good looks went I'd be shagged.

ELLIE [*to* P.J.]: If I didn't know better I'd say it was Hallowe'en. Do you think she was run over?

P.J.: By the look of her, more than once.

[BEA *is circling round* TISH *with a glass of brandy*.]

BEA: Will this do?

JOHN: Where are you going?

BEA: I'm trying to find out if she has a windward side.

JOHN: Give it to me.

TISH [*pointing at the television set*]: What's that yoke?

JOHN: It's a television.

TISH: A what?

JOHN: Take just a sip of this.

TISH [*darkly*]: Did you put somethin' in it?

JOHN: Of course not.

TISH [*grinning*]: You chancer. [*She tastes it.*] It wouldn'ta been the first time.

JOHN [*reaching for the glass*]: There, now.

[TISH *drains it and hands it to him.*]

ELLIE: Ask her what she's doing here.

JOHN [*smiling*]: That's not quite how it's done. Where disorders of the mind are involved, the patient must be led gently. [*He shoots his cuffs and addresses* TISH *soothingly.*] You do realize we want to help you?

BEA: Watch this: it's his Claude Rains imitation.

TISH: Where's me ma? Why isn't she with me?

JOHN: We're going to find out.

TISH: It's gone dark out. I dunno what road I'm on.

JOHN: You're with friends. Can you tell me what day this is?

TISH AND ELLIE [*together*]: It's Saturday.

ELLIE: Sorry.

JOHN: Excellent. And the month and year?

TISH: Has he a slate loose?

JOHN: Just bear with me. This month is what?

TISH: It's August.

JOHN: Splendid.

TISH: ... Nineteen-forty-nine.

JOHN: Very g ... [*He breaks off.*]

   [BEA *laughs, thinking that* TISH *is trying to be funny.*]
Could we be serious?

TISH: Missus, are you laughin' at me?

BEA: You told him the year was ...

TISH: If you want to make a jeer of someone, make a jeer of someone else, don't make a jeer of me.

BEA: I assure you ...

TISH: There's something wrong about this place, there's somethin' wrong about all of youse.

JOHN: Why do you say that?

TISH: Dunno. It looks queer. It's all ... wonky. The way youse is dressed.

JOHN [*to the others*]: Disorientation. She may be concussed.

TISH [*staring at* JOHN'*s crotch*]: Them trousers.

JOHN: Oh yes?

TISH: There's not much room for improvement. [*Looking at* ELLIE] And the get-up of your wan. And her [BEA] with the greeny stuff on her eyes, like she was in a concert. [*Looking at* P.J.] And your man there ... Starve-the-Barber. No, it's all wrong. Tell me what way is the bus and I'll go home. [*In sudden panic*] Me handbag

... where's me bag? Have I me few shillin's? [*She snatches up her handbag and roots through it.*]

JOHN: I think she should stay.

ELLIE: John!

JOHN: She's obviously in shock ... she may be injured. [*To* TISH] Would you like to tell us your name?

TISH: Miss Murphy. [*Counting*] It's all there ... eight and a kick.

JOHN: Try to think. What's the last thing you remember before you came here?

TISH: I was ... [*She stops, confused.*]

JOHN: Could you have received a blow?

TISH: Beg your pardon?

JOHN: Could you have been hit on the head?

TISH [*at once*]: It was in the stomach. [*Her memory clears.*] *That's* what happened me!

JOHN: Go on.

TISH: I was standin' outside the Pav.

JOHN: The ...?

TISH: The picture house ... the Pavilion. It's where you can see who's comin' off the mailboat. I mean, the hard times that's in it, I do go down there on business. And the mammy was in the bushes over the road. Like, she'd never be far off, like, on account of there's them 'ud rob you, or maybe worse. It's a hard old station.

JOHN: I know, yes.

TISH: Gettin' soaked to the skin when the weather's wet and gettin' made a mock of be the cornerboys when it's dry. I never tamper with no one ... you ask who you like, you ask the polis. I keep meself to meself ... got enough to do pullin' the divil be the tail without bein' made a mock of.

JOHN: Tell me what happened?

TISH: When? Oh ... pawr-don. I was outside the Pav. And this young lad, this little get, comes up to me. I know him well to see of an old date: always pimpin' and pryin' and folleying me ... never out of the corner of me eye, and hoppin' off like a hare when I look straight at him. Only this time he comes up to me. A tinker

the like of him ... 'claire to God, he draws out and hits me two
pucks in the stomach.

[P.J. *rises, staring at her in horror.*]

'Dirty Tish,' he shouts at me. 'Dirty Tish.'

P.J. [*shrilly*]: Tish?

TISH: And the next thing I know, I'm ... [*Glaring at* P.J.] Is he
makin' a jeer?

ELLIE [*fuming*]: I might have guessed.

P.J.: It's her. I don't know how, but it is.

TISH: Beg your pardon?

ELLIE [*to* P.J.]: How dare you?

P.J.: I'm going mad.

ELLIE: How dare you put that woman up to this?

P.J.: Eh?

ELLIE: First, you make up that pack of lies; then you pretend to be
having visions of mailboat piers; and then she walks in. Do you take
us for fools?

P.J.: It *is* her: I swear to you. Tish ... don't you know me?

BEA: If he calls her 'mother', I'll scream.

ELLIE: *That's* how she got in. He gave her a key ... it was planned.

JOHN: I believe you're right.

ELLIE: It was rigged. The beret, the hoop earrings: for God's sake,
look at her. It's a hoax. Next, he'll tell us she's been wandering
around in a stupor ever since he was that high. Thirty years!

TISH: Me? Does she mean me?

BEA [*to* P.J.]: Yes, love, it's a bit Irish.

TISH: Thirty years? Oh, Jasus ... where's there a lookin' glass? [*She
begins to search frantically in her handbag.*]

ELLIE: You can drop the act. We're not impressed.

BEA [*to* TISH, *indicating a wall mirror*]: Try that one.

ELLIE [*to* P.J.]: Whoever that woman is and wherever you found her,
get her out of here. You've embarrassed me and you've embarrassed
John and Beatrice. Of all the ...

[TISH *has dashed over to the mirror. She gives a sigh of relief.*]

TISH: Thanks bit o' God. I'm no different: there's not a blemish.
The fright she gev me ... I thought maybe I'd turned into an oul'
bag o' bones like your woman in that fillum, 'Lost Whores'.

BEA: 'Lost Whores'?

P.J.: I think she means 'Lost Horizon'.

TISH: But I'm still in me prime.

P.J.: Tish, it's unbelievable ... you haven't changed.

ELLIE: The joke is over!

TISH [*to* P.J.]: Do I know you?

P.J.: Better than you think you do.

TISH [*coyly; pleased*]: How would I? ... Sure you're a toff. Where was it?

P.J.: I'm the little boy who punched you.

[TISH *grins, then stops grinning. She gives a cry of fear.*]

TISH: Keep him away from me.

P.J.: I mean, I *was*.

TISH: He's in the jigs ... don't let him come near me.

P.J. [*to* JOHN]: You tell her.

JOHN: Really, P.J., first you make this unfortunate creature your accomplice, and now you poke fun at her. It does you no credit.

P.J.: John, as God is my ...

JOHN: Enough is enough. [*To* TISH] Would you mind if I looked in your handbag?

TISH: Would I what?

JOHN: To help us to help you.

TISH: You damn well won't.

JOHN: And perhaps you'll accept this for your trouble.

[*He produces a pound note.* TISH's *eyes are at once fixed on it.*]
I know it's an imposition. Yes? [*He puts the banknote into her hand and takes the handbag.*] Aren't you good! Thank you. [*To* P.J.] And this is where *you* begin to look foolish for a change.

TISH [*muttering*]: What's in there is private property. Youse have no business meddlin'.

[JOHN *brings the bag to a table and takes out the contents, one article at a time.*]

JOHN: Let's see, now. A door-key ... cigarettes ... matches ... packet of ... [*He stops, embarrassed.*]

BEA: Packet of what?

[TISH *angrily snatches the packet from* JOHN's *hand and bears it away.*]

JOHN: Nothing.

ELLIE: Well, go on. What else?

JOHN [*delving further*]: Here's something ... it's a book of ... I don't believe it.

BEA: Let's see.

JOHN: Talk about relics. It's a ration book. Well, I never! 'Valid for year ending December, Nineteen-forty-nine.'

BEA: Good Lord.

ELLIE: So it is. Look, Bea ... clothes coupons. Do you remember?

BEA: Actually, no.

TISH: Youse is easy amused. And them coupons is counted. [*She sits, one leg swinging, and disassociates herself from the proceedings.*]

JOHN: The things people hang on to! What else? Lipstick ... compact ... and a prayer book!

ELLIE: No!

P.J.: She never missed Mass ... I remember that.

ELLIE: No one is talking to you.

JOHN: It's a bit dog-eared. [*Opening it*] Well, no wonder. 'To my daughter, Patricia, for her Confirmation ...'

BEA [*touched*]: Ah ... poor thing.

JOHN: '... On the twenty-fifth of May, Nineteen-twenty.'

ELLIE: When, did you say?

JOHN: On the ...

[*As the fact of the year sinks in, he looks at* TISH, *who is unconcernedly singing to herself.* ELLIE *grabs the book from him.*]

TISH [*singing*]:

   'Don't sit under the apple tree

   With anywan else but me,

   Anywan else but me, anywan else but me,

   No, no, no ...'

BEA: But if her confirmation was nearly sixty years ago ...

ELLIE: Bea, no one is that well preserved. It's not her prayer book, it's her mother's. Ask John.

[JOHN *is beginning to crack up. He looks at her blankly.*]

I'm telling Bea that it can't possibly belong to ... What's up?

[JOHN *takes the purse from the handbag and empties the coins on the table.*]

P.J.: Found something?

JOHN: Pre-decimal.

P.J.: Come again?

JOHN [*becoming agitated*]: It's old coinage ... obsolete. Thruppenny
bits ... a sixpence! [*Holding up a coin*] This one is Nineteen-forty-
seven, and it's brand new.

ELLIE: Well, she hoards things. Why are you so ...

JOHN: It's in mint condition. [*He finds a cardboard stub.*] Look ... look
here. Train ticket Dalkey to Dun Laoghaire. Are you blind?

BEA: You're being rude.

JOHN: I'm sorry ...

BEA: Polite people wait till they're in the car.

JOHN: I'm trying to say that the fare on this ticket is twopence.

BEA: What of it? Maybe it's a special offer like midweek excursions.
Maybe pros get reduced rates.

[*JOHN looks at her.*]

Well, how do I know?

P.J.: Is that the lot?

JOHN: I think so. [*Searching the handbag*] Odds and ends. A mirror.
Broken comb. Photogr ... [*He takes a photograph from the handbag
and looks at it.*]

P.J.: Any joy?

[*JOHN thrusts the photograph at him abruptly, walks away and pours
himself a drink.*]

BEA [*nervously, to JOHN*]: Is something wrong, petal?

ELLIE [*to P.J.*]: Well, tell us.

P.J.: It's a picture of her and an old woman. She's wearing the clothes
she has on. [*He crosses to TISH.*] When was this taken?

ELLIE: I want to see it.

TISH: That's me in O'Connell Street.

P.J.: I know it is.

TISH: The day of the mammy's birthday. We had an outin'.

P.J.: When was that?

TISH: 'Scuse me for breathin'. It was last year.

P.J.: Thanks. [*He hands the photograph to ELLIE.*] Take a look at the
other people ... how they're dressed. And that large object in the
background is the Dalkey tram.

BEA: Tram?

P.J.: The trams stopped running in Nineteen-forty-eight.

TISH: Last year, yeah. It's all buses now. The pair of us went to the Theatre Royal. It was massive. All the motts showin' their legs, and your man croonin'.

[*Lilting to herself*]

'I'll walk alone,

Because to tell you the truth

I am lonely;

I don't mind bein' lonely . . .'

ELLIE: But if that's thirty years ago why hasn't she changed?

[JOHN *clears his throat.*]

JOHN: I mentioned earlier that one of our ministers heard a certain theory and had to be certified. You'd better know now what it is. If you pack too many people into a lift you'll snap the cable. Well, according to a Harvard scientist, a past pupil of Einstein's, that's what's happening. He believes that so many people are longing for the simplicity of bygone days that Time has been ruptured. His theory is that people who can't cope with the present, who want no part of it, are disappearing back into the past.

ELLIE [*in disgust*]: You're worse than he is. [*Meaning* P.J.]

JOHN: Also that the reverse is happening. People we remember and want to see again are popping up in the here and now. They're appearing by the score . . . elsewhere by the hundreds. That's why there's a concentration camp in County Kerry.

P.J.: Sweet, merciful, all-loving –

JOHN: I'm told there are already no less than fifteen Humphrey Bogarts down there, thumping hell out of each other.

ELLIE: It's lunacy. The world's gone mad.

JOHN: Anyway, that's why there's to be a ban on old films and such: to try and close the floodgates.

P.J.: You mean, to stop people from living in the past?

JOHN: In a very literal sense, yes. And of course that would account for the disappearance of Bishop Lucey and the deputy for Leix-Offaly. They weren't exactly what you'd call progressives.

ELLIE: But who believes such nonsense?

JOHN: A moment ago, I, for one, became a convert.

ELLIE: John!

BEA: I'm a bit lost. Do you mean in the religious sense?

JOHN: Bea, let's not be credulous. I'm talking about travelling through time.

ELLIE: I'm asleep, it's a nightmare.

JOHN: Ellie, the proof is in this room. [*He indicates* TISH, *who has fallen asleep.*]

BEA: She's nodded off.

P.J.: Poor soul. She's been on her feet all day at the mailboat pier.

ELLIE: Now stop that! Bea, tell them it's rubbish.

BEA: You know me: if it saves thinking, I'll believe anything. But, P.J., you distinctly told us that she was the most beautiful creature. A stunner, you said.

ELLIE [*clutching at straws*]: Yes! What about that?

P.J.: I have lousy taste.

ELLIE [*to* JOHN]: What's past is dead and gone and over and done with. You talk as if she's come here by way of the Naas Road.

JOHN: The American scientist, Dr Schlepper ... he believes that all along we've mistaken the very nature of time itself. According to him, it's our consciousness of a given moment – we call it the present – that's on the move. Time isn't. The past is still there, like a page in a book after we've read it.

P.J.: I see.

BEA: You do?

P.J.: What I'm having trouble with is the fifteen Humphrey Bogarts.

JOHN: Ah! That's an interesting theory ...

ELLIE: Well, I don't want to hear it. What I do want is that woman out of here.

P.J.: Why?

JOHN: She has a point. We'd better send for the Collection Squad.

P.J.: For the what?

JOHN: It's the same as the Special Branch, except that they don't beat you up. They'll come and have her shipped off to Kerry.

P.J.: John, you can't.

JOHN: It's the humane thing to do. These poor creatures are wandering about, lost and confused, frightened by fast cars, jet aircraft and pop groups. They have no proper money and no jobs. Who's to look after them? No, she'll be better off.

P.J.: In a camp?

JOHN: It's not so bad. They have Glenn Miller concerts, and the Al Jolsons are forming a choir.

P.J.: You seem to be well informed.

JOHN: I am. But I didn't believe any of it until now. Well, the Government can't keep it a secret much longer. Only yesterday they turned down a request from the Rathmines and Rathgar Operatic Society to have one of the Carusos released from Kerry for 'The Desert Song'.

ELLIE: Will you please ring that number?

JOHN: Of course.

P.J.: We might at least offer her a cup of tea first and a sandwich.

JOHN: That's an idea. She may not have eaten in quite a while.

P.J.: Twenty-eight years.

ELLIE: I blame you for this.

P.J.: What did I do?

ELLIE: Who conjured her up?

P.J.: You won't believe she was conjured up.

ELLIE: No, I will not. But if I did believe it I'd blame you. [*About to enter the kitchen, she hangs back.*] Bea, do you want to come?

P.J.: Yeah, go with her. Maybe Jack the Ripper is in there.

BEA: Now that's cruel. You know quite well that Ellie is highly strung. [*To* ELLIE] Of course I'll come with you, dear ... don't mind him. [*Then*] You go first.

[ELLIE *and* BEA *go off through the dining area.*]

P.J.: The miracle of the loaves and fishes pales by comparison with my wife's talent for having her cake and eating it.

[JOHN *is gathering up* TISH's *effects and replacing them in her handbag.*]

JOHN: Your friend there ... is she still alive?

P.J.: Seems to be: she's making noises. [*Then*] I see what you mean.

JOHN: Is she?

P.J.: I heard a rumour. Someone said she's living in England. She got married. She's white-haired and respectable.

JOHN: How did she ever get married?

P.J.: I dunno. Unlucky, I suppose.

[*He is dejected.* JOHN *pats him on the shoulder.*]

JOHN: Look here ... I won't send for the Collection Squad until she's had food. I gather they arrive like greased lightning. It's the danger to health.

P.J.: The which?

JOHN: People like her ... their first impulse is to head for home. They turn the knob and walk straight in. To date, it's caused more than one coronary.

P.J.: It would do, yes.

JOHN: That's why I asked if she was still alive. I'm glad she's in England: it wouldn't do if she ran into herself.

P.J.: Bit embarrassing.

JOHN: Indeed.

P.J.: She could drop down dead.

JOHN: Easily.

P.J.: And she might never get over it.

[*He splutters into his glass.* JOHN *eyes him austerely.*]

[*Wiping his eyes*] Sorry.

JOHN: P.J., there is nothing funny about the trauma induced in a woman who is confronted by her younger, pre-menopausal self. God knows what Sigmund Freud would have said.

P.J.: Ask him when he gets here.

[JOHN *is visibly annoyed.*]

Hey, he could, you know. What if Tish gets nostalgic for *her* good old days? And the people she conjures up ... suppose they don't like it here, either? And if *they* start living in the past as well ...

JOHN: In that event, before the year is out you'll be seeing the Last Supper in your breakfast room.

P.J. [*sobered*]: There'll be more of them than of us.

JOHN: And so much for the Pill.

P.J.: Multiplying like rabbits. We could starve.

JOHN: There's no 'could' about it, matey. [*He helps himself to the potato crisps.*] And Ireland will be the first to go under. Living in the past is our speciality.

P.J.: What'll we do?

JOHN [*shrugging*]: Same as always ... blame the British.

P.J.: The evening started out so pleasantly. We had a nice dinner, and I was looking forward to that film on the box. I can't even remember what it was, now. [*Remembering*] Oh, yeah ...

JOHN: Well, let's not meet our troubles half ...

> [*There is a bugle call from outside. It is the 'retreat'; French army version. It is repeated, then the last note dies away.*
> *Unnoticed by the men, the noise awakens* TISH.]

P.J.: What the hell was ...

> [ELLIE *comes in.*]

ELLIE [*to* P.J.]: Now stop that, do you hear? Stop it. [*She returns to the kitchen.*]

P.J.: It must be the Carnahans again. Funny way to call people to supper.

JOHN: I imagine one gets very engrossed playing Strip Monopoly.

P.J.: True.

JOHN: But turning to a more cheerful subject ...

P.J.: Good lad.

JOHN: ... Are you chasing my wife?

> [P.J. *is too stunned to reply.* TISH *looks on, wide-eyed.*]

When I was in the kitchen a while ago I was eavesdropping, so I couldn't help overhearing.

P.J.: Am I chasing your ... ?

JOHN: If you're going to take offence I'll be sorry I asked.

P.J. [*indignant*]: Beatrice and me?

JOHN: In fact, I do apologize. The question was anti-social.

P.J.: You accuse me ...

JOHN: I was making small talk.

P.J.: ... of running after your ...

JOHN: Now let's watch the adrenalin.

P.J.: I have never laid a finger ...

JOHN: Don't worry about it.

P.J.: As God is my ...

JOHN [*the perfect host*]: It's my pleasure.

P.J.: Will you let me get a word in? [*Lowering his voice*] I do not chase. My life with Ellie is not exactly one of domestic bliss, and to run after other women you need to be happily married; otherwise you can't concentrate.

JOHN: That makes sense.

P.J. [*richly amused*]: Me chasing Beatrice!

JOHN: You were playing footsie in the restaurant. Yes?

P.J. [*half-admiringly*]: You don't miss much. X-ray eyes, what?

JOHN: Actually, it was my foot.

P.J.: Shit.

JOHN: What I'm driving at is: like many women her age, Beatrice is enjoying a late vocation as a man-eating tigress. I'm the one who suffers. If I don't let her off the leash, I get mauled, and if I do let her off the leash I get migraine.

P.J. [*sympathetic*]: There's never a happy medium.

JOHN: There could be. [*Hesitant*] I know this is an imposition ...

P.J.: Say it.

JOHN: What she needs is having something to look forward to. And when I felt your toes curling around my instep in the Mirabeau, it occurred to me. Assuming, if I may, that your intentions towards her aren't of a ... an acrobatic nature.

P.J.: No way.

JOHN [*smiling his gratitude*]: Then I wondered if you could oblige me by keeping her on a slow simmer, as it were ... without actually bringing her to the boil. It would make life at home that much easier.

P.J.: Well, I'm blowed.

JOHN [*a small laugh*]: I hope not.

P.J.: That is one hell of a compliment.

JOHN: Balderdash.

P.J.: It is. You're trusting me to ...

    [*He sees that* TISH *is awake and staring at them.*]

    Look who's awake. Feeling better?

TISH: Youse is lovely. The pair of youse is lovely.

JOHN: Thank you. We were ...

TISH: I never heard such dirty talk. Married men, makin' little of women behind their backs. Call yourselves the quality.

P.J.: Tish, what's wrong?

TISH: Miss Murphy in your mouth. Him, askin' you to simmer his wife for him. Well, it's a misfortunate day for poor people like meself if it's youse we have to look up to.

P.J.: What we were discussing was ...

TISH: With the soft pink hands on youse that never saw dirt. If any man, I don't care who he is, said to my face things about his wife like what you said about yours, I'd reef him.

P.J.: We said nothing.

JOHN: It's no use. Don't argue.

TISH [to JOHN]: What are you smirkin' at?

JOHN: Do you mean me?

TISH: Go on, say it. Say what's in the back o' your mind, an' see what it gets you.

JOHN: Let's not get heated.

TISH: Don't you look down on me. I have me business to mind, but any man I ever went with, it was for money! No one ever trick-acted with me ... no, nor set his foot inside my house. I'd live on dry bread first. An' many's a time, bad as I needed the few shillin's, there's men I said No to an' sent home to their childer or walked them to the chapel gates. I've wiped away more tears, Mister, than you'll cry in two lifetimes. And I'll say this to you free o' charge: if there was a man worth marryin' an' he was gent enough to ask me, I could say Yis to him an' tell him he was the first and not go red in the face while I was sayin' it. Put that in your saucepan and simmer it!

P.J. [to JOHN]: Do you know, I can't think what I ever saw in her.

[ELLIE *and* BEA *come in bearing coffee and sandwiches.*]

ELLIE [looking at TISH]: What's all the row about?

JOHN: Row? There's no row.

BEA: You've been making more noise than fifteen Humphrey Bogarts.

ELLIE: Why was she yelling?

JOHN [a diversion; to P.J.]: Humphrey Bogart ... yes: you asked how that was possible. Now if you can envisage time as a kind of ...

[P.J. *is flinching painfully, shielding his eyes.*]

What is it?

P.J.: The sun is blinding me.

JOHN: The sun is?

P.J.: The heat ... I'm roasting. Turn it off.

JOHN: The heat?

[*There is a crash from the hall, and* HARRY STANDISH *comes staggering in. He wears the uniform and full marching pack of a ranker in the French Foreign Legion. His rifle has bayonet fixed. His face is caked with sand. He is in his late 20s. He fetches up against the back of a chair and leans on it in utter exhaustion.*]

HARRY [*gasping*]: Pardonnez-moi, mesdames ... messieurs. Je suis désolé de vous déranger.

ELLIE [*finding her voice*]: I've afraid you've mistaken the house. The fancy-dress party is over there.

HARRY [*he is British*]: My God, you're English.

BEA: We're Irish, actually.

HARRY: Yes? Well, at least you're white ... that's something. [*He lurches to the drinks table, picks up the water jug and drinks from it.*]

TISH: Who's your man?

ELLIE: He's in the wrong house and he's so drunk he can't walk straight. [*To* HARRY] Excuse me, but ...

P.J.: I think the people you want are the Carnahans.

[HARRY *drains the jug.*]

HARRY: Rotten manners, I'm afraid. Terribly sorry. Stumbling on this oasis was a ... stroke of luck. Not on the maps. They came at us in the dark, you see, shouting prayers to Allah. Filthy heathens. Captain LeBlanc tried to parley with them ... they shot him where he stood. It's not playing the game. Every man wiped out, except for me.

ELLIE [*her voice trembling*]: John ...

JOHN: I'll have them here in ten minutes. Now stay calm. [*He goes out into the hall.*]

BEA [*to* HARRY]: Where exactly are you trying to get to?

HARRY: Sidi Ben Abba. Do you know it?

BEA: It rings a bell. I think it's in Glenageary.

ELLIE [*urgently, beckoning*]: Beatrice ...

[BEA *watches in fascination as* HARRY *takes off his pack, sits and begins to remove a boot.*]

P.J.: Ellie ... that film I was looking forward to ...

ELLIE: Don't say it, because I won't listen.

P.J.: But it's him, it's him. My God, it's happened again.

BEA: What has?

[HARRY *pours a stream of sand from his boot on to the carpet.*]

Oh, have you been down on the beach then?

[JOHN *comes back.*]

JOHN: Sorry ... your phone seems to be out of order.

ELLIE: It can't be; I rang the Carnahans.

HARRY: They cut the wires.

P.J.: Who did?

HARRY: The Tuaregs. They may not be Englishmen, but they aren't fools. Well, it seems that wiping out the column isn't enough for them: now they're going to get tiresome.

JOHN: Not to worry. I'll nip up to the phone box in the village. Back in two ticks. [*He goes out.*]

HARRY: Don't go out there. Are you mad? ... the sandhills are crawling with them.

[*The front door slams, off.*]

Too late. [*He salutes the departed* JOHN.] The gallant fool. For his sake I hope the fiends don't take him alive.

P.J.: There's something I think we should explain.

ELLIE: Don't say anything.

P.J.: This may come as a shock, but ...

[*There is the half shot, half whine of a rifle being fired some distance off.*]

BEA: He'll really have to get that exhaust seen to. [*Eyeing* HARRY *from head to toe*] Do you know, if you lose at Strip Monopoly you're going to be the hit of the evening.

HARRY: Madame?

[JOHN *returns, a hand cupped over one ear. He is in a blazing temper. He walks towards* P.J.]

BEA: That was quick.

ELLIE: Wouldn't the car start?

P.J.: What's up?

JOHN [*pointing at* TISH]: I don't mind you conjuring up her: it's your business. I don't even mind him. [*Meaning* HARRY] What I do object to is going for a civilized drink in Killiney and being shot by an Arab.

[*He drops his hand, the better to grab* P.J. *by the jacket, and we see that there is blood on his ear.*]

[*Curtain*]

ACT TWO

P.J., JOHN *and* HARRY *are sitting in silence, nursing their drinks.* JOHN *is wearing a makeshift bandage which gives him the rakish look of a buccaneer.*

Thirty minutes have passed.

P.J.: Speaking of Arabs, there's a story about this cannibal restaurant in New York. Well, they say that New York has every kind of restaurant under the sun, so there's this one that serves up people. Anyway, this woman with a blue rinse walks in and looks at the menu. It says: 'Englishman, five dollars; Frenchman, five dollars; Australian, five dollars; Arab, seven dollars fifty.' So she calls the waiter. 'Tell me,' she says; 'how is it that Englishmen, Frenchmen and Australians are all five dollars, but the A-rab costs seven dollars fifty?' And the waiter says to her: 'Madam, have you ever tried to clean an A-rab?' [*Pause. To* JOHN] How's your ear?

JOHN: It hurts.

P.J.: Could have been worse.

JOHN: How, worse? Do you realize I've been marked for life? The whole lobe is shot away.

P.J.: Still, it's not as if you wore earrings.

JOHN: It's typical of you to get philosophical about other people's lobes. If you were a lobe short we'd soon hear all about it. This mutilation has cost me my livelihood.

P.J.: Have a jar.

JOHN: You think I exaggerate? How can I hope to be all-wise and Godlike to people who walk into my consulting rooms, take one look at me and say: 'Hey, where's your ear?'

[P.J. *tops up his glass.*]

I shouldn't have this, I'm in shock. [*Accepting it*] I don't care any more.

P.J.: Look, don't get peeved ...

JOHN [*truculent*]: Why?

P.J.: What you told us, you weren't coming the hound? I mean, that Arab *was* on a camel when he shot you?

JOHN: How many more times? . . . Yes.

P.J.: One hump or two? [*As* JOHN *glares at him*] I'm trying to picture it.

JOHN: I didn't wait to do a hump-count. I saw this long-necked slobbering thing with knobbly knees standing over me.

P.J. [*his W. C. Fields bit*]: Never mind your love-life, stick to the camel.

JOHN: Now I'm warning you . . .

HARRY: You're deuced lucky you weren't bitten. They're the filthiest creatures . . . riddled with venereal disease.

JOHN: I didn't know that.

P.J. [*as before*]: And the camels aren't too healthy either. [*At once*] John, I'm not getting at you. I'm in shock, too; this is how it affects me.

HARRY: In my small experience, when one goes abroad there's not much that isn't filthy. Take the men in our regiment: scum, nearly all of them, and I speak with charity. Dagos, frogs, huns, niggers and wops . . . and only one or two English chaps.

P.J.: I wonder how many of them are there.

HARRY: In our company alone there's . . .

P.J.: No, I mean Arabs in our garden.

JOHN: All I can vouch for is the one who shot me. But surely if there was a gang of them they'd have launched an attack by now.

P.J.: Maybe.

JOHN: Or do they always wait until dawn?

P.J.: You're thinking of Apaches. No, use your loaf, these Arabs are in unfamiliar territory. There's greenery instead of sand, and they're bound to be taken aback if they see a 59 bus go by. Also, on this estate alone there are thirty houses. For all we know, they could be slitting throats over at the Carnahans'.

JOHN: That's a point.

P.J.: In their get-up someone could mistake them for guests, let them in, and before you know it the house is crawling with camels.

JOHN: Horrible.

P.J.: It's what I call getting VD the hard way.

JOHN: And we could be next.

P.J.: It depends on the luck of the draw. There's a Jewish couple at 'Mountain View': they'll put up a fight. No, as I see it, by the time they work their way through the estate it'll be broad daylight, and even in Killiney a herd of camels isn't likely to go unnoticed.

JOHN: Then we have a chance?

P.J.: If we sit tight.

JOHN [*cravenly*]: Maybe if we said a little prayer ...

P.J.: John, you're going to pieces.

JOHN: Am I? Yes, you're quite right ... there's no God, how can there be? If there was, He'd have at least sent us Apaches.

P.J. [*raising his hand*]: Quiet!

JOHN: What is it?

P.J.: I heard a ...

> [*An* ARAB *appears at the window, trying to see in, his shape and face swimming indistinctly and wraithlike in the perspex.*]

You ... bugger off. Hoosh ... private property. Get away from here ... shoo.

> [*The* ARAB *scuttles away.* HARRY *has dropped on one knee behind a chair, his rifle aimed.*]

Bloody nerve.

HARRY: Would you mind awfully closing the curtains. And I wouldn't recommend showing myself, if I were you.

> [P.J. *pulls the curtains shut.*]

JOHN: That wasn't the one who shot me. So there *is* a gang of them. Hundreds!

P.J.: John, don't yell. Do you want to alarm the womenfolk? ... I mean, the girls.

JOHN: Frankly, I don't give a continental. They want equal rights, don't they? Well, let them be as frightened as I am.

P.J.: Now, look. Have you ever seen a film where you could tell one Arab from the next? No, you never did. So why couldn't he have been the one who shot you?

JOHN: Because he wasn't on a camel.

P.J.: Maybe it humped off. [*Quickly, as* JOHN *starts towards him*] I didn't mean that.

[BEA *comes in from the hall.* HARRY *at once comes to attention.*]

BEA: You were shouting loud enough to ... [*Seeing* HARRY] Hello
... to wake the dead. What's going on?

JOHN: Arabs.

P.J. [*covering up*]: It's my fault: I made a joke, and John got narked.
How's Ellie?

BEA: Fine. All she needed was a lie-down: she got over-excited. She's
much better, practically her old self again.

P.J. [*hollowly*]: Oh, God.

BEA: What's-her-name ... Miss Mailboat Pier is taking good care of
her. But honestly, P.J., making fun of John after what he's been
through. Poor lamb.

JOHN: It throbs.

BEA: I know, pet. Did you hear about Van Gogh's landlady?

JOHN: Eh?

BEA: She was cleaning his room. She looked on the floor and said:
'What's this 'ere?'

[JOHN *gives a yell of rage, picks up the nearest chair and raises it
high above his head.* BEA *cries out in fear and retreats to the door.*]

P.J.: John, for God's sake.

BEA: I really do not know what's got into him this evening. He
wouldn't want to lose an ear-lobe every day. [*She goes out.*]

P.J.: John, put the chair down and sit on it. This isn't like you.
Where's the voice of sanity? What happened to the man in charge?

JOHN: In charge of what? They're going to wipe us out.

P.J.: Not a chance.

JOHN: They will: they'll slaughter us and rape the women. She'd
enjoy that.

P.J.: A few hours from now it'll be a normal grey wet August
morning, and the only sign of what's happened here will be the
camel manure in the garden.

HARRY: If they do attack ...

P.J. [*for* JOHN's *benefit*]: Which they won't.

HARRY: If they should, the important thing is to give 'em billy-o.
Put the kybosh on as many of the beggars as possible, and there's
a good chance we'll earn their respect and they'll kill us outright.

JOHN: Is he on our side?

HARRY: It's not amusing being captured by the Tuaregs: they aren't sportsmen. When they take a prisoner, their idea of a jape is to tie him down stark naked on a sandhill until the sun burns the flesh from his bones.

JOHN: You hear him?

P.J.: John, in our climate you could last indefinitely.

HARRY: That's true ... I keep forgetting. You did explain it that I'm not there any more and it's not then, either. Queer, that.

P.J.: I must say, you took it calmly.

HARRY: Being British helps, you know. Mind, I don't quite get the hang of it about Time doing a somersault and all that. But I do know I must be in Ireland: you haven't dressed for dinner. And I don't have to be told it's no longer Nineteen-twenty.

P.J.: No?

HARRY: Well, if it is, you've both got rotten tailors. Besides, how else can one explain that lady visitor of yours in the beret? I mean, she's showing rather a daring amount of lower limb. The woman of the future, eh?

JOHN [scowling at P.J.]: It depends on your viewpoint.

HARRY: She's dashed attractive.

P.J.: Who ... Tish?

HARRY: Rather.

JOHN: Good God.

HARRY: Would it be bad form to ask if she has an attachment?

P.J.: Frequently.

HARRY: Bit of a flirt, eh? Do you know, it's been eighteen months since I've seen a white woman.

JOHN: I can believe it.

[HARRY goes to the window, lifts the curtain and peers out cautiously.]

P.J.: He fancies Tish.

JOHN: You didn't know that Beau Geste was a raving lunatic, did you?

P.J.: With her face, she's lucky he's a leg man.

HARRY [returning]: Not a sign. Either they've sheared off or they're lying low behind the privet. Hard to tell. Well, what's been happening?

P.J.: Pardon?

HARRY: Since Nineteen-twenty. Been many changes?

P.J.: Oh, yes. There was a second world war ... you missed it.

HARRY: By jove.

P.J.: And there was ... [*To* JOHN] What else?

JOHN: Well, science hasn't done badly. Sulfa drugs ... heart transplants.

HARRY [*polite amazement*]: Heart transplants ... Good Lord.

P.J.: Hydrogen bombs.

JOHN: Space satellites.

P.J.: And there's been a man on the moon.

HARRY: On the moon ... well done!

P.J.: It's gospel.

HARRY: I believe you.

JOHN [*determined to impress him*]: Nuclear submarines. Supersonic aircraft. Half the world turned communist.

P.J.: East-West confrontation.

JOHN: Britain a minor power.

HARRY: Ha-ha.

JOHN: What's funny?

HARRY [*patting his shoulder*]: Let's not get carried away.

P.J.: It's the truth. The Empire has packed it in.

HARRY [*chuckling*]: You Irish ... irrepressible.

P.J.: I'm saying that countries like India and Kenya got their independence, their freedom. John, tell him.

HARRY: Got their freedom?

JOHN: From Britain.

HARRY: Sorry, not possible.

JOHN: Why isn't it?

HARRY: Because the expression 'freedom from Britain' is a contradiction in terms. [*He goes imperturbably towards the drinks table.*] Mind if I have a spot of this?

P.J. [*seething*]: I'll fix him.

JOHN: He's unfixable.

P.J.: You watch me. [*To* HARRY] And there's something I forgot. Five years ago, the entire population of the United States was wiped out by leprosy. Word of honour.

HARRY: Canada's all right, though, is it?

> [P.J. *capitulates.* JOHN *gives him a 'You see?' look.*)

[*Drinking*] Cheers. I hope you didn't mind my catching you out just now. Not quite the done thing from a guest who's been rescued from a sticky wicket. After all, if it hadn't been for ... [*To* P.J.] you, was it? ... I'd still be in Morocco fighting off the Tuaregs.

JOHN: You still are.

HARRY: Don't follow.

JOHN: You're still in Morocco.

HARRY: I see.

JOHN: As well as here.

HARRY: How damned interestin'. [*To* P.J.] Known him long, have you?

JOHN: I'll show you.

> [*He takes hold of* HARRY *and faces him towards opposite walls in turn.*]

There is where you were born. Over here, you die.

HARRY: Where's Morocco?

P.J.: Don't confuse him.

> [JOHN *begins to point out successive places along an imaginary line which extends from one wall to the other.*]

JOHN: Here you get your tonsils out. Here's puberty. Here you meet a girl with whom you have nothing in common. Here you marry her. [*Moving on*] Your parents die. The company you work for goes bust. Here, the male menopause. Here, people in their twenties start calling you 'sir'. Here you get the old age pension. Here it's all over.

P.J.: Time goes fast when you're enjoying yourself.

JOHN: Think of a photograph album with a picture in it for every split second you've lived. Well, when P.J. dragged you into the present, all he did was tear out one of the snapshots. The other photos are still there.

HARRY: And I'm in Morocco?

JOHN: You've probably been killed by now.

HARRY: Killed?

P.J.: You still have your health. Be thankful.

JOHN [*to* HARRY]: You see, it's all perfectly simple, except that in your case it's not simple, it's impossible, because being a character in a book, you don't exist, and yet you're here, and so are the Arabs and so are their poxy camels, and if by some miracle I survive tonight, then first thing in the morning I'm having myself committed.

[BEA *comes in with* ELLIE *and* TISH.]

P.J.: John, pull yourself together.

BEA: Now ... look who's as good as new!

HARRY: Your husband's been most amusin'. I should say he's one Irishman who's definitely kissed Barney Stone.

BEA: I wouldn't be at all surprised.

P.J. [*to* ELLIE]: How do you feel?

ELLIE: So much fuss. I was on edge to begin with, and the sight of blood was the straw that broke the camel's back.

[JOHN *laughs mirthlessly.*]

Sorry, John.

BEA: Blood! I'm so selfish ... I never thought.

JOHN [*magnanimously*]: It doesn't matter ... don't mention it.

BEA [*who was talking to* ELLIE]: Your carpet.

ELLIE: What?

BEA: He bled on it.

ELLIE: Oh, never mind.

TISH: Youse won't get bloodstains out. Them's worse than purple pencil.

ELLIE: For heaven's sake, what's a few specks on a carpet?

BEA: There's one ...

ELLIE: Where?

[*The ladies examine the spot.*]

JOHN [*bitterly*]: When you come to the ear-lobe, it's mine.

P.J. [*trying to get attention*]: Girls, if I could ...

ELLIE: That's not blood, it's blackcurrant.

BEA: Is it?

ELLIE: And that's all there is.

BEA: I will say this for John: he's fanatically tidy.

P.J.: Girls ...

BEA: Do you know, after he takes a bath he washes the soap.

P.J.: Excuse me, but while Ellie was feeling under the weather we had a pow-wow and got the benefit of Mr Geste's expert advice on the subject of desert warfare.

[*All look at* HARRY, *who assumes that* JOHN *is the person referred to.*]

HARRY [*laughing*]: He's an expert now and no mistake.

P.J.: No, I mean you.

HARRY: Me? My name's not Geste.

P.J.: Why isn't it?

HARRY: Because it's Standish ... Harry Standish. What makes you think I'd have a Froggie name like Geste?

P.J.: Harry Standish?

HARRY: Sorry!

P.J. [*to the others*]: I never even heard of him.

ELLIE: Well, trust you to invite a gatecrasher.

P.J.: Who did?

ELLIE: You did.

P.J.: Don't talk balls. If I invited him, how can he be a ...

HARRY: Did I damage your gate coming in?

ELLIE [*ignoring* HARRY]: Even when he does something that's wrong he still can't do it right.

P.J.: There's been some sort of mix-up, I grant you. I don't know how. But before you start getting hypercritical you might at least give credit where it's due. I got us real Arabs, didn't I?

JOHN: Yes, let's not take that away from him.

BEA: Did you say 'Arabs', with an 's'?

P.J.: What?

BEA: More than one?

P.J.: We don't know ... [*As* ELLIE *opens her mouth in alarm*] we don't think so. What I was trying to say is, to be on the safe side it might be as well if everyone camped here for the night.

ELLIE: Because he's still out there?

P.J.: In case he is.

BEA: How will we know if it's safe?

P.J.: Nothing simpler. Tomorrow morning, if they don't kill the milkman, we're in business.

JOHN: That seems fair.

ELLIE: He's so impudent. [*Clarifying*] Our milkman is.

TISH: Well, amn't I nicely circumstanced, me that never dossed anywhere, except in me own bed. Be tomorrow the whole town will have it that I was off out carryin' on with someone. There goes me good name.

BEA: She's very difficult.

TISH: At least, Missus, I was brung up proper. No Arabs ever cem to our front door. Maybe we were hard put to have two ha'pennies to rub together, but no one belongin' to me ever went next nor near an Arab ... no, nor bade one of them the time of day, not unless he was where he had a right to be, in a crib at Christmas.

HARRY: Hear, hear: one must have standards.

ELLIE: I'm trying to think. There's the single bed in Emma's room ... then there's the spare room ...

P.J.: That's plenty: the men will have to stay up, anyway.

HARRY: I suppose there are no weapons in the house? A shotgun?

P.J.: Nothing, no.

JOHN: In the boot of my car ...

HARRY: Yes?

JOHN: But what's the use? I'd never get near it.

HARRY: Perhaps I could.

P.J.: It's too much of a risk. If the Arabs don't get you the camels will.

JOHN: A fate worse than death.

HARRY: But by jingo, it's worth trying. D'you know, I think I'll have a shot at it. [*Handing his rifle to* P.J.] Would you mind awfully holding this?

JOHN: You'll need the key of the boot.

HARRY [*taking it*]: Top-hole. [*He moves to the door to the hall.*]

BEA [*to* JOHN]: It's your car, why don't you go?

JOHN: Because one ear is my limit.

HARRY: If I keep low and move fast it shouldn't take more than a jiffy. [*Looking out*] I say, what luck: the moon's gone in. It's as black out as a dago's armpits.

BEA: He's too much, he really is.

HARRY: Well, standing here won't get the baby washed. Here goes for England, home and beauty, eh? Tally ho.

P.J.: Are you positive your name isn't ...

    [HARRY *has already dashed out.*]

  Well, whoever he is, that's what I call true grit.

JOHN: You know, when the chips are down you've really got to hand it to the British.

P.J.: You're right. As thick as two planks.

ELLIE: I'll be living on Valium after this ... I know I will. And it's not as if this was a low-class neighbourhood. I could show you our rates bill.

P.J. [*to* JOHN]: But you, you're a crafty sod. I didn't know you owned a gun.

JOHN: A gun?

P.J.: In the boot of your car.

JOHN: Who said it was a gun?

P.J.: Then what is it?

JOHN: My bow and arrows.

P.J.: Your ... ?

JOHN: Never go anywhere without them. The bow is collapsible, you know ... ideal for travelling.

P.J.: You let him go out there for a ...

    [*There are two rifle-shots from some distance away and the tinkle of broken glass in the room.*]

ELLIE: Oh, my God, listen.

P.J.: Down ... will everybody get down?

ELLIE [*dropping to her knees*]: In Killiney ... this is disgraceful.

P.J.: Take cover behind something ... a chair, a chair.

ELLIE [*bad-tempered*]: All right, all right! [*She crawls behind an armchair.*]

P.J.: Tish? Where's Tish?

TISH [*from an unknown location*]: I'll tell you this, Mister ... tomorrow morning there'll be more summonses in this house than there's snuff at a wake.

P.J.: Wherever she is, she's all right. Bea ... get behind this.

    [*He moves the armchair behind which* ELLIE *is sheltering, so that it is now in front of* BEA.]

BEA: Bless you, darling.

ELLIE: Well, honestly.

226

[JOHN, *also on his knees, reaches over and pulls the chair away from in front of* BEA *so that it is now providing cover for himself.*]

BEA: You rotten sod.

[*Everyone flinches as three more shots are heard whining against the outside wall of the house.*

The front door is slammed shut, off, and HARRY *comes in, out of breath, and carrying a bow and a quiver of arrows. He espies* JOHN *and goes over to him.*]

HARRY [*with icy disdain*]: Yours, I think. [*He gives him the quiver and bow and walks away scornfully.*]

P.J.: It's gone quiet again ... yes, it's a definite lull. [*To* HARRY] That was very heroic of you.

BEA [*rising*]: Yes, it was. And you must forgive my husband: he's a stickler for etiquette ... he always brings a bow and arrow with him when we go out to dinner.

JOHN: You may be glad of these yet, so there's no need for ... Jesus.

[*A rug has risen from the horizontal.* TISH *appears under it.*]

I thought it was a camel.

TISH: I'm goin' to summons youse and [*She points out*] I'm goin' to summons them. I'm not thick, you know ... I didn't come down in the last shower. I know what a solicitor is for.

BEA: If you don't, who does?

TISH: And you needn't try to soft-soap me, either.

ELLIE [*her manner cool*]: Beatrice, if you're finished with that chair my husband very kindly offered you, would you mind coming with me while I make up the extra beds? [*She gives* P.J. *a venomous look.*]

HARRY: I should keep down if I were you, when crossing the hall.

P.J.: Now what have I done?

ELLIE [*bent double*]: Don't pretend you don't know.

BEA [*following her at a crouch*]: They always act the innocent. They couldn't stand up straight to you if you paid them.

[ELLIE *and* BEA *go out, which is what* P.J. *has been waiting for.*]

P.J. [*to* HARRY]: So break it to us. How many are out there?

HARRY: Do you mean Tuaregs? I saw nary a one ... they were shooting from cover. But I did see twenty or so camels around a waterhole.

P.J.: Around a what?

HARRY: Over that way.

P.J.: That must be the Fitzgibbons' swimming pool.

[*He notices that* JOHN *has taken out a pocket calculator and is working it.*]

What are you doing?

JOHN: I'm trying to calculate how many Arabs there ... [*He breaks off.*] I'm losing my reason. I was counting the legs of the camels and dividing by four.

HARRY: If you ask me, our dusky friends will stay put until first light and content themselves with keeping us pinned down. Then, as soon as dawn comes ...

P.J.: Go on.

[HARRY *takes three bullets from his ammunition pouch and stands them upright on a table.*]

HARRY: I think it would be as well to set these aside, for the ladies. One each.

JOHN: Well, that's the limit.

HARRY: As a last resort.

JOHN: You look to him for advice, and what does he do? He hands out souvenirs.

P.J.: John, what he's trying to tell us ...

JOHN: I don't want to hear it. Wherever I go, at every turn ... gross incompetence. If the truth were told, he probably didn't lock the boot of my car after him.

P.J.: Will you calm down?

JOHN: If my spare wheel is gone tomorrow I'll know who's to blame. [*Pointing at* HARRY] Catch him losing his no-claim bonus ... oh, no: he won't, but I will. And it's not just stupidity, you know: part of it is deliberate. [*His hysteria begins to mount.*] I get it all the time: jealousy and malevolence. Yesterday – I'll give you an example – yesterday, I gave my new receptionist a five-pound note and asked her to go out and get me five singles. She came back with five bags of chips. In my consulting room, and while I was treating a case of anorexia nervosa ... chips! Don't tell me that was accidental.

HARRY [*with disgust*]: The fellow's in a blue funk.

JOHN: That's what you'd like, isn't it? That's what those bullets are for. You want me to get hysterical; and then you can spread the word and I'll be a laughing-stock all over Africa. Well, you're not getting the satisfaction.

TISH [*to* P.J.]: In the fillums they always give them a slap on the face.

P.J.: You're right.

JOHN: Yes, you want my name to be mud in every oasis in Morocco. Well, hard luck!

[P.J. *has marched purposefully up to* JOHN, *ready to slap him.*]

P.J.: John ...

[JOHN *turns and slaps* P.J.'*s face.*]

JOHN: You irresponsible fart ... this is all your fault.

P.J.: That hurt.

JOHN: You did this. We're going to be slaughtered by a horde of maniacs in bedsheets, and you brought them here. Another man, a man in his senses, a man of culture and refinement, would have conjured up Deanna Durbin and we could have had a little sing-song. But not you. And why? ... because you're sick ... sick!

[*He begins to whimper.*]

TISH: Ah, the poor bugger.

P.J.: Do you want a hankie?

JOHN: I'll never ... forgive you. [*Wiping his eyes*] Sorry.

P.J.: Losing an ear-lobe would upset anyone.

JOHN: I'm not afraid of dying ... honestly. It's just that in my case it's such a tragedy. [*He blows his nose.*] Are the girls coming back?

P.J.: No sign of them. We'll go into the kitchen; you can give your face a rub.

[*He leads* JOHN *upstage.*]

JOHN [*still sniffling*]: I've never once hit another human being in anger. We don't even slap hysterical patients any more ... we give then an injection instead, because ...

P.J.: I know. Because it calms them.

JOHN: No, because you can put it on the bill.

[*He and* P.J. *go into the kitchen.*]

HARRY [*to* TISH]: I'm wretchedly sorry you had to see that.

TISH: Doesn't bother me.

HARRY: No?

TISH: Men is always cryin'. If they're not cryin' because they can't do it, they're cryin' because they did do it.

HARRY: Do what?

TISH: Beg your pardon?

HARRY: Crying because they did do what?

TISH: You must be new in the navy.

HARRY: The navy? The ships of the desert are more in my line. [*He unleashes a laugh which is half Old English Sheepdog.*] Rather good, what?

TISH: You're a howl.

HARRY: Look here, might I say something? We're in a hellishly tight corner, and I consider that you are being an absolute brick.

TISH: Oh, yeah?

HARRY: What I mean is, those heathens must have seen my uniform just now, so they know I'm in here. That means we're for it. And yet you haven't batted an eyelid.

TISH: It has feck-all to do with me.

HARRY: But if those brown Johnnies should attack ...

TISH: Looka, mister, they can be any colour they like ... I don't ask them to go with the wallpaper. Maybe they have a bone to pick with youse, but the way I look at it, what's a Arab to you is a man to a woman and what's a man to a woman is a customer to me.

HARRY: A customer? Oh, I see.

TISH: High time, too.

HARRY: You're in trade, are you? Got a little shop?

[*As* TISH *stares at him,* P.J. *returns.*]

P.J.: He's out of the woods. He had a little cry over the double sink.

HARRY [*still to* TISH]: Well, good for you. I daresay that nowadays for a lady to be in commerce is quite pukka. Not like when I was a boy ... seventy-five years ago.

TISH: Beg your pardon?

HARRY: Oh Lor', the fun we all had on Mafeking Night. And it seems like only yesterday that the pater took us up to town for the old Queen's diamond jubilee.

TISH [*to* P.J., *her voice trembling*]: Mister ...

P.J.: It's all right: there's a perfectly unbelievable explanation.

HARRY: Do you know, I've just twigged ... assuming I'm still alive, I shall be eighty-six next birthday. [*To* TISH, *solemnly*] Would you credit it?

TISH [*with false heartiness*]: And fresh and well you're lookin'.

HARRY: My family ... I suppose the last trump has sounded for all of them by now.

[*A trumpeting noise.* JOHN *has walked in, blowing his nose.*]

Did I tell you why I joined the Legion? I took a jewel, a sapphire. Only it wasn't: it was an imitation. My aunt – Aunt Patricia – had sold the original. Except that it wasn't hers to sell. She put the fake jewel in its place, and the truth was going to come out and there'd have been the devil of a scandal. So I took the imitation and skedaddled. Family honour, you know.

P.J.: Hang on a tick ... are you positive your name isn't ...

HARRY: I've never told that to a living soul. Except once, to a retired officer in Marrakech. English chappie, name of Wren. Rum sort of fellow ... kept saying he was going to put it in a book.

P.J. [*to* JOHN]: *That's* why he's here. He's the original.

HARRY: Of course he was just pulling my leg.

P.J.: The man who inspired it ... well, I'm buggered.

HARRY: Eh? Ha-ha, you wait till the Arabs get here. Which reminds me: it's time we stood sentry. If one of you gentlemen would ...

JOHN: What does he mean, wait till the Arabs ...

P.J.: John, I'm trying to listen.

HARRY: If one of you would mount guard at the front of the house, I shall station myself at a rear window. Agreed?

JOHN [*to* P.J., *plaintively*]: They wouldn't, would they?

HARRY [*to* TISH]: Dear lady, I know that I presume on an all too short acquaintanceship, but if you would consent to place yourself under my personal protection I should be most fearfully bucked. [*He salutes her and goes into the kitchen.*]

JOHN: Well, that takes the biscuit.

P.J.: What does?

JOHN: What he said. I know they're uncivilized, but I assumed they'd at least behave like normal decent human-beings to the extent of raping the women and letting it go at that.

TISH [*to* P.J.]: Mister, let them in, quick.

P.J.: Let who in?

TISH: Them!

P.J.: The Arabs?

TISH: They're not Arabs. They're from the loony bin, lookin' for him. [*She indicates* HARRY, *off.*] Let them in.

P.J.: John, explain it to her.

JOHN: Well, if it comes to a choice between an honourable death and degradation, I know which one I'll pick. By God, I do.

P.J.: John . . .

JOHN: Only if word of it ever gets out I'll be ruined.

P.J.: Tish didn't ask to come here; but since she *is* here she's a guest. I think we owe her the common courtesy of telling her what's happened.

JOHN: His house is surrounded by nancy boys on the rampage and he talks about etiquette. You tell her, then. Try it.

TISH: Tell me what?

P.J.: Tish, I know this will come as a shock, but be calm. The fact is, you're in Nineteen-seventy-seven.

TISH: I see.

P.J.: Nineteen-seventy-seven.

TISH: Yis.

P.J.: You accept that?

TISH: I'm not thick.

P.J.: Good.

TISH: But what's the name of the road?

[JOHN *laughs*. P.J. *tries again.*]

P.J.: Nineteen-seventy-seven isn't the house number, Tish: it's the year. Due to a little mix-up in time, you've been moved twenty-eight years into the future.

[TISH *regards him beadily. He is emboldened to press on.*]

And, of course, the future for you is the present for us; only according to Dr Schlepper you're still living in the past as well, so it isn't as complicated as it may seem. Come to that, you're not only living in the past and present, but you're also living in England, very hale and hearty for your age, you'll be glad to hear, and we'd be only too delighted, wouldn't we, John, to chip in with the boat fare so's you can drop in on yourself. And at least you can console yourself that you're better off than he [*Indicating* HARRY] is. Don't mind that rubbish about him being eighty-six next birthday. I mean, he was probably killed in Africa half an hour ago in Nineteen-twenty, so compared with him you're laughing, right?

TISH [*to* JOHN]: Mister . . .

JOHN: What?

TISH: Let them in.

P.J.: Tish, it couldn't be simpler. You . . .

JOHN: Let me do it. [*To* TISH] Go and find my wife, Beatrice. Ask her to tell you how you got here this evening. Will you do that for me?

TISH: Ask her how I got here?

JOHN: She'll make it all crystal clear . . . I guarantee. Go on.

[TISH *looks at him uncertainly and goes out.*]

P.J.: What did you do that for? How can Bea explain it?

JOHN: A few months ago I finished a consultation in London a day earlier than expected and caught a Starflight home. I was turning into Mount Merrion Avenue at one-thirty a.m. when I saw Beatrice. She was limping along, wearing high heels and a dress with a neckline which was not so much glad as verging on the ecstatic. In one hand she was swinging a piece of material which on closer inspection turned out to be a brassiere. I drove her home, and there we had a full and frank discussion, no holds barred, at the end of which I unequivocally accepted her explanation that she had been on a charity walk and had lost her way. Not only did I believe her, but I sponsored her retroactively for fifty pence a mile.

P.J.: What about the bra?

JOHN: She said it had been choking her. So you see, if Beatrice can't explain it convincingly to your friend from the mailboat pier, then no one can.

P.J.: I'll buy that.

JOHN: Although I wish you hadn't promised her a trip to England. In the event that she and Lawrence of Arabia manage to survive tonight, it's Kerry for both of them.

P.J.: Oh, let them go.

JOHN: And risk prosecution? ... no, thank you. It's the Collection Squad for them and the RSPCA for the camels.

P.J.: John, be big. Do you remember at the end of 'Stagecoach', where the marshal turns a blind eye and lets the Ringo Kid and the town brasser go free? Sends them off into the sunset. You think he's going to arrest Ringo; instead, he ...

JOHN: Don't reminisce about any more old films!

P.J.: Sorry.

JOHN: We can't afford sentimentality. What's occurred here is probably happening all over the country. For all we know, Parnell may at this moment be addressing a monster meeting, in O'Connell Street.

P.J.: At this hour?

JOHN: Tomorrow then.

P.J.: In that case, there'll soon be more people *in* that concentration camp than out of it.

JOHN: It's the end of the Kerry jokes, I'll tell you that.

P.J. [*decisively*]: Well, it'll have to be stopped.

JOHN: And I suppose you know how?

P.J.: By law, that's how. People will have to be told not to think about old times.

JOHN: Ha-ha.

P.J.: Why not?

JOHN: I'll give you a demonstration why not. Don't think about naked women.

P.J.: All right.

JOHN: Good. What are you thinking about?

P.J.: Naked women.

JOHN: You see?

P.J.: Bugger it.

JOHN [*wincing*]: I wish you'd find a happier turn of phrase. [*He looks about him.*] Now ... where are they?

P.J.: What are you looking for?

JOHN: One of us had better stand sentry, and since I'm not likely to sleep tonight it may as well be ... Ah! [*He finds what he is looking for: his bow and quiver.*]

P.J.: John ...

JOHN: If I had any guts I'd save the last arrow for myself.

P.J.: The people who disappeared ...

JOHN: Well?

P.J.: Where do you think they went to?

JOHN: I told you: they're in the past.

P.J.: Well, I was there; I grew up in it and I didn't see them. I mean, in Nineteen-thirty-two was there an elderly gentleman who turned up at the Eucharistic Congress and said: 'Hello, I'm Bishop Lucey and I'm a refugee from contraception'?

JOHN: No, there was not.

P.J.: He could hardly have passed unnoticed.

JOHN: P.J., you cannot go barging into the past as if it was a pub. If you did that, you'd change it just by being there, and you can't change what's already happened.

P.J. [*not getting it*]: Sorry.

JOHN: Suppose you went back thirty years, met me as a child and gave me a thump in the face that disfigured me for life. But I'm not disfigured, am I! So how can I be both ugly *and* handsome?

P.J. [*nodding*]: Got you.

JOHN: No, my theory is: those people have gone back to a single remembered moment in time. And they're caught inside of it, like a pea in a deep-freeze.

P.J.: Like a ... ?

JOHN: No, a garden pea ... P-E-A.

P.J.: Oh.

JOHN: Poor devils. Stuck there ... watching themselves holding a first-born, winning a prize at school, making love.

P.J.: And it's permanent?

JOHN: Forever is a better word.

P.J.: The world's longest orgasm ... my God.

[ELLIE *comes in.*]

ELLIE: Is he boasting again?

P.J.: John has a theory that ...

ELLIE [*ignoring him*]: John, there's a bed made up, and I've lent Bea a nightdress.

JOHN: No sleep for me, I'm afraid. [*Modestly heroic*] At times like this someone has to man the barricades.

ELLIE [*polite dismay*]: What a shame.

JOHN: Can't be helped. Men have always done the fighting and they always will ... do. Stay cheerful, I'll be close by, in the hall. [*To* P.J.] We ought to have a prearranged signal, though, in case they attack. Any ideas?

    [P.J. *looks at him stonily.* JOHN *comes back to reality.*]

I suppose a scream is as good as any.

    [*He goes out.* ELLIE *begins to pick up the used glasses.*]

P.J.: Quite an evening. [*Silence*] I say, it makes a change from the usual Saturday. [*No answer*] That fellow from the Foreign Legion has fallen for Tish, do you know that? Of course there's a hell of a difference in age. I mean, he's eighty-something and she's in her sixties. Then there's the question of social status. It reminds me of 'Waterloo Bridge', where Vivien Leigh is a ...

    [ELLIE *flings a glass to the floor violently. It does not break.*]

What's up?

ELLIE: This is not one of your bloody films.

P.J.: I know it isn't: if it was a film the glass would have broken. Why are you narked?

ELLIE: Why? People from thirty and fifty years ago walk into my living room, and you ...

P.J.: No, this started months ago.

ELLIE [*feigning innocence*]: Oh?

P.J.: I remarked on it earlier.

ELLIE: To outsiders: so you did.

P.J.: What I told them was, we don't get on, we store up grudges. Do you think that's news to them?

ELLIE: It is to me.

P.J.: Now come on ... !

ELLIE: Come on where? I'm a liar, is that it?

P.J.: Now wait ...

ELLIE: Am I being called a liar, yes or no?

P.J.: Yeah, sure, definitely. I'm saying you're a liar, so now you can chalk up one for your side. Just tell me one thing: what score are we aiming for, and when do we stop?

ELLIE: Don't think I don't know what you're up to. You want a row, now, with the house full of people.

P.J.: I don't want a row.

ELLIE: You mean, you don't, but I do?

P.J.: I never said that.

ELLIE: I see. So what it boils down to is: you're accusing me of unjustly accusing you of accusing me of wanting a row?

P.J. [*his head swimming*]: Pardon?

ELLIE: You're not all there, you know that?

P.J.: That's very possibly true, but in my lunatic way I'm trying to find out why, for the past God knows how long, whenever I say a word to you, you jump down my throat.

ELLIE: I do what?

P.J.: You do, you take offence.

ELLIE: Me?

P.J.: Offence, yes.

ELLIE [*thundering*]: I never take offence . . . how bloody dare you?

P.J.: There's no need to . . .

ELLIE: The . . . the nerve. Telling me that I . . .

P.J.: Don't get offended.

ELLIE: I damn well will get offended. How dare you say that I take offence? You lying sod.

   [JOHN *puts his head in.*]

JOHN: Did you call me?

ELLIE AND P.J. [*together*]: No.

   [JOHN *withdraws.*]

P.J.: Ellie, will you sit down? Just for a minute. Will you do that much?

ELLIE [*sitting, near tears*]: God knows I do my best, and all I ever get from you is accusations.

P.J. [*placatory*]: You're too sensitive.

ELLIE: It's always my fault. My fault, never yours.

P.J.: Ellie, about the Arabs . . .

ELLIE: No, you're perfect!

P.J.: There *is* more than one. The garden is full of them.

ELLIE: Well, let them get an earful . . . I don't care.

P.J.: That's not what I mean. There's a remote possibility that we may be the first people in the history of Killiney to be wiped out by Moslems.

[*She half rises.*]

I'm positive it won't happen. If you ask me, the going will be too soft for the camels.

ELLIE: But ...

P.J.: Don't get flustered. They're nomadic, so try and think of them as no more than African tinkers. Hang on to that. But just in case the old sweepstake ticket does come up, I thought you and I ought to get things sorted out between us.

ELLIE: There's nothing to sort out.

P.J.: Ellie, you live on your nerves.

ELLIE: Then stop tormenting me.

P.J.: Is it to do with Emma?

[*She shakes her head.*]

Will we tell her she can come home?

ELLIE: No.

P.J.: If it's not Emma, is it something *I* did? Or didn't do. Is it Beatrice?

ELLIE: Bea? What about her?

P.J. [*retreating*]: Nothing.

ELLIE: Why would it be Beatrice?

P.J.: Yes.

ELLIE: I said, why would it be ...

P.J.: Exactly; I agree with you. So that eliminates her.

ELLIE: Are you and Beatrice having it off?

P.J.: John's in the hall.

ELLIE: Are you?

P.J. [*a thumbs-up sign to* JOHN, *off*]: Fight the good fight!

ELLIE: I asked you a ...

P.J.: No. As God is my ...

ELLIE: Because if I thought for one instant that you and she were ...

P.J.: Look. She flirts and likes to play footsie. She keeps saying 'Ring me, ring me', as if she was a prize at a Hoop-La. I mentioned her because I thought maybe you'd copped on to her and got the mistaken idea that the tapes had gone up.

ELLIE: That would be the last straw.

P.J.: I'd never do that to you. It'd be the end of us.

ELLIE: It certainly would, if your carryings-on cost me one of the few friends I've got left.

P.J.: Beatrice is as safe as ... [*He breaks off.*]

ELLIE: Well?

P.J.: As houses.

ELLIE: She had better be.

P.J.: And thanks a bundle.

ELLIE: What for?

P.J.: The compliment.

ELLIE: When?

P.J.: You're a charmer, you know that? Well, don't worry about it. When I do start screwing women I'll make sure they're not friends of yours. I mean, I don't want to cause you annoyance. I'll pick up some scrubber in a pub on the North side. All righty?

ELLIE: P.J., do whatever you like.

[*He looks at her. The indifference in her voice tells him that she means it.*]

I don't care.

[*From outside a voice wails 'Allah!' twice.* P.J. *looks towards the source of the voice.*]

P.J.: Do you hear them? [*Addressing the voice*] Ne-e-eh, what's up, Doc?

[*He picks up one of the empty glasses, sniffs at the dregs and takes it to where the drinks are.* ELLIE *has been looking at him steadily, making up her mind to speak.*]

ELLIE: The week after my father died ...

P.J. [*cutting in*]: If losing bloody Beatrice is more important to you than ...

ELLIE: You've been persecuting me to tell you. Now listen.

[*He waits.*]

The week after he died I was in the town going somewhere, and I started to cry. In the street, with people looking at me. So I went into a cinema where it was dark. And I sat next to you. Well, where else would I meet you, only at some crappy film?

P.J.: It wasn't crappy. It was 'She Wore a Yellow ...'

ELLIE: Who, except you, cares what it was? I was in bits from losing him, and you were kind to me, good to me. I had no one. And the pair of us, we did this ... what they used to call a steady line. And you asked me and asked, and when the time came there were things I couldn't feel, but there were things I did feel, and I thought that would be enough. So I said yes. Only now half my life is gone, and it is *not* enough.

[*The same voice outside the house calls out 'Allah!' once.*]

P.J. [*yelling back*]: Bugger off!

ELLIE: That day we were sent for, to the school, and Sister Benedict showed us the letter she found in Emma's locker, and we were told that at the age of fifteen that child was as much of a virgin as I am ...

P.J. [*unwilling to hear*]: All right.

ELLIE: You turned your back then, like you're doing now. To me, it was one more part of the times we live in. Our daughter, it was terrible, but there it was: you coped with it. At least *I* did, I tried to. You ... what did you do? Sent her down the country to the Land of Oz. Ask the Wizard for a new maidenhead and stick to the Yellow Brick Road. Then you went on about how it couldn't have happened in the old days, how wholesome life was then, like an ad for cornflakes. God Almighty, you're forty years old and you still think sex is a kiss, then 'The End' comes on the screen, the lights go up and everybody heads for home. According to you, there's ...

P.J.: Don't overdo it. I get the message, I'm with you.

ELLIE: That's the whole point. You were never with me. That's why I don't care.

[*Pause. He nods, accepting this, and goes to pour himself a drink. During the following he grins to himself.*]

Anyway, you yourself would be the first to point out that indifference is par for the course. I mean, seeing as how we're married. [*Then*] Are you grinning?

P.J.: I was thinking of you in that cinema. It's demolished now. It was dark, I kept trying to see what you looked like. You were crying, and the usher said to me: 'Whatever you're doing to that young one, stop it.' That girl ...

240

ELLIE: What girl?

P.J.: You. Then. She was nice. I wish I could ... [*A thought occurs to him.*]

ELLIE: You wish what?

P.J.: Not a thing.

[*The thought grows into an idea. He walks away from the drinks table. He begins to hum softly to himself: 'She Wore A Yellow Ribbon'. He is concentrating, hard. She looks at him with vague disquiet.*]

ELLIE: Do you want that drink or don't you?

P.J. [*under his breath*]: 'And when I asked her why she wore that ribbon ...'

ELLIE: What are you doing?

[*He shakes his head, not wanting to be distracted.* HARRY *comes from the dining area.*]

HARRY: Hello. Terribly sorry to barge in, but there's some news from the front.

ELLIE [*still looking at* P.J.]: The front is out that way.

HARRY: Ha-ha, witty as well as charming. [*Calling towards the hall*] I say, could we rally round, d'you think?

ELLIE: Has something happened?

P.J. [*singing*]: 'Far away, far away ... far away, far away ...'

ELLIE: Will you stop that?

[JOHN *comes in.*]

JOHN: Is there good news? Have they slaughtered your neighbours?

HARRY: No, they're still out there. Listen.

[*They listen.*]

P.J. [*singing*]: '... Far away, far away, I wear it for my sweetheart who is ...'

ELLIE: Shut ... up!

JOHN: I can't hear a thing.

ELLIE: It seems quiet to me.

HARRY: That's just it ...

P.J., HARRY AND JOHN [*together*]: ... It's too damn quiet.

JOHN: Sorry.

ELLIE [*to* P.J.]: You do what you're doing.

P.J.: Certainly.

HARRY: I don't like it. Just now one of them was calling out to

Allah, and that wasn't exactly their version of evensong: it means they're massing for an all-out att ...

[BEA *comes in. She has changed into a rather seductive nightdress with matching negligee.*]

BEA: Did I hear someone say 'Rally round'?

JOHN: Good God.

BEA [*to* ELLIE]: You told me to help myself from your wardrobe, so I took the first thing that came to hand.

ELLIE: That was at the very back.

BEA: I played Lucky Dip.

JOHN: They're only murderous Arabs, you know: it's not formal.

ELLIE [*embarrassed*]: P.J. bought it for me in London.

BEA: Really?

ELLIE: One day when he was ...

P.J.: Drunk.

ELLIE: ... there on business. I've never worn it.

BEA [*nodding*]: I don't get away from home much, either.

JOHN: Please. [*To* HARRY] You were saying?

[HARRY *is staring at* BEA, *who affects to be suddenly aware of him.*]

BEA: Heavens, are you still here? [*Keeping her negligee open*] Don't look: I'll go crimson.

JOHN [*to* HARRY]: You were telling us about the Arabs?

HARRY: Yes, I'm afraid we've had our innings. They're going to launch an all-out nightdress.

JOHN: Pardon?

BEA: Is P.J. ill? He's gone pale again.

P.J.: I think I've done it ...

BEA: Oh, yes?

P.J.: Except this time it's different. It's gone dark and I'm in a ...

[*There is a loud cry in Arabic, off. It is at once a prayer and a call to battle. It dies away.*]

JOHN: I suppose that couldn't have been the Gardai?

HARRY: It's the signal. The swine are as good as on top of us. We must barricade the door. Use the sofa, chairs, anything ...

P.J.: But where is she?

ELLIE: Where's who? Wait, he's right: that Tish woman isn't here.

P.J.: No, I don't mean her: I mean ...

BEA: Well, we were in the spare bedroom. She got all hot and bothered at first ... I mean, when I explained to her that it really is Nineteen-seventy-seven. Then I mentioned to her how the price of everything has gone sky-high since her day, and that seemed to cheer her up. I can't think why.

[*There are rifle-shots from a distance and the sound of tinkling glass.*]

HARRY: They've started. [*Thrusting his rifle at* JOHN] I'll go and fetch her. Hold this.

JOHN: Bea, you take it.

BEA: Me?

JOHN: I don't want to offend them. [*He sits on the sofa.*]

ELLIE: It's all right ... I see her.

[TISH *hurries in. The rifle-fire and the sound of ricochets continue sporadically, off.*]

HARRY: Thank God you're safe.

JOHN: Safe!

TISH: Couldn't even get the drawers offa me in peace. If this is Nineteen-seventy-seven, youse can keep it.

HARRY [*pointing at the corridor, opposite*]: They're attacking from down there. [*To* P.J.] Quick ... give me a hand.

P.J. [*moving to help*]: I know something happened ... I felt it.

HARRY: Take that end.

[*They begin to shift the sofa on which* JOHN *is sitting.*]

JOHN: What's up? Where are you taking me? No, please don't give me to them!

P.J.: John, get off.

ELLIE: It's not good enough. First the burglars, and now this. It's more than our share.

BEA: What do you think they'll do to us?

TISH: Whatever it is, you're dressed for it.

[HARRY *and* P.J. *have dragged the sofa against the living-room door.*]

HARRY: It's no use: this won't stop them, not a hope. Listen ...

[*There are cries, off, and the noise of wood splintering and of breaking glass.*]

They're smashing in one of the windows. I'm rather afraid it's all up with us.

JOHN: No! [*He climbs on the sofa and yells into the hall.*] There's no need for violence. We're your friends. This is Ireland of the Welcomes!

HARRY: They don't savvy the lingo.

JOHN: Eh?

HARRY: They speak Arabic.

JOHN [*yelling*]: Cead mile failte!

P.J. [*putting his arm around* ELLIE]: Hang on, love ... at least we'll go together.

ELLIE: Job's comforter! [*She breaks away.*]

TISH: I don't folly this at all. Dev promised us we'd stay neutral.

JOHN: Beatrice ...

BEA: I'm here, sweetness.

JOHN: Go out and be nice to them.

BEA: Are you mad?

JOHN: Now she gets fussy.

HARRY: Look here ... there is one slim chance. I'm the chap they want. If I go out by the front door and draw their fire, it may give the rest of you time to make a run for it from the rear.

BEA: But you'd be killed.

HARRY: Well, that's Kismet for you.

BEA [*appealing*]: John ...

JOHN: My wife is right. You mustn't do it.

HARRY [*pleasantly surprised*]: Thanks. Thanks for that, old man, but ...

JOHN: I mean, don't go out the front, go out the back. My car's in front: we can get away in it.

HARRY: Oh. I see your point.

JOHN: It's a good job someone here has kept his head.

[*Another crash, off.*]

HARRY: Well, no time to waste.

[*He looks soulfully into* TISH'*s eyes and kisses her hand.*]
Goodbye.

TISH [*pleased, embarrassed*]: Chancer!

JOHN: We're a bit pressed for ...

HARRY: 'If I should die,
　　　Think only this of me,
　　　That there's some corner of a foreign field ...'

JOHN: He'll be here all night. [*To* HARRY] Please?

[HARRY *reaches the rear of the room in one bound.*]

HARRY: '... That is forever England!'

JOHN [*agonized*]: Oh, Jasus.

[*There is a sob from* BEA *as* HARRY *delivers a last salute before his suicide mission. As he turns bravely to go there is a faint bugle call, off.*]

P.J.: What the hell is that?

HARRY: D'you know, it sounded like a ...

[P.J. *holds up his hand for silence. The call is repeated, closer now. There is a distant rumble.*]

BEA: Do Arabs have a bugler?

HARRY: No, and it's not our chaps. It's a call I've never heard before.

[*He goes to the window and pulls back the curtains.*]

JOHN: Careful, it could be a ...

[*The call comes again. The rumble is now identifiable as the sound of galloping horses.*]

HARRY [*looking out*]: Well, I'm jiggered.

JOHN [*approaching*]: What? Where?

P.J. [*realizing*]: Oh, no ... it can't be.

JOHN: My God, it's the United States Cavalry!

P.J.: Oh, shit.

[*The ladies rush to the window.*

P.J. *remains where he is, disgusted.*

During the following, distorted shapes go rushing past the window. Shots are heard.]

HARRY: I say, they're routing the Tuaregs.

TISH: Look at them scatterin'.

BEA [*to* ELLIE]: They're ruining your lovely lawn.

HARRY: The wogs are showing the white feather. The beggars are running like billy-o. [*Waving his kepi*] Hurrah! Hurrah! Go to it.

JOHN: P.J., you're missing it ...

HARRY: Look at that ... oh, well played, sir.

JOHN: ... It really is the bloody US Cavalry. And there's one of them out in front waving ...

[*A look of incredulity comes on his face. He staggers away from the window towards where* P.J. *is. The bugle call – the 'Charge' – comes once more, but fainter now, and the shots and the sound of hoofbeats die away.*]

HARRY: How astonishing. They just drove the wogs before them.

BEA: I think they're heading down Killiney Hill Road.

BEA: Ellie ...

BEA: I know. We're alive.

HARRY: Stroke of luck, I call it.

P.J. [*to* JOHN]: What's up with *you*?

JOHN: I caught sight of the man leading the charges.

P.J.: Oh, yeah?

JOHN: It was John Wayne.

    [P.J. *nods, not at all surprised.*]

HARRY: But where on earth did they come from?

ELLIE: Who cares!

HARRY: Odd-looking uniforms. In my day we favoured khaki.

BEA [*to* TISH]: Are you all right, dear?

TISH: It was massive.

BEA: Wasn't it!

TISH: The way they scattered.

BEA: Yes.

TISH: Like shit off a shovel.

BEA: The very phrase I had in mind.

TISH: It was like in a fillum.

BEA: A film? [*Realizing*] 'She Wore a ...' [*To* P.J.] It was you. *You* did it!

JOHN: Him? How could P.J. have ... Of course! He conjured them up. You bloody genius.

P.J.: Actually, I ...

HARRY: Good Lord. [*Wringing* P.J.'*s hand*] Now that's what I call using the old bean. Well done. Stout fella.

BEA: P.J., you saved our lives. We can never repay you. [*She kisses* P.J.]

JOHN: But there's a small deposit.

BEA: Ellie, he did ... he saved us.

ELLIE: P.J., I may have my faults – you keep telling me I have – but at least I can give credit where it's due. Here ...

    [*She is about to kiss him. He looks at her, his face woebegone.*]

Why are you so ... [*She realizes the truth and draws back from him. Slowly*] My ... God ...

JOHN: Beatrice ... home! It's all hours and I have to get a tetanus injection.

BEA [*looking at her watch*]: Good grief, so it is. Didn't the evening fly? [*To* ELLIE] Darling, don't mind if we rush off. The babysitter will tear us limb from limb. And bless you for asking us back ... it was fabulous.

JOHN: Beatrice ...

BEA: I'm coming, petal. [*To* ELLIE] Now do we owe you a dinner or do you owe us? You owe us ... well, in that case don't be silly. We'll see you soon. [*To* JOHN] I'm ready, sweetness.

JOHN: Are you?

BEA: I just said I ... [*She notices what she is wearing.*] God Almighty, I'm starkers. Still, at this hour who'll notice? The neighbours will, and they'll think we've been swapping. I won't be two ticks.

ELLIE: I'll go with you. [*To* P.J.] You were trying to get *her*, weren't you?

[P.J. *says nothing.* ELLIE *goes out angrily with* BEA.]

TISH: It's time I was off, too.

P.J.: Off where?

TISH: Below to the town. It must be full of Yanks now.

P.J.: You can't go there. John, give me some money.

JOHN: What?

P.J.: I saved your life. Now give me some money.

[JOHN *produces some notes.* P.J. *adds whatever money he has.*]

[*To* HARRY] Will you look after her?

HARRY [*pleased*]: Me?

TISH: Him? Don't make me laugh, I'll burst me stitches.

JOHN: P.J., you're breaking the law.

P.J. [*to* HARRY]: Will you?

HARRY: With a heart and a half, if the lady will do me the honour. And you have my word that any man who dares lay a finger on her will answer to me.

TISH: Do you hear him? I'll starve to death.

P.J. [*giving* HARRY *the money*]: Take this. I don't know how far it'll last you, but try not to be picked up. You and Tish are illegal immigrants.

HARRY: Don't worry: I know how to be inconspicuous. You're a white man. [*To* TISH] Shall we?

TISH: But where are we goin'?

HARRY: To foreign parts. Wherever there are wogs, dagos or nig-nogs, there will always be honest work for English hands. Absolute equality, that's the thing; and throughout the ages we have always defended to the death the sacred right of every black man, no matter how lowly, to be equal to every other black man. Perhaps we'll go to Kenya. By jove, what a welcome the darkies will give us. [*To* P.J. *and* JOHN] Gentlemen ....!

P.J.: Goodbye, Tish.

TISH: Amn't I in nice company? No matter, it's the oul' dog for the hard road. I'll make an honest pimp out of him yet if it kills me.

[TISH *and* HARRY *go out.*]

JOHN: That was highly irresponsible.

P.J.: What matter? I couldn't let the chance go by: it was just like the end of 'Stagecoach'.

JOHN: Well, with the United States Cavalry looking for rot-gut and scarlet women in the streets of Dalkey, I daresay one more couple at large won't make much difference. I think we behaved rather well under stress. We kept our heads, no undue panic ...

P.J.: John ...

JOHN: Of course this is only a reprieve. We're doomed, you know. The whole world is. In a matter of months ... weeks ...

P.J.: John, I wasn't trying to conjure up the US Cavalry.

JOHN: You mean someone else did?

P.J.: It was an accident. The first time I met Ellie was at a western. It was her I was trying to get, but something went wrong. Instead I got the film:

JOHN: Lucky for us.

[P.J. *shrugs.*]

Not that I don't think the world of Ellie, but why do you want two of her?

P.J.: The other one was different. I wanted to get to her before time did.

JOHN: Every man to his taste, but I certainly wouldn't want to call up a second Beatrice. I'm fond of her, but one can have too much of a good thing.

P.J.: I suppose.

JOHN: That wasn't the happiest choice of phrase.

P.J. [*sipping his drink*]: Whatever I do, I make a botch of it.

JOHN: Nonsense.

P.J.: It's true. If there's someone I don't like and I try to snap my fingers in his face, my hands are wet. Whenever I want to drive home an argument and make a dramatic gesture like this ...

[*To illustrate, he flings his arms wide. The drink goes over* JOHN.]

... it goes wrong. I don't know how, but it does. Do you know the story of my life? You're not listening.

JOHN: I am, I am.

P.J.: I was in a public-house toilet. On the wall in front of me, over the urinal, someone had written 'Look up'. I did. Further up the wall they'd written: 'Look higher'. I did. On the ceiling were the words: 'You are now peeing on your shoes'. I was.

[ELLIE *and* BEA *return. The latter has changed into her original clothes.*

ELLIE *gives* P.J. *a cold look. He sits out of the way.*]

BEA: Now then, I'm as ready as I'll ever be. Where are the others?

JOHN: They left.

ELLIE: Do you mean without saying 'Thank you'? Well honestly.

BEA: Aren't some people the limit? And I, like a fool, thought he was rather dishy. Well, it goes to ... What's that smell?

JOHN: Eh?

BEA: It's you: you pong like a distillery.

JOHN: Had an accident.

BEA: Give me patience. Listen ... Ellie wants to know if we're free for dinner next Saturday.

JOHN: No reason why not.

ELLIE: It's a place that does Irish cooking.

BEA: *Is* it? My God. It was only yesterday when an Irish seven-course dinner was a boiled potato and a six-pack. [*She shrieks with laughter.*] P.J. told me that joke, didn't you, you ...

[*She has turned to address* P.J. *who is no longer in the room.*]

Where is he?

JOHN: He was right there.

BEA: He must have slipped out.

ELLIE [*going upstage, calling towards the kitchen*]: P.J., are you in there? Answer me.

JOHN: Probably he went to bed.

ELLIE: I was facing the hall ... he couldn't have. P.J., it isn't funny, now stop it. Will you come when you're called?

JOHN: I'll find him. [*He goes into the hall. Off*] P.J., your presence is requested ... we're going home.

BEA: He was sitting there.

ELLIE: I know he was.

BEA [*looking under a cushion*]: P.J.? I'm going mad. Darling, people don't disappear into thin ...

ELLIE: He's gone.

BEA: Don't be ridiculous.

ELLIE: Then where is he?

BEA: If John dared to play a trick like this on me, I'd kill him. I would: I'd ...

[JOHN *returns.*]

JOHN: Well, he's either hiding or he's stone deaf.

BEA: John, Ellie's upset.

ELLIE: He's gone back. I know he has.

JOHN: Gone back where?

ELLIE: To her. To that cinema. To that little bitch.

BEA: *What* little ...

ELLIE: The house is empty ... can't you feel it? He's there now, with her. God, how I hate her.

JOHN: Ellie, calm down.

ELLIE: How dare he!

JOHN: The three of us are going to comb every inch of this house.

ELLIE: It's no use.

JOHN: And we'll find him. He can't have disappeared: I'll tell you why. In every case where it's happened there's always been a kind of two-way traffic. It's true. Whenever someone vanishes, his place is taken by someone who pops up from the ...

[*The front door slams, off.*]

There ... you see. It's him. He slipped out without us ...

ELLIE [*relieved*]: P.J. ... thank God. I thought you'd ...

   [*Two* DECORATORS *come in. They wear dark overalls stained with whitewash. One is large and fat, wears a toothbrush moustache and a bowler hat. The other is small and thin, wears a bow tie and a bowler hat. They are carrying buckets and brushes, and the smaller man is shouldering a step ladder. The* FAT MAN *simpers archly on seeing the company. He twiddles his tie at them.*]

FAT MAN: Pardon us, I'm sure. [*To the* THIN MAN] Come, Stanley. [*They pass through the room.*]

[*Curtain*]

Also by Hugh Leonard in Penguins

HOME BEFORE NIGHT

A delightful evocation of his Dublin childhood in the thirties and forties, Hugh Leonard's autobiography is like an Irish *Cider With Rosie* – crammed with people and conversations, rich in poetry, full of love, laughter and rare pleasures.

'Entrancing ... the playwright author's gift of language and apparently total recall make his account of growing up in the thirties and forties absolutely irresistible' – *Sunday Telegraph*

'Impossible to put down ... a brilliant, multi-faceted gem' – *Hibernia*

'An unqualified delight ... (he has) a marvellous eye for character, the ability to weave show-stopping funny stories into larger narrative, and to recreate the past with the sensuous immediacy of childhood' – Irving Wardle in *Books and Bookmen*

'Superb ... moving and very funny' – William Trevor